Russian Blood

Alex Shoumatoff

Russian

Blood

A Family Chronicle

Vintage Books

A Division of Random House, Inc.   New York

First Vintage Books Edition, July 1990

Copyright © 1982 by Alex Shoumatoff

All rights reserved under International and Pan-American copyright Conventions. Published in the United States by Vintage Books, a division of Random House, Inc., New York. Originally published, in hardcover, by Coward, McCann & Geoghegan, New York, in 1982.

A considerable portion of the text originally appeared in *The New Yorker*.

Library of Congress Cataloging-in-Publication Data
Shoumatoff, Alex.
Russian blood : a family chronicle / Alex Shoumatoff. — 1st
Vintage Books ed.
p.   cm.
Includes bibliographical references.
ISBN 0-679-72578-4
1. Shoumatoff family.   2. Avinoff family.   3. Shoumatoff, Alex—
Family.   4. Soviet Union—Nobility—Biography.   5. Soviet Union—
Social life and customs—1917–   6. Russian Americans—Biography.
7. United States—Biography.   I. Title.
[CT1217.S56S56   1990]
929.7′7—dc20   89-40092
                                                    CIP

BOOK DESIGN BY CHRIS WELCH
Manufactured in the United States of America
10   9   8   7   6   5   4   3   2   1

*To Nani and the memory of Mopsy—my
remarkable grandmothers—the strong bridges on
which our family crossed to the New World*

Contents

Russian Blood

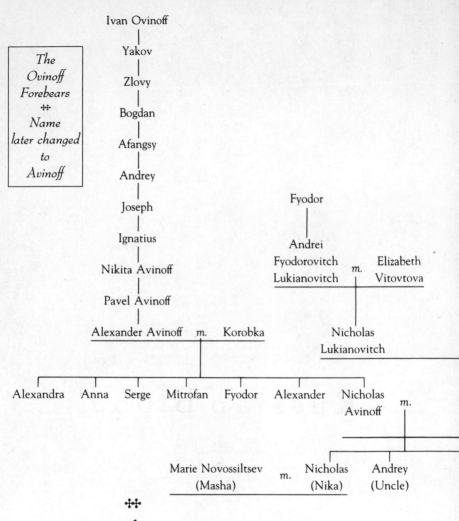

Ivan Ovinoff

Yakov

Zlovy

Bogdan

Afangsy

Andrey

Joseph

Ignatius

Nikita Avinoff

Pavel Avinoff

Fyodor

Andrei
Fyodorovitch   *m.*   Elizabeth
Lukianovitch   Vitovtova

Alexander Avinoff   *m.*   Korobka

Nicholas
Lukianovitch

Alexandra   Anna   Serge   Mitrofan   Fyodor   Alexander   Nicholas
Avinoff   *m.*

Marie Novossiltsev   *m.*   Nicholas   Andrey
(Masha)   (Nika)   (Uncle)

✠

The
Avinoff-Shoumatoff
Line

✠

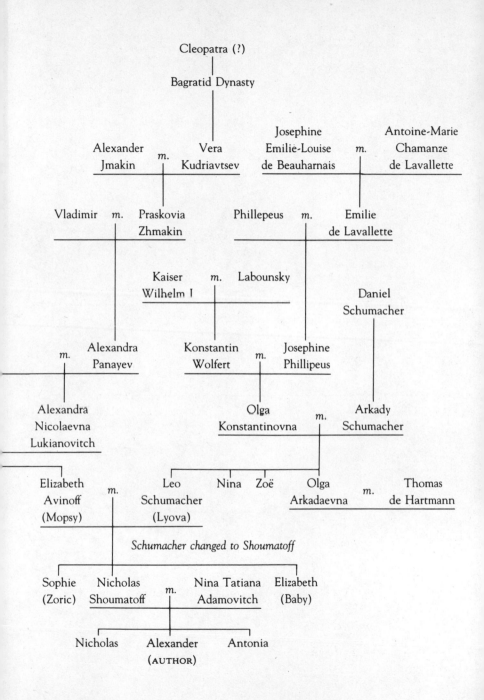

Part One

Mopsy
Leaves Us

We all knew it was coming, but when it came none of us was ready. I'd kept in close touch, talked with her several times a week and driven down to see her whenever I could. It wasn't as if I had to drag myself to Locust Valley. She was fun to be with, "cozy" (the quality that mattered most to her in people). Then one day she just got up from her easel and went into the hospital. Of course we knew she had to die sometime. She was almost ninety-two.

We went back together as far as I can go. Roaring Gap, North Carolina, summer 1950. Mopsy (Her younger daughter, reading about Flopsy, Mopsy and Cottontail in a little book by Beatrix Potter, decided she should be called Mopsy, and that became her family name. Her real name was Elizabeth Shoumatoff. Her friends called her Ellie.) was going to this resort in the Blue Ridge Mountains to paint a number of prosperous southerners—tobacco Reynoldses, Chathams of Chatham blankets, stocking-company Haneses. At the spur of the moment she decided to take me, then her youngest grandchild, along. I was four, just getting the world into focus. I vaguely remember a man in Elizabethan duds handing out samples of a new cigarette (Sir Walter Raleigh, Cavalier?) in front of the Greystone Inn as we went in to dinner.

I clearly recall a drive we took one Saturday morning to Elkin, at the foot of the mountains. I'd complained of a toothache, and the nearest dentist was in Elkin.

Starting in 1941, Mopsy drove a succession of Cadillacs. This Cadillac had big fins because it was the fifties, and made no noise. With the windows up and the air conditioner on, it almost seemed as if we were gliding down to Elkin. Serenely negotiating switchbacks, Mopsy was telling me a story about a witch called Goody Grum, who always said Hoity Toity. I was sitting beside her like a little conspirator, hanging on every word. Anyone who was ever painted by her when they were children can vouch that she was a mesmerizing storyteller. Goody Grum was a character in a British magazine called *Chatterbox*, which Mopsy subscribed to when she was a girl in Russia, but I didn't learn this until much later. I didn't think of Mopsy as being Russian when I was growing up. She was always low-key about the past. There was nothing foreign about her. She didn't have an accent, as my other grandmother, also Russian, did. She spoke a cultivated, continental, neutral sort of English—not American, not English, not Russian, sprinkled with cozy Mopsyisms. "By the by." "Anywho."

Sometimes there would be an opening in the lush Appalachian foliage, and we could see down to the hazy plain where we were headed, or across to the next rib of the Blue Ridge, where there was an abandoned road, probably the old road to Elkin, with grass growing through its cracks. We rounded one bend in time to see a man walking on the abandoned road across a gully slightly below us. "Look, Mopsy," I pointed excitedly. The man was dressed in rags. He had over one shoulder a stick with a bundle hanging from the end of it. Mopsy explained that he was a hobo. I still dream of that hobo from time to time, and nothing in the rest of my life has surpassed the bliss of that spin to Elkin. But when I asked Mopsy about it years later, she couldn't remember it at all.

She developed a special relationship, almost a pact, with each of her four grandchildren. With my sister, it began when she was sitting for the second of the four portraits Mopsy did of her. Tonia was a snow-blond five-year-old, and Mopsy told her how when she was a girl she would get up at six in the morning to weed the garden, and would read the Saints' Lives by candlelight long after she was supposed to be asleep, because she wanted to be good like them. Only the servants knew about her private devotions, and she had sworn them to secrecy. Years later, when Mopsy was invited by Princess Joan of Luxembourg to paint her children,

Charles and Lotti, she took along Tonia and her other grand-daughter, Victoria, and Tonia got to experience her grand-mother from the vantage of young womanhood. It was one of Mopsy's last trips. She was in her late eighties, and in great form. After a sumptuous luncheon (seven plate changes, sculpted potatoes) they were all getting up from the table when Mopsy felt her legs starting to give. Fortunately two men in green livery who had been standing against a wall came up and caught her under either arm. "I beg your pardon," she said to them with her most gracious smile. "I must have caught that heel of mine again." That was Mopsy's only concession to time, an occasional loss of equilibrium, a breakdown of the inner ear.

I first noticed the problem in 1971, at a cocktail party for Svetlana Stalin, who had just defected. It was an emo-tional meeting for Mopsy: Svetlana, after all, was the daugh-ter of the man responsible for the numerous arrests and probably the execution of her oldest brother. Svetlana turned out to be a small woman with a round, compelling face. "Often I think how could it have happened that I was the daughter of such a monster," she was telling Mopsy. "But he was a wonderful father. I only saw that side." Mopsy was listening with her usual rapt attention (she always made you feel important by *really listening* to what you said) when all of a sudden, for no apparent reason, she just fell. "I'm an expert at falling," she laughed as we helped her to her feet. "All I need is a flat surface. I don't even need steps."

Back in their rooms, Mopsy, Tonia, and Victoria told *faits divers* and laughed for hours. Mopsy knew hundreds of them. She collected them. One of her favorites concerned a parrot who greeted people with the words, *charmante soirée.* "One evening, just before a large dinner party," she told her granddaughters that afternoon, "the parrot was attacked by the cat, who pulled it from its cage and took it under the couch. The parrot's mistress was ushering in guests at the time. Just as everyone had seated themselves they heard an awful screech coming from under the couch. The mistress pushed the couch aside just in time to see the parrot being swallowed by the cat. As the last of its head disappeared inside the cat's mouth, the parrot squawked out *charmante soirée* and was gone."

Something prompted Victoria to whisper *charmante soirée* to Tonia as we stood in the Locust Valley Cemetery, listening to the minister say a few last words over Mopsy's ashes. It was a cold, crystal-clear December morning, with limitless horizons. The ground was bare, except for a light dusting of hemlock needles, and the leaves of the rhododendrons, curled and folded like umbrellas, were trembling. There were already three stones in the family plot. One said Andrey Avinoff, 1884–1949, and after his name were the initials of his two honorary doctorates, and Dostoevsky's famous remark, "Beauty Will Save the World." He was Mopsy's brother, a remarkably versatile man who saw the writing on the wall and left Russia in the summer of 1917. He made his mark here as an artist, a scientist, and a museum director. We knew him as Uncle. Another stone said Marie Avinoff, 1882–1975. That was Mopsy's sister-in-law, Masha. She married Nika, the oldest brother, who refused to join Mopsy and her husband on the last trans-Siberian express out of Petrograd in the fall of 1917, before the Bolshevik coup d'etat. Someone had to stay and pick up the pieces, he told them. He helped organize the flow of coal and firewood into Moscow. The Soviets praised him for his dedication and arrested him seven times. During the Yezhov purge of November

1937, he was taken away an eighth time, and Masha never saw him again. He was probably liquidated along with the sixty thousand other victims of that purge. Masha herself did time in the Lubyanka and Butyrka prisons, was exiled to central Asia, and finally released in a small town near the Polish border, a few months before it was overrun by Nazis. After the war she joined Mopsy on Long Island. We became good friends, sharing a love of Pushkin, Goethe, and Flaubert, whom she could spout at length (it was how she had kept her sanity), switching from Russian to German to French without breaking stride. She was a huge, imperious woman, a Scherbatov on her mother's side and a Novossiltsev on her father's. There was a certain way she looked at you, a wistful, whimsical expression, her eyes contriving to seem at once full of sorrow, mischief, boredom, and disdain, which I've often seen in émigrés of that generation.

The third stone was Baby's. It said Elizabeth Bossi, March 19, 1973. Baby was Mopsy's youngest daughter, the one who named her Mopsy. They were very close, more like sisters or college roommates than mother and daughter. They made each other laugh. Baby was killingly funny on a regular basis, and she could be scathing when she wanted to be. Nothing was sacred to her. She was also a beautiful woman, twice married, engaged numerous times; she once stood up a fiancé at the licensing bureau. Mopsy grew tired of having to meet prospective mothers-in-law. Baby was an intensely *human* person, if that means anything. At the New York University Hospital, where she raised money and handled publicity, she was adored. But there was a dark side to her, too. Ten days after the death of a close friend—she had been drinking steadily—she went out the window of her apartment on East Sixty-sixth Street. She was fifty years old.

My brother claims that as the minister was saying "and may the light eternal shine on her," a ray of sunlight came down through the trees on Mopsy's remains, and he no longer felt cold. I didn't notice the ray, but there is a family tradition of such synchronicitous natural displays. On the day Uncle died, a good friend of his was walking in the Ojai Valley in California, when she was suddenly covered with butterflies. Knowing how closely he identified with butterflies, she suspected that he was leaving the world, and when she returned to where she was staying, there was a telegram from Mopsy confirming her premonition. Uncle himself was painting a landscape, and something had just made him put in a dead tree, when he got word that his brother-in-law, Mopsy's husband and my grandfather, had drowned. On a Fourth-of-July picnic on Jones Beach of all things. And my mother claims that at the moment of Mopsy's death—5:03 P.M. the previous Sunday—there had been an unusually spectacular sunset. I didn't catch the sunset either, but I remember— my wife and I were spending the afternoon with some Brazilian writers—suddenly just after five o'clock I went pale and for several moments I was completely out of it, dead to the world. It was noticeable enough for my wife to become worried. At the time I attributed my malaise to overeating and drinking. Now I wonder.

The minister, who was Episcopalian, gave a final blessing, and then we drove to the Our Lady of Kazan Church in Sea Cliff. It was a small wooden church in the style of North Russian wooden churches of the seventeenth century. It was hard to believe that it had started as a garage, as one of the members told me. The beams were lovingly carved in folk motifs, and there were numerous little alcoves with icons and blazing rows of candles. Mopsy had been adamant about not having the full, three-hour Orthodox funeral, in which she would have been displayed in an open coffin. Instead, there was a beautiful hour-long *panehydre*, to "give rest to this soul which had gone to sleep, half-august, half-abject," as the four-part male chorus sang.

Mopsy's faith was the center of everything. It was the one thing that never changed, that insulated her from the slings and arrows of fortune. In every room of her house, generally in the upper right-hand corner as you entered, there was an icon. And every morning, before she was brought her soft-boiled egg, her hot milk and coffee, her toast with Tasmanian honey, and her *New York Times*, she would sit up in bed and read the appropriate entries in both the Daily Word and the Russian Saints' Calendar. There was always a light burning in a little red glass, called a *lampada*, before the several dozen images of her bedroom *kiot*, or corner stand of icons. "The light is a constant source of prayer for everybody," she explained to me once. I had asked about the icons. They were powerful friends, if you believed in them. She had four Virgins. The small, Italianate one, painted on mother-of-pearl, she'd gotten at a monastery near her country house a few days before she left Russia. The Bogoroditsa, Our Lady of the Sign, she'd had in her room since childhood. The seventeenth-century Our Lady of the Burning Bush was entirely covered in silver except the painted face and hands. Its job was to protect the house. The family icon, said to have been given to a fourteenth-century ancestor by two angels, also depicted a standing Virgin. Once I brought the family icon into the living room to look at it in the light. Mopsy was smoking a cigarette. "Please put it back," she asked me. "I can't smoke with it around." She had three icons of St. Spiridonius ("If you want money, pray to him, and the money will come"); one of Panteleimon, the patron saint of physicians; one of Tsilimel, the healer; one of Selica, the patron saint of babies; one of St. Barbara, the patroness of "someone who doesn't want to die suddenly." This last was one of three small traveling icons that had belonged to the late tsar. Uncle had gotten them from his friend Victor Hammer, the art dealer. Beside the *lampada* were some sprigs of pussywillow, which, because of the unavailability of palm fronds in Russia, had always been used at Palm Sunday there. There were several crosses on the table of her *kiot*, too. One was made of olivewood and was a present from her old schoolmate, Valya Svetkova, who became Sister Barbara, Mother Superior of the Mount of Olives Convent in the Garden of Gethsemane. She was Mopsy's best friend at the Pension Constant in St. Petersburg, when they were sixteen.

Mopsy never started a painting without a prayer, and if it was an important one, she would always begin it on a Saturday. "When I was a girl, illustrating stories that I read, like *Quo Vadis*, Mother said, 'You must pray to St. John the Divine. He helps artists.' I did for a while, but then I switched to St. Alypius. I thought he'd be a more reliable saint for help. He was the first Russian artist. He lived in Kiev during the twelfth century, and his bones are buried in the catacombs there. He died in the middle of painting an icon, and an angel came and finished it for him." During her last year, Mopsy still painted daily, but sometimes, when she wasn't feeling up to par, when she was feeling decrepit and her head was heavy, she'd ask St. Alypius to take over. The work was as fine as ever, or better. There was a picture in her studio of St. Alypius at his easel.

Mopsy had given an icon of the Virgin of Kazan to the church at Sea Cliff. She was an important behind-the-scenes patroness, and at odd moments like Friday afternoon she would sometimes go there to pray. She didn't attend the Sunday services. As a rule, she didn't have much to do with the Sea Cliff colony, whose five hundred souls form one of the largest pockets of White Russians in the East. There was a woman in Sea Cliff from whom she bought *pelmene*, Siberian meat dumplings that are a sort of cross between won ton and ravioli. And sometimes, when she was having a party, or on the help's day off, Nadya Vladimirovna, a former cabaret and opera singer, would come over from Sea Cliff and serve the meals. But Mopsy and Uncle had adapted more successfully than most of their ex-compatriots. They were "good sports" about the Revolution. They took the break in their destinies as a challenge and, right at the beginning, got down to the business of becoming American. By the thirties they were off and away, while many of their fellow-exiles were still huddled together and living in the past.

I noticed at the church several similarly resilient Russians whom I'd met at Mopsy's house. Old Storozhev stole up to the iconostasis with a large flower arrangement. His father, a local priest in Ekaterinburg, had conducted the last service for Nicholas II and his family, on the evening they were shot. Prince Serge Troubetzkoy, a cousin of Masha's, was standing unobtrusively at the rear. He had that special attentiveness one meets in Russians of the old school. Mopsy had been very fond of him. Katya Alexeyeva was there, too. Her father had been a classmate of Uncle's at the Imperial Law College. Except for them, and a few other old Russians whom I didn't know, most of the fifty or so people in the church were there for the first time. For their benefit the handsome, bearded young *batyushka* conducted the key parts of the service in English. He described how vigilantly Mopsy had listened to his prayers when he visited her at the hospital, and how, "in that ancient Orthodox gesture of faith," she had reached for the cross around his neck. He and my father had been the last ones to see her alive. My brother and I had gone down on the previous Wednesday. My cousin Victoria had called and said she was going fast, we'd better come right away. Mopsy had entered the hospital four weeks earlier to be treated for some kind of intestinal blockage. The doctor had operated and found cancer. The cancer was inoperable. He had estimated that she could still live a year, at the outside, and had started her on chemotherapy. By the time we got there she was unrecognizable. Her mouth was dry and cracked, scalded and dyed purple from gentian drops applied to relieve an irritation that was due either to the chemotherapy or to a protein deficiency. It was just hanging open, and there were tubes running into her nose. "Who would have thought it would end like this?" she had managed to say to Victoria a few days before. *

Now she was scarcely able to speak, and had trouble recognizing people. The room was dark, and a handsome black nurse, who must have had a lot of deathbed experience, because she projected just the right amount of strength, forbearance, and tenderness, was sitting beside her. Mopsy was lying on her back with her eyes closed. Her breathing was terribly congested. I won't soon forget the sound of her breathing. It was obvious from it, and from the deflated condition of her body, that she wasn't going to make it. We stood for several minutes, trying to adjust to the sight, not knowing if we should disturb her. Finally I put my hand on

---

* Her last words were to the nurse: "Would you please fix me up. I may have a visitor soon and I want to look nice."

hers—the delicate, liver-spotted right hand, with the long fingers and the crook at the first joint of the forefinger, where she had held the brush that had produced so many paintings. She opened her eyes, and seeing two blurred figures standing over her, slowly recognized that it was us. She smiled, or rather her large, soft, warm brown eyes shone. I tried to think of something to say. You've meant so much to me. I'll never forget you. But they all seemed lame and graceless, and I couldn't bring myself to say anything. My brother, who knows how to say the right thing, said, "You've brought happiness to so many *thousands* of people." She raised her hand slowly and made a thin space between her thumb and forefinger, as if to say, "So little, I've done so little in my life." A bit later she raised her hand and blessed us, making the sign of the cross in the air, as she had so often before, standing in front of her house as we backed down the driveway. My brother noticed that she was trying to tell us something. We leaned close. Her whispered words were scarcely audible. *"Do skorovo. A bientôt."* Then a kind of glaze crept over her, and the room was silent except for the struggle of her breathing.

About twenty of us, relations and close friends, went on to the house, where her oldest daughter, Zoric, had arranged for there to be food and drink. I spoke with John, who tended the rose garden, who filled with thistle seed the clear plastic cylinder that hung from the birch tree and brought goldfinches all summer long, who was on call whenever a fuse blew, a pipe burst, a door stuck. "I was with her forty-three years," he told me. "She always said, 'If anything happened to Johnny, I'd sell the place.' " John had started working for her when she was still living at Hidden Hollow, a big house with an undulating slate roof at the bottom of the hill. After

Uncle died—her children had already gone off on their own—she didn't need all that space, and being a great believer in simplicity, she bought this ranch house. It was an unusually tactful ranch, sitting in the shade of its low roof, with brown shingle siding, a varied border of evergreen shrubs, ivy climbing the brick entry. The commercial strips and the coagulated expressway for which Long Island is known were only minutes away, but Mopsy's lot, on a quiet, secluded street in Locust Valley, was like an oasis. When the country was in its terrible sixties, and I was in my terrible twenties, I used to go to Mopsy's to escape from the wildness and craziness. That she was there, serenely turning out one exquisite portrait after another, was important to me, and to the others who drew on her energy.

The house grew. A studio, a guest room, a wing for Masha, when she arrived from Paris, quarters for the cook-housekeeper were added. The house grew, yet it remained cozy. Its décor was a study in quiet good taste. Mopsy broke away from the cluttered, fruitcake richness of the interiors she had known as a child, but there was still, not surprisingly, a distinctly Russian flavor to the house. There was a lot of malachite, the opaque green stone with black swirls—a semiprecious form of copper ore—that was quarried extensively in the Urals during imperial times and carved into all kinds of objects. Mopsy had a replica of the famous statue of Peter the Great on his rearing horse that overlooks the Neva River in Leningrad. Its base was malachite. So was the base of her bronze head of Nicholas the First. When Masha's first cousin, Sophie Troubetzkoy, was visiting a few years back, she noticed the head of Nicholas and came out with a flabbergasting bit of gossip: that he wasn't the son of Emperor Paul at all, but of a handsome admiral named Klokachov. "Now you mustn't spread that around," Mopsy had warned me. "It would shake the world. If it's true, then the Romanoffs . . . aren't the Romanoffs!"

Mopsy also had a mantel clock, an urn, and a tabletop of malachite. The shelves in the glass cabinet of her antique secretary contained an assortment of prerevolutionary bric-a-brac: Fabergé eggs, lacquered boxes with miniature Russian folk tales painted on them, silver cigarette cases, mother-of-pearl opera glasses, one of twelve cups that Alexander the First had made in Paris for his generals. Most of the pictures in the house were flowers with butterflies that Uncle had done. He was considered by such discriminating observers of art as John Walker and Helen Clay Frick as the finest flower painter of this century.

"His art was the art of a high culture, such as Russia had, for a limited number of people who were, in a sense, dilettantish," Walker said. "It bore no relation to the art that was being done by the significant artists of the twentieth century. But in just sheer technical bravura of the type that he practiced—accurate delineation, fairly dry wash, and so on, no one could surpass him."

Over the mantel was an Old Dutch bouquet he had been working on when he died. Only the butterflies—a tiger swallowtail and a tortoiseshell—and the flower heads had been painted in. On other walls hung his roses with butterflies, his orchids with butterflies. The hallway leading to the dining room had some of his Jamaican landscapes—tree ferns and waterfalls, air plants and languidly flapping heliconiine butterflies, and the sun-drenched hillsides of the Cockpit Country, frothing with rain forest. Uncle and my father had been, during the thirties, the first lepidopterists to set foot in the

Cockpit Country of west-central Jamaica. They had charmed the Maroons, descendants of escaped slaves who had fled there in the eighteenth century, and the Maroons were not usually receptive to "outers." One of the new butterflies they caught was named for my father, Shoumatoff's hairstreak. Butterflies were more than a hobby for Uncle; they were his lifelong passion. Before the Revolution he had financed forty-two collecting expeditions and had himself trekked into the remote fastnesses of Ladakh and western Tibet in search of new species. By 1917 he had more than eighty thousand specimens in his collection, one of the largest ever made by a private individual. Uncle continued to do important lepidopterological work here, but perhaps it would have been even more important if he hadn't been separated from that fabulous collection.

Mopsy didn't share Uncle's scientific interest in butterflies, but she liked to have them around. They had warm associations. She had butterflies on her mailbox, on her soap and towels, on her matches and ashtrays, on her curtains, table-mats, toilet-seat covers and china. In the dining room there was a triptych of Uncle's in which the Uranea moth, a black, day-flying species with swallowtails and opalescent green bars, and several spectacular tropical butterflies are gliding over a crumbled, vine-smothered ruin. The paintings were inspired by a poem called "Butterflies," by a friend of Uncle's, Haniel Long. Mopsy recited it to me once. I could tell from the tremble in her voice how much it moved her.

> *There will be butterflies*
> *There will be summer skies*
> *And flowers upthrust*

> When all that Caesar bids
> And all the pyramids
>   Are dust.
>
> There will be gaudy wings
> Over the bones of things
>   And never grief
> Who says that summer skies
> Who says that butterflies
>   Are brief?

There was even a small clouded sulphur in the house, pains-takingly painted in watercolor from a specimen caught and mounted by the artist, who is identified by the austere initials, A. S., and was none other than me, aged ten. How hard I'd tried to reproduce the basal smudges on its lemon wings, and in the end, by painting over them too many times, made them dull and muddy, *trop lâché*, nothing like the vibrant, fresh colors of Uncle's insects, but still not bad for a kid.

Most of the people who had come back to the house were in the dining room, eating and drinking, laughing (some of the women through tears) and telling Mopsy stories. Zoric was sitting in a daze, exhausted by everything she'd had to attend to the past week. The atmosphere in the dining room was almost festive. Though no one came out and said it, we all knew that gaiety was the correct response. She would have liked it that way. And hadn't she had a long, marvelous life and gone peacefully to her reward? If there was a hereafter (and she was convinced that she would soon be reunited with her mother, Uncle, Baby, Masha, all her departed friends and dear ones), we all would have nominated her for a high place in it. I couldn't accept that her consciousness had ended. It must still be functioning somewhere, in some form, at the very least, within all those she had touched. Even now, eight years after her death, she still appears at off moments in my waking hours. This room, for instance, was so permeated with her laughter that I could almost hear her joining in whenever one of the clusters of conversationalists, remembering a funny story about her, bubbled into merriment. Her laughter was a wild release that involved her whole being and everyone within hearing range. Like the mad gobble of a pileated woodpecker erupting in the woods, once you had heard it, you didn't forget it.

I could see her now at the head of the dining room table, presiding over the party she always gave on Russian Easter, beaming benevolently over the tall cylinders of *kulich*, the pyramids of *paskha*, the piles of painted eggs, the platters of roast ham and turkey galantine. I had had a presentiment the previous Easter that this would be our last one with her. On the way home I had asked my brother and sister who was going to kiss us three times on either cheek after Mopsy died, and say *Christos voskresye*, Christ is risen, to which the proper rejoinder was a hearty *voistinu voskresye*, Indeed he has risen. Where would we get *kulich*, the golden pastry filled with bits of dried fruit and tasting somewhat like the Italian *panettone*? Or even more ambrosial *paskha*, the rich, soft, sweet cheese filled with raisins and pistachios? Without Mopsy to pull it together for us, this last vestige of Russianness would undoubtedly slip out of our lives, or at best would become an empty ritual.

I sat with Edith, the last of her cook-housekeepers, a sunny blond Norwegian woman of about fifty. She'd been with Mopsy four years, driving her to look at the sea or to buy a new house plant (something rare and striking was always in bloom at the living room window, and there was an exuberance of potted vegetation in almost every room), drinking a split of champagne with her at the cocktail hour if there wasn't company, sharing the same life without closing the distance defined by their relationship, gradually becoming, as all the women who worked for Mopsy did, her confidante. "I think I came to know her as well as anybody," Edith said. She was taking it pretty badly, looking out the window with eyes swollen from crying. "There are people here who wouldn't have entered the house if she were alive," she said bitterly. She was referring to a family, one of whose daughters Mopsy had painted a few years back; although they still hadn't paid for the portrait and no one had invited them, all four of them were whooping it up in the dining room. "But I suppose it's all right. She would forgive them." Then Edith looked at the bare trees bordering the lawn and said, "I'm so glad she got to see the leaves this fall."

I talked, too, with Nora Harris, who had lived across the street for more than thirty years. She asked who was going to see that Mopsy's memoirs were published, what would happen to her little silver paintbox, would there be a retrospective at the Frick or at Knoedler's? Mopsy never had a real show. Once a few of her portraits were displayed at a local gallery, along with work by Uncle, Zoric, Victoria, and my brother. The exhibit was called "Three Generations of Shoumatoff Artists." But she did that as a favor to the owner. Only a handful of her more than three thousand portraits are on public view. The Locust Valley Public Library has one she did of its founder. The Frick Collection has a small watercolor of Henry Clay's wife. The White House has her portraits of Franklin Roosevelt and Lyndon Johnson (she was approached about doing Nixon, but refused). The famous unfinished portrait of Roosevelt—he went into a coma during the second sitting and died from a cerebral hemorrhage a few hours later—hangs in the Little White House in Warm Springs, Georgia. That painting thrust her into the loathsome glare of publicity. There was even speculation that she was a Soviet agent (she had a Russian name, right?) and had done him in.

People were always after her for the details about the relationship between FDR and Lucy Rutherford. Lucy, who had arranged the portrait, died in 1949, but Mopsy never betrayed that friendship. As a friend and as a businesswoman, she had total discretion. She never used an agent. Work came to her strictly by word of mouth. She gracefully side-stepped the hustle of having to "make it" as an artist, yet at the height of her career, she was making up to ten thousand dollars a week. That career spanned sixty years. During it she got to be on intimate terms with Firestones, Fords, Mellons. She documented that well-established, subtly interconnected group who pretty much ran the show in this country during the first half of the century, and whose offspring still have a good deal to say about what goes on; she became one of the two or three most sought-after portraitists of that era. Having a watercolor by Madame Shoumatoff in your living room was a sign of good taste and of membership in a very exclusive group. There were two portraitists Mopsy most admired: Madame Vigée-Lebrun, the court painter of Marie Antoinette and Catherine the Great; and Peter Sokoloff, who painted the notables during the reign of Nicholas I. The cultural niche she eventually filled here was comparable to theirs. Like them, she painted the good families, the captains of industry, the heads of state. It was a Sokoloff portrait of Masha's grandmother, a Princess Scherbatov, that got her started. Masha asked her to copy it. Soon she was doing enlarged miniatures, in the manner of Sokoloff, of her family and friends, so detailed that every hair was visible. She worked best in watercolor, and gradually perfected a technique of laying color on color that was unique in the history of the medium. No other aquarellist approaches her control, comes close to her skin tones or her eyes. She captured the essence of the person through the eyes. Her eyes are uncanny. They seem to jump from the paper.

Whether it was art that she was doing is an interesting question. I don't think she herself cared. She didn't keep up with what was going on in the art world or try to be associated with it. She didn't worry about being contemporary. Both she and Uncle were throwbacks to a more pictorial, representational endeavor that has largely been displaced by the camera. The photograph is more accurate, but something has been lost: the patience, the care, the coming to terms with the subject that their sort of painting required. Mopsy and Uncle were deeply perceptive in a way I don't expect people will ever be again. Certainly in their dedication, and their concern with technique, they were artists. And Mopsy wasn't concerned just with the painting, but with the total presentation. She was fussy about the matting, and supervised the framing to the utmost. "A frame, like a good dress, must not be noticed," she told me once. And while she was still able, she would always go to the subject's house, not only to see where the portrait was going to hang, but to examine the habitat.

I was once asked by someone who didn't know her if there was any sadness to the fact that someone whose family had owned two villages and thousands of acres had been reduced to making flattering portraits of rich capitalists. I explained that it wasn't like that at all. Her work wasn't a chore to which she had been degraded. There was a high purpose to it. It was almost like icon-painting. She gave her subjects a radiance and a graciousness that they might only have had once a year. She brought out a side of them that they may not even have seen in themselves, but they recognized it instantly, and were grateful to her. If that was flattery, she was guilty of it. To me it was legitimate. What nicer gift could you make to someone? Her deft little cosmetic touches were harder to defend against the charge of flattery, but on the other hand, *they* were art. She was known to give tactful nose-jobs when the situation was utterly hopeless, or (as in the case of her last portrait of me) more chin than you really had to make up for a deficiency. But that was part of her positive outlook. On her living room coffee table there was an ivory carving of three little monkeys covering their ears, eyes, or mouth with their hands. Hear no evil, see no evil, speak no evil—she fended off tragedy with brilliant success by the simple expedient of snubbing it, of refusing to admit that it even existed.

✣   ✣   ✣

Most of the Mopsy stories that were being told in the dining room I'd heard at one time or other. For the past two years I'd been collecting every bit of information about her that I could. She, of course, was my main informant. This had been my way of preparing for her death. I had felt uniquely placed and chosen, as the writer in the family, to document the beautiful, charming world of which she was the only survivor, before it slipped out of our ken forever. Sometimes I would feel pleased with myself for beating death to her wonderful memories. But now I could see the futility of that:

the memories she had left me were like the transparent cas-
ings that cicadas leave fastened on the sides of trees; the
creatures had flown away irretrievably. There was so much
more she'd promised to tell me; now I'd never know. I felt
deserted by her dying. But she had been as much help as she
could.

Part Two

Shideyevo

Uncle had an interest in genealogy. In a fine, elegant hand—his own calligraphy—he had made long charts, mapping his antecedents to well before Christ. He was quite certain he was related to Cleopatra—collaterally, through her brother—and when Mopsy was going through his effects after his death, she found a sheet of paper, folded into an inch-and-a-half square, on which he had written, "These people could be our ancestors." Inside were two ancient, small gold coins, stamped with the faces of a man and a woman. Scrutinizing the fine Greek print with a magnifying glass, Mopsy realized that the man was Jesus Christ, and the woman the Virgin Mary.

I didn't think much about my ancestors until I had children, and saw that I was part of a progression. Uncle was acutely aware of that progression because he had no children, and he knew that when he died, an old boyar name dating to the previous millennium would become extinct. Mopsy had given up the Avinoff name by marrying. Nika and Masha had been childless, and Nika was almost certainly dead. So that left Uncle. The name Avinoff comes from the Russian word for barn, *ovin*, which may in turn have derived from *ovis*, the Latin word for sheep. When Uncle met a man named Barnes in Boston in 1916, he astounded the man by clapping him on the shoulder and saying, "But you're my relative!" The Ovins and the Ovinoffs were a leading family in the city of Novgorod. Uncle always said that one of the four men—Sloven, Krivich, Mer, and Chug—who brought Rurik from across the Baltic Sea in 854 was an Ovin. Rurik was one of those marauding Scandinavians (variously called the Normans, Vikings, Varangians, and Rus) who traveled by water and had by that time already reached the farthest corners of the known world. Sloven and the others belonged to a tribe of semi-nomadic Slavs, hunters and fishermen from Neolithic times, who lived along the Volkhov River. They had to pay tribute to the Scandinavians whenever they passed through and were constantly at war with other tribes in the vicinity. Rurik came at their invitation to stabilize their lives. He built a "new city" of wood—Novgorod—just below where the Volkhov River comes out of Lake Ilmen. He gave them laws. He was the Father of Russia. Anybody who was anybody in Old Russia was descended from Rurik. The Obolenskys, the Scherbatovs (Masha's people), and ten other families were princely lines issuing from Rurik. My mother can trace herself to him through one of her great-grandmothers, a woman named Vsevolodsky.

Too far north to attract the Mongols, and on a well-traveled river road to Byzantium, Novgorod was beautifully sited. In 907 Rurik's grandson Oleg, vastly overestimating his strength, sent ten thousand Novgorodians to attack Constantinople. The Byzantines repelled them with ease, and retaliated by gradually undermining their faith, which took about a century. "The Greeks led us into the buildings where they worship their god," emissaries of Vladimir, the Prince of Kiev, reported in 980, "and we knew not whether we were in heaven or earth." Kiev was the sister city of Novgorod, and eight years later everyone in both cities was baptized. Many Novgorodians were confirmed pagans and had to be forced to enter the Volkhov. The stone idol of Perun, the sun god, was taken from its place and thrown into the river. Volos, the pagan patron of cattle, was renamed St. Vlasii but allowed to keep his function. From then on the people of Novgorod worshiped icons, and each street struggled to put up the handsomest onion-domed church.

By 1100 the city was making alliances with other commercial powers along the Baltic. One of their ambassadors, I found out in Novgorod, was an ancestor, Felix Ovinoff. His seal appears on a diplomatic document found in Lübeck, Germany, and dated May 7, 1338, and on a trade agreement with the Swedish island of Gottland. His stone house was on Ilinsky Street, near the Church of the Transfiguration. It was excavated in 1962, and a cache of Arabic coins was found in the basement.

When Novgorod became an independent boyar republic in 1138, it was one of the most powerful cities in medieval Europe. Thirty thousand people were crowded within its walls, and its territory extended north to the White Sea. The open land was divided into ten military-financial districts called *tma*, or "thousands," which were in turn subdivided into *sotnya*, or "hundreds." The *sotnya* fanned out from Novgorod for a radius of several hundred miles and were run as feudal estates by a few families, one of which was the Ovinoffs. The chronicles of Novgorod have much to say about a certain Gregory Kirilovitch Ovinoff. In 1417 he was elected to the position of *posadnik*, or burgomeister. In 1433 he built the stone church of St. John Christatome. In 1435 he fought with Sigismund, the Grand Duke of Lithuania, with whom he made peace a year later. He owned a silver cup that is famous in the history of Russian decorative art, and is now one of the treasures of the Moscow Kremlin. In the Novgorod Kremlin there is a large icon called "Praying Novgorodians," which has a full-length portrait of a man beneath whom is the name Gregory Kirilovitch Posakhno. The man has high cheekbones, a long beard, a long coat of chain mail, and is leaning on a crooked staff. Posakhno, which means "crooked staff," was Gregory Ovinoff's nickname. His cousin, Shepelo Osipovitch Ovinoff, was nicknamed Skovorodnik, which means "the frying-pan man." The Ovinoff *sotnya* extended to the Gulf of Finland and included the land on which, three centuries later, Peter the Great would build his Peterhof and Tsarskoye Selo palaces. (A point that I couldn't resist making to the relentlessly anti-capitalist guide, a prim blonde named

Tanya, who escorted my wife and me to the Peterhof. Gesturing at the palace's gold cupolas, which had red stars on them instead of Orthodox crosses, I said in the most offhanded tone I could muster, "You know, we used to own this place." She blanched and disapproved of me even more.)

Gregory Ovinoff had three sons—Zachary, Cosmo, and Ivan. The first two were elected *posadniks* after him, but by the time they took office, the republic was in trouble. Moscow to the south and Lithuania to the west were beginning to eclipse Novgorod as military and commercial powers, and some form of appeasement was necessary. The boyars inclined to Lithuania, while the peasants and the clergy, despising Catholicism, favored alliance with Moscow. In 1471 a force of Novgorodians engaged some Muscovites at Sholon. Cosmo Ovinoff was taken prisoner and exiled to the government of Kolonye, but after several years he was allowed to return to Novgorod and resume his duties as *posadnik*. In 1475 he and his brother received a visit from the Grand Duke of Moscow, Ivan the Third. On January fourteenth of the following year Ivan returned, and the brothers Ovinoff gave a solemn dinner in his honor. Later they gave him forty sable furs, five measures of Dutch linen, thirty sovereigns, one barrel of red wine, and one of white. But under the show of hospitality, there was a lot of tension. The *vieche* (the republic's most advanced feature, an assembly in which every class was represented) was split into two factions. One was for consolidation with Moscow, the other against. Those who favored independence were led by a woman named Marfa Posadnitsa (which simply means "the woman *posadnik*"). She may have been married to Zachary or Cosmo. In any case, they all wanted Novgorod to stay free. May 31, 1477, was "a day of unrest," according to the chronicles. Zachary and Cosmo were seized in the archbishop's yard by pro-Moscow crowds, dragged to the Great Bridge, and thrown into the Volkhov River. This was the preferred method of execution in Nov-gorod. To be thrown into water was considered shameful, and because the clothes of the period were heavy and no one could swim, fatal. If the victim sank right away the watchers said he had been heavy with sin. If he floated back to the surface, it was said that he was such a sinner the river wouldn't take him. The middle of the Volkhov is deep and never freezes. Sir Donald Mackenzie Wallace, who spent a few years in Novgorod at the end of the last century, noted a "curious bubbling" there. The Great Bridge was destroyed in the last war, to slow advancing Germans. Only its stumps remain.

What happened to the third brother, Ivan Ovinoff, is not told in the chronicles. Shortly after the execution of Zachary and Cosmo, Ivan the Third came in force and de-clared Novgorod an appanage of Moscow. He ordered the great bell that called the citizens to the *vieche* to be taken to Moscow. It was an important symbol and, according to legend, unable to bear the disgrace, it fell from the wagon on the way to Moscow and shattered into a multitude of small bells. Ivan banished a hundred boyar families. The Ovinoff estates were given to one I. A. Bistukhov. The widows of Zachary and Cosmo fled to the government of Kostroma, northeast of Moscow, where they had kin. It was left to Ivan the Terrible (grandson of the Third) to finish off Lord Novgorod the Great, as the city was called, a century later. He invited all the remaining boyars to a solemn feast, then had them thrown off the Great Bridge. When the purge was over, something like five thousand Novgorodians were dead. A dove flying over the St. Sophia is said to have turned to stone at the sight of such carnage. The petrified bird is still there, frozen to the tallest cross.

In Kostroma, there is a big lake called Galitch. Another branch of the family lived on its shore. Several books about the icons and monasteries of Old Russia describe a vision boyar Ivan Ovin had one Sunday when he was walking along the lake. The incident took place while Dmitrii Donskoi was the Grand Duke of Moscow, around the time of the Battle of Kulikovo, which was fought to rid Russia of the Tatar yoke. That would make it about 1380. It was a time when miracles occurred with some regularity. Two young men, far too handsome to be from earth, met Ovin in the road and gave him an icon. "This icon is from your late wife, who wants you to build a monastery here," they said. Ovin did as he was told. In late imperial times, the Paisievsky Monastery, as it was called, was for men of the third *chin*. There were thirteen *chini* in the Imperial Table of Ranks. Upon reaching the tenth *chin* (collegiate secretary, lieutenant, midshipman), you were admitted to the nobility. The third *chin* was made up of privy councillors, lieutenant generals, and vice-admirals.

The main attraction of the Paisievsky Monastery was its wonder-working icon. It was called the Avinovskaya icon. Until the Revolution a photograph of Mopsy's parents, Nicholas and Alexandra Avinoff, stood on the altar below it. The Avinovskaya icon is of the Bogomateri, or Mother-of-God type. To the left it shows the Virgin Mary, in red and blue robes, standing on a golden pedestal and holding her baby. The child neither grazes her cheek nor gazes adoringly at her, but coolly, detachedly, like a miniature adult, faces the spectator. This attitude is known as the Hodigitria position. The Virgin and Child were depicted by Russian iconographers in some three hundred positions. The three most common ones, still known by name to most Russians, were Eleousa, Hodigitria, and Orans. In the upper right-hand corner of the Avinovskaya icon, set off from the rest of the picture by swirling ochre nimbuses, is a second representation of Christ as a bearded man, sitting on a dais with a lighted candle in his left hand, and the first finger of the right pointing didactically. Fluttering to his right are three blue-winged cherubs. To his left are three pink-winged cherubs. Shimmering behind the Virgin is a golden city with many cupolas. At the bottom of the icon, on the shore of a lake, is the city again, with a stout kremlin wall and fewer domes. This is Kitezh, which is said to have sunk spontaneously into Lake Galitch rather than let itself be taken by the Mongols. Later the city rose out of the lake and was physically translated into heaven. The legend inspired Rimsky-Korsakov's choral opera, *The Tale of the Invisible City of Kitezh.*

In 1433, during a battle between the Prince of Galitch and Grand Duke Vasily the Blind, the Avinovskaya icon was taken to Moscow, where even though under heavy guard, it managed to slip away and return to the Paisievsky Monastery. From then on its reputation was golden. It became the goal of pilgrimages, and several miraculous healings were credited to it. In Moscow I tried to find out what had happened to it. Since the Revolution there had been no word of its fate. I applied to Intourist, the state tourist monopoly, for an excursion to the Paisievsky Monastery, but was told that Lake Galitch was off the authorized tourist route, that I would need a special visa requiring several days to process, that I would have to return the same day because there were no hotels out there, that it would take sixteen hours to drive there and back, and that I would probably not find a guide willing to go with me. I went to the Tretyakov Gallery and met with the curator of its icon collection, a cultivated, silver-haired woman named Nadezhda Rosanova. She remembered having passed along Lake Galitch fifteen years before, "but there was nothing. No monastery. No icon. Many of our treasures, as you know, perished in the Revolution. My own feeling about your icon, I'm afraid, is that it is nowhere." It was lucky that there was a copy of the Avinovskaya icon in Mopsy's house, which she took to America.

During the sixteenth century there isn't much about the Ovins except their names. But they are great names: Yakov, Zlovy, Bogdan, Afanasy. At the beginning of the seventeenth century the first Avinoff appears. His name was Andrey, which was also the name of the last. The new spelling is probably a geographical adaptation. Vowels don't travel well, especially unstressed *o*'s to central Russia, where the national tendency to pronounce them like *a*'s is intensified by the flatness of the regional accent.

This Andrey Avinoff, a landowner in the village of Kosimov, had a son Joseph who had a son Prokofii whose brother Ignatius (bear with me) fought in the Crimean War of 1687– 88. Ignatius's son Nikita had three sons. Gregory had no children, and neither did his brother Peter; but Ivan Nikitich, a clerk in the Moscow Chancellory, had Andrey and Paul before dying at a ripe age in 1777. Paul died a young man in 1786, but left a son, Alexander, who was born on March eighteenth of that year, for whom big things were in store. Alexander Pavlovitch's widowed mother took him to be brought up by an uncle who entered him in the service of Catherine the Great. He was ten and a page in her court when the empress died.

At the age of nineteen, as a visiting Russian midshipman, young Avinoff was present at the Battle of Trafalgar. On June 4, 1819, he signed on as senior officer of the *Discovery*, a Russian ship whose mission was much like that of Darwin's *Beagle* a few years later, to sail around the world, mapping unknown coastline. Setting forth from Kamchatka, she headed north through the Bering Strait and proceeded into the Arctic Sea, but at the seventy-second parallel encountered solid ice, and unable to find a passage to the Atlantic, she turned back. Even so, they were at sea for a year. A second expedition was mounted with Avinoff in command. Its mission was to map the Alaskan coast between capes Newenham and Derby. Much of the Pacific Northwest was first charted by Russians, and as a result the shoreline of Alaska bristles with names such as Tolstoy Point, Kotzebue Sound, Golovin Bay, Cape Romanzof. Just below the sixtieth parallel, east of Nunivak Island, an insignificant nub of land juts into the Etolin Strait. Its name is Cape Avinof. (Note the single *f*, a simple attempt at transliteration. The double *f* would not come into vogue until the 1920s, when it was adopted by thousands of exiles, the Shoumatoffs and Uncle among them, who were gallicizing, teutonizing, or anglicizing their names. Vladimir Nabokov called the double *f* a "continental fad" and wouldn't have anything to do with it.) On recent maps, instead of Cape Avinof, the word Kipnuk is likely to appear. Kipnuk is the largest of five native villages on the cape. It is the only one with an airstrip, map status, and a telephone number, which I dialed one morning, direct from Westchester County. An Eskimo man answered. He sounded unimpressed by my claim to be the great-great-grandson of the man for whom Cape Avinof was named, and when I asked about the population of Kipnuk, he became suspicious. "I'm not going to tell you anything unless you send me a hundred thousand dollars first," he said. "We're no dumbbells out here."

In spite of several bad storms Avinoff managed to finish the survey and to deliver ship and crew safely to the port of Petropavlovsk. The rest of his naval career was full of glory. He died on September 30, 1854. Apparently he felt that having restored the family to some prominence, he was entitled to alter its coat of arms, for he substituted its princely crown and mantle with a Navy cannon and phoenix rising out of flames, which Mopsy, his granddaughter, thought was hideous.

Between cruises he fathered ten children. The photograph of him and his wife with the seven who reached adulthood (missing are Ivan and Michael, who died young, and Vassily, who drowned in the harbor of Piraeus) is a classic mid-nineteenth-century family group. The men are all in uniform, the most splendid of which, of course, with its admiral's epaulets, is that of the paterfamilias, a small, intensely fit-looking man with stylish white muttonchops. The oldest daughter, Alexandra, married a Major General Ridinger. Anna, her sister, stayed single. She had plenty of admirers, but somehow frightened them whenever they were about to propose. Her last beau had a wooden leg. Anna lived with her brother Serge, who was caught when he was a general with the wife of his regimental commander. There was a divorce, and Serge married the woman. Later, in the Caucasus, he made a fortune in real estate. His brother Mitrofan married and had two daughters. The first married Eugene Anichkov. Their daughter Elizabeth, a vivacious beauty in the last days of St. Petersburg, was shot in a detention camp on the Yenisei in 1942. Her cousin Vasily was shot in the

Lubyanka Prison in 1927. By chance, Alexander Solzhenitsyn obtained photographs of them. Their appealing faces,
randomly selected from the hundreds of thousands who died
in the purges, are reproduced in *The Gulag Archipelago*, "so
that at least these deaths would have left a small scar on our
hearts." Mitrofan's other daughter, Lila Mitrofanovna, married a man named Badminsky, who was one of the tsarevitch's
many doctors. Mopsy remembers him visiting the house and
telling of Rasputin's astonishing power to stop the boy's at-
tacks of hemophilia. Fyodor, Alexander Avinoff's next
child, married the daughter of Admiral Vasiliev, his father's
commanding officer on the first voyage of the *Discovery*, but
ran away on his wedding night. The woman may have been
well-connected, but her ugliness was inexorable. "I can't see
her in a night bonnet," Fyodor sobbed to his mother. He
became a gentleman-in-waiting at the court. Mopsy remembered him as "just a playboy." Alexander, or Sasha, another
son, married Florence Washington Wright, a second great-
niece of George Washington. They met at a lavish ball in
Philadelphia that was given in 1863 for officers of the visiting
Russian Navy. A few months earlier, the finest ships in the
Russian fleet had suddenly appeared in New York and San
Francisco harbors. The Americans had interpreted it as a
gesture of support for the Union, and given the Russians a
tumultuous welcome. In fact, as documents released years
later would reveal, the ships were sent there because Alexander II feared they were about to be trapped in their home
ports by the combined navies of Britain, France, and Austria,
who were upset with the tsar's treatment of the Poles during
their recent rebellion. Sasha and Florence honeymooned at
Niagara Falls, which were "big," he reported to the family
when he returned with her to St. Petersburg. Several years

later, in 1867, Sasha's life was cut short by pneumonia. Florence went back to Philadelphia, but corresponded with her sister-in-law Anna for fifteen years. There were no children from the union. In fact, of all the admiral's sons, the only one who would perpetuate the Avinoff name was Nicholas, his last child, who in the photograph is still in the velvet and ruffles of boyhood. Nicholas was Mopsy's father.

In 1730 the Russian empire extended only to the northern edge of Little Russia, as the Ukraine was then called, to where the wooded steppe gave way to billowing feathergrass. Crimea still belonged to the Tatars, who periodically swarmed into Little Russia from their villages near the Black Sea. To defend the empire from their raids, Empress Anna ordered a fortified barrier to be put up along its southern border. Known as the Azov line, it was a kind of Chinese wall, with ramparts that extended for hundreds of miles, and twenty regiments of Cossacks stationed along it. By 1774, the Tatars had been tamed, and the border of Russia pushed to the Black Sea. In January 1787 Catherine the Great, with Prince Potemkin, her favorite, set out on their famous grand tour of the newly acquired territory. Both were getting on, and were no longer interested in each other physically. She had already started taking other, younger men, but kept him on because he was good company and knew about matters of state. The imperial party traveled in fourteen maisonettes on runner, Henri Troyat tells us. Each was pulled by eight to ten horses, with three windows on each side, and furnished with divans, pillows, rugs, and tables. Following the maisonettes were sixty-four more modest sleds, and preceding them was a cloud of servants and advance-men who billeted houses, erected wooden palaces, and hastily filled them with furniture, prepared feasts, roused the local populace to turn out and cheer the empress, lit bonfires to point the way across the desolate white expanse, and even, at Potemkin's insistence, threw up false villages here and there, charming little *trompe-l'oeils* to make the steppe seem more prosperous than it was.

Following the old Azov line, the maisonettes were gliding one day through the district of Kobelyaki, in the government of Poltava. The now abandoned ramparts had been built along the high right bank of the Orel River, a tributary of the Dnieper, which had created a small, hourglass-shaped lake as it drifted through the marshes below. Beyond the marshes the view stretched for miles to a distant cluster of hills. Admiring the view, Catherine gave it, and all the people in it, to one of her deserving senators, a man named Nicholas Alymov.

But Alymov already had an estate, and didn't need another one. So on the eve of his marriage, he gave it to his future brother-in-law, Andrei Fyodorovitch Lukianovitch. Andrei Fyodorovitch was Mopsy's great-great grandfather. The Lukianovitches were an old Ukrainian family. During the seventeenth century, they fought with the Cossacks against the Poles. Fyodor Lukianovitch, Andrei's father, owned a village with a grist mill and eighty-five souls in 1740. He became a burgomeister of Poltava and in 1785 was admitted to the Russian nobility. Andrei Fyodorovitch was born in 1786. He was a cavalry officer in the Napoleonic wars. The woman soldier, Nadezhda Durova, who is a Ukrainian folk hero, was one of his adjutants. Canvassing the libraries of Poltava, I found half a page on him in Mordzalevsky's *Little Russian Genealogy*, and in I. F. Pavlovsky's *Poltavians* his portrait was reproduced. The long, thin face was framed with sideburns, the eyes were small and clever, the right hand clasped a scroll. Elegantly sheathed in a frock coat, with a frilly jabot at the throat, he looked to be well over six feet tall.

In 1806 Andrei Fyodorovitch married Elizabeth Vitovtova, the daughter of a Lithuanian count and a Baltic baroness. Her mother, *née* Baroness Mengden, was a great-niece of Count Ernst Johann Biron, the German lover of Empress Anna and, according to John Stuart Martin's A *Picture History of Russia*, "a polished sycophant incapable of any thought save for his own income and pleasure." During the ten years they ruled jointly, "Russia suffered internally from fires, storms, epidemics, taxation, persecution, famine. (Above, right): Anna, with Biron at her right elbow, shooting animals at the Peterhof zoo. The 'sport' was to have game chased past her majesty by hounds." Andrei's marriage produced three children, Nicholas, Alexander, and Lyuba.

In 1820 Andrei Fyodorovitch left his regiment (the Hussars) to become the governor of Simbirsk, a sleepy province on the Volga. After six uneventful years there he retired to his land on the Orel, where he built one of the most impressive manor houses in southern Russia, called Shideyevo. The name came from *shado*, the old Tatar word for ramparts. The architect was Korinfsky. The style was a neoclassical variant known as Russian "Empire." The north and south facades were supported by a dozen massive white columns— almost mandatory props for the house of a *grand seigneur* in retreat. A large green cupola with a belvedere gave the structure a Slavic character, and sometimes attracted itinerant pilgrims, who from a distance mistook it for a monastery. One wing was a church, the classical simplicity of whose lines was modeled on the Church of the Imperial Stables in St. Petersburg. The walls were whitewashed stucco over brick and four feet thick. The rooms were huge, with parquet floors. Footsteps echoed in them. Andrei Fyodorovitch had their walls painted with sepia frescoes of Bacchanalian scenes. Since his days as a young officer, he had been addicted to practical jokes, and he booby-trapped the house with secret closets, hidden doors, *trompe l'oeils* with receding corridors and enticing flights of steps. His favorite prank involved a big haystack next to the house. When visitors from afar arrived, he would take them immediately on a lengthy tour. He would lead them into the dining room so they could see that nothing had been prepared for them to eat. After a complete inspection of the house, he would start on the grounds. "And you *must* come and see my haystack," he would say. Groaning, they would follow along. Slyly, triumphantly, he would fling open a door in the haystack. Inside, on a long table, was a fabulous feast. Candles blazed. A liveried serf stood behind each chair. The guests would gasp and shriek with delight.

Andrei Fyodorovitch's *joie de vivre* became well-known in that part of Little Russia, and numerous poets, artists, musicians, and entertaining parasites enjoyed his hospitality. The writer Ivan Kotlyarevsky came often and gave readings of his ribald parody of the *Aeneid*. It was the first significant literary work in the Ukrainian tongue. The characters were all local nobles (including Fyodor Lukianovitch) or Cossacks. Kotlyarevsky may even have written *Natalka Poltavka*, the first play in Ukrainian, while at Shideyevo, basing its heroine on one of the comely yard servants. The play was definitely performed there, in the large ballroom. The spectators sat in a gallery with an orchestra and a choir made up of serfs. In one skit improvised for an evening's diversion, the flippant conduct of a young man named Justin Petrovitch, who was fresh out of military academy and staying at Shideyevo for a while, was investigated. On another evening a dozen colored lithographs relating the life of Louis XIII and Mademoiselle de Lafayette, which hung in the red drawing room, were brought to life as *tableaux vivants*. In the final lithograph Mademoiselle de Lafayette had become a nun. The king was on his knees before her. She was pushing him away. A cross was required: in the picture she was holding a cross. One of Lyuba Lukianovitch's young friends (Mopsy told me this) ran into the church and snatched the cross from the altar. That night the girl died inexplicably. Everyone agreed it had to do with the terrible sacrilege she had committed. Lyuba ended up marrying a man named Ustimovitch, who one evening, Mopsy also told me, when they were playing cards on the balcony, became blind with rage. A nurse had come out with their baby, and tripping, let it fall from her arms to the flagstones. "I'd rather be blind than see such a thing," Ustimovitch said. When he stood up at the end of the game, he found that he couldn't see, and he remained blind for the rest of his life.

Mopsy told me, too, that Andrei Fyodorovitch's former aide-de-camp got drunk once, tried to ride his favorite dog, Hermide, and broke its back. Andrei Fyodorovitch had the man flogged. In Mopsy's day there was a dog named Hermide. It was a tradition. August nineteenth was St. Andrew's Day, the name day of both Uncle and Andrei Fyodorovitch, and it was celebrated with cannonades and fireworks. Perched on the edge of a precipice, the five cannon commanded a fine view of the valley. Near them stood a pavilion where the children would play with their nurses and, seated attentively on banquettes, receive instruction from their governesses and tutors. At the head of steps that led from a flower garden to a vineyard were two stone statues, Polovtsian idols from the eleventh or twelfth centuries. Around eight feet tall, the weathered figures had caps like mushrooms and squatted with their hands folded in their laps. In 1843 the brilliant Ukrainian poet and painter, Taras Shevschenko, visited Shideyevo and made a drawing of the two idols; the Orel valley and the lake, with its whimsical crook, are in the background. The lake was deep and cold and was called the *liman*. Shevschenko was a freed serf. He not only attacked serfdom and celebrated peasants, but published in Ukrainian without the protection of a pseudonym. For any of these offenses, under the repressive regime of Nicholas I, he was asking to be packed off to Siberia, but somehow he never was.

By 1845 twenty years of boisterous revelry had caught up with Andrei Fyodorovitch. He was so crippled with gout or, as he insisted, rheumatism, that he was confined to a chair, his legs wrapped in a plaid blanket. Having exhausted his governor's pension, he had been forced to mortgage the estate with its two hundred and fifty-five registered souls, and only the personal intervention of the Minister of the Interior, an old friend, saved him from ruin. A year later he died, and Shideyevo passed to his son, Nicholas, who seemed to be pursuing a fairly sober career in the capital: graduated, University of St. Petersburg, 1823; *junker*, Preobrazhensky Regiment; resists Decembrists in Palace Square and St. Isaac's Square (the Decembrists were a high-minded band of noble dissidents who were agitating for a constitution); for this is awarded Cross of St. George and exempted from one of his twenty-five years of military service; 1831, Order of St. Anne, third class, followed by Orders of St. Stanislav and St. Vladimir; 1840, writes biography of General Vistrom, gets four thousand roubles for it; 1843, writes history of war of 1828 against Turkey, in which he had fought; 1843, clerk in Ministry of Finance; 1844, chief of fourth department in Ministry of Salt Mines and Mineral Resources; 1846, head of ministry; later that year, puts out two more volumes on war with Turks; 1854, permanent state councillor. Nicolai Andreyevitch was much too busy to get down to Shideyevo, and he left the estate in charge of his maiden aunt, Elena Fyodorovna. His father had had five sisters. Barbara, Uliana, and Nadezhda were triplets. Elena, born in 1771, was the oldest. They'd all been quite beautiful in their youth, but only Uliana married. The others had been so smitten with Prince Potemkin, with whom they had danced during Catherine's visits, that they had stayed single. When Elena Fyodorovitch was in her eighties, word reached her nephew that she was critically ill. Rushing to her side (Mopsy again is my source), he reached Shideyevo late at night, and hearing there was little hope, went straight to bed. The next morning, prepared for the worst, he went into the dining room, and there was Elena Fyodorovna, in the pink of health, devouring a watermelon and a plate of crayfish. She lived a few years more, finally succumbing to homesickness after Nicholas moved her to his brother's estate in the village of Mirgorod, where Nicolai Gogol grew up. After Elena Fyodorovna left, Nicholas asked a neighbor named Kisiliov to look after the place, but he couldn't have known the man very well, because Kisiliov helped himself to everything that was portable.

When he was forty-eight Nicholas married a woman named Alexandra Panayeva. She was just eighteen, and a good catch. The Panayevs were a cultured and talented family. Alexandra's father was one of four brothers. The oldest,

Alexander, was a boyhood chum of the writer Sergei Aksakov and appears in many of his stories. Ivan, the next, was a lyrical poet whose reputation was eclipsed by that of his son, also Ivan, a socialite journalist and novelist who in 1847 took over, with the poet N. A. Nekrasov, *The Contemporary*, a review started by Pushkin, which, until it was banned in 1864, was the most influential periodical in Russia. Then there were Vladimir and Pyotr. Vladimir was the father of Alexandra. In his youth, during romps on the steppe with his brother Alexander and Aksakov, he had collected butterflies; at the University of Kazan the three of them were shown how to dry and mount their specimens by the eminent entomologist, Eversmann. Vladimir tried his hand at poetry, but his idylls were too academic to attract much of an audience. He entered the Civil Service. On April 10, 1830, he was running the Department of Appanage in the Ministry of Court in St. Petersburg, when a maladroit twenty-two-year-old, with a comically long nose and chronically suppurating ears, joined the department as a clerk, copying statements of accounts, underlining titles, stitching leaflets together, making notes on the roomful of cowed functionaries bent over equally dull tasks, whom he would later satirize. His name was Nicolai Gogol.

By the time of his death in 1859, Vladimir Panayev was a privy councillor and secretary of state under Alexander II. In charge of acquiring art for the Hermitage, he managed himself to amass a large collection of oils by European masters. There is a portrait of Panayev's children in the Tretyakov Gallery: Pyotr, Vera, and Alexandra are in the foreground, holding toy swords with the glazed, self-absorbed look of little children. Behind them, on a lower lawn that recedes to a lush glade, are his oldest daughter, Nadezhda, not quite of marriageable age, and his son Alexander, a wan, melancholy young man. It was painted by A. G. Venezianoff in 1841, I was told in the director's office, and presented to the People by Nicholas Avinoff in 1928.

It was through Panayev's wife, a woman named Praskovia Jmakina, that Uncle thought he might have been related to Christ and Cleopatra. She was a descendant of the Bagratid dynasty of Georgia, one of the most complete and widely branching Indo-European genealogical trunklines. The Bagratids were said to be descended from King David of Israel. Through David they even claimed to be "heirs of our Savior Jesus Christ," and in turn-of-the-century St. Petersburg, Fitzroy Maclean tells us, "at least one elderly Princess Bagratid would wear mourning on the feast of the Assumption of the Virgin Mary on the grounds that it had been a family bereavement."

Now that he was married, Nicholas Lukianovitch began to spend his summers at Shideyevo. In a photograph of his wife when she was around fifty, she is wearing a white bonnet. Her face has great strength, and at the corners of her mouth there is a slight smile. Mopsy told me that her grandmother was a deeply religious woman, almost a fanatic, and that this fanaticism was a Panayev family trait. One of her cousins had not exactly pushed his brother through some ice, but had not done all he might have to pull him out, either. The brother died, and he felt so guilty that he vowed to stand on all fours for a year. The penance was performed in the yard of his house. Servants fed and cleaned him, and during the winter sheltered him with a tent. When he was told that the year was over, he tried to get up, but found that he was completely paralyzed. Alexandra herself, while stopping short of wearing horse-hair shirts, gave all her clothing away except for two dresses (the bare minimum that a woman of her station could get by with), and just before her death made a pilgrimage to Jerusalem from which she returned distressed by how the Holy Land had been commercialized.

Her first act, on taking possession of Shideyevo, was to have the frescoes painted over. Only the tearful entreaties of her little daughter, a few years later, saved the false perspective in the entrance hall, which looked like a long passage with a series of diminishing arched doorways. Alexandra brought up her daughter, who was also named Alexandra, as a Christian of the first century. Mirrors were removed so that little Alexandra could not be distracted by her reflection. The girl became deeply religious, and gave up all social activities. Surrounded by members of the church except for a few young friends from equally pious families, she prepared to take the veil. But one day an old schoolmate of her mother's at the Smol'ny Institute, Anna Avinoff, came to tea at their house in St. Petersburg, bringing her younger brother Nicholas, who was an officer in the Preobrazhensky Regiment. It was difficult for sheltered Alexandra to be unimpressed by Nicholas Avinoff's uniform alone: the green tunic, the white trousers, the black jackboots and helmet with white feathers cradled under his arm. After a few more visits he proposed. She accepted. Her mother was beside herself. Her father was no longer alive, but perhaps he would have been happier to see his daughter married, and to a member of his own regiment, than condemned to be a nun. "I don't think it was a very happy union, but it was a smooth one," Mopsy recalled of the relationship that produced her.

Mopsy was born on December 18, 1888, and christened Elizaveta in Kharkov, the first big city in the Ukraine, coming from Moscow. Her father was the commander of an infantry regiment there.

Life in Kharkov for the Avinoffs was very gay. There were families with children the same age: the Kanilevskys, the Novossiltsevs, the Buddes. "Games, dancing lessons, parties at the house of an extraordinary hostess, Madame Kharina"— this was Mopsy talking of one hundred years ago—"we had a French governess called Madame and an old nurse, Tatiana Ivanovna. Uncle had a collection of queer articles. He kept them in a glass jar that he called a museum. It was the first time I recall hearing that word, which was later to play such a big part in his life. The articles in his museum were the yolk of a very hard egg, the claw of a chicken, and the hook from a corset. Each was carefully placed on cotton. I was most impressed by this collection and, as a matter of fact, by everything Uncle did." Uncle was four years older than Mopsy. Nika, born in 1881, was the first child.

In the autumn of 1893 their father was promoted to colonel and named commander of a brigade of sharpshooters in Tashkent. The trip to remote Uzbekistan took several months. First the Avinoffs took a train to Vladikavkaz. Then they went by stagecoach over the Caucasus, whose snowpeaks and gorges were stupendous. A detachment of soldiers escorted them for the length of the Georgian Military Highway until Tbilisi. The mountains had not been pacified, and there was danger of being set upon by bandits. From Tbilisi they took a train to Baku, then a ship across the Caspian to Krasnovodsk, then another train across the black-sand desert plains of Khiva and Bukhara to Samarkand, the city of Tamburlaine, whose glamorous mosques, inlaid with turquoise and lapis lazuli, had given rise to a saying that in other places, the light descends, but in Samarkand it ascends. At Samarkand the railroad ended, and they hired a tarantass to take them across the red-sand desert of Murzarabat. The tarantass was a large carriage that rode on poles instead of springs, with a high seat for the coachman, then an open section, then a coupé, with a small booth in back for the maids. Soon after crossing the Syr Darya, they reached their destination. Tashkent was half-European, half-Oriental. Most of its roofs were mud and smothered with poppies. At a certain time of year, when the poppies bloomed, the whole city turned red.

The Avinoffs took a house on Kauffman Boulevard. That summer they suffered terribly from the heat. My father remembers hearing, as a child, how his grandparents sat in barrels of water in Tashkent and played cards. The game was *bintz*. Among their new acquaintances were the Kerenskys. Kerensky was superintendent of schools for the district of Ekaterinburg. His son Sasha, a schoolmate of Nika's, would become a grandiloquent socialist and form the Provisional or, as it would even be known, Kerensky government after the abdication of Nicholas II. But in Tashkent he still belonged to a conservative, almost monastic family who were such staunch monarchists that when Alexander III died later that year, Mopsy remembers seeing them all walking along the Salara Boulevard in deep mourning.

Sasha had a younger brother, Kolya, who was Uncle's age. That summer the Avinoffs took Kolya with them when they went to the Chimgan Mountains, fifty miles north of Tashkent, to escape the heat. Like the local nomads they all lived in a felt yurt in a lush pasture above the treeline. The smoke went up through a hole in the roof. The air outside was crisp and filled with butterflies. Uncle was already collecting butterflies seriously. He had caught his first specimen when he was five. His cousin Lila, visiting Shideyevo, was making a watercolor of some flowers and asked him to bring her a butterfly to copy. He ran into the garden and came back breathless, carefully grasping a beautiful white one, a cabbage. The next morning, not having finished the painting, Lila asked him to catch her another one. It had to be white, she insisted. This was no easy task, but at last he saw another cabbage and caught it with his hands. As he presented it to Lila he noticed that its markings were different from the first—a remarkable observation for a five-year-old. "That's all right. I'll manage," Lila said. But Uncle was puzzled.

A few summers later, when he was eight, Uncle had read Sergei Aksakov's enchanting boyhood memoir, *The Butterfly Collectors*, one of whom was his great-grandfather, Vladimir Panayev, and been moved by it to start his own collection. His tutor, who had an interest in natural history, helped him assemble the necessary equipment. The first day they caught twenty specimens. Now he was ten, and he found willing accomplices in Kolya Kerensky and the son of Pfaff, his piano teacher. The three boys spent hours running up and down' the slopes of the Chimgans, disregarding time and space. Uncle had only one book with him, Berg's *Butterflies of Europe*, which didn't show the numerous satyrids and lycenids of alpine Uzbekistan. One morning he netted a day-flying sphinx moth that looked almost like the *Macroglossa croatica* in the book. That evening, in the yurt, he painted over the discrepancies. When he had grown up, he realized that he had caught a great rarity, *Macroglossa ducalis*. This was the only deliberate falsification of his scientific career.

At nine Uncle was already painting accurate watercolors

of butterflies. These paintings were a far cry from his first effort, which his mother kept in the old Karelian birch bureau at Shideyevo, a drawing made when he was four of three hills with three disproportionately large birds sitting on them. Uncle saw that something was wrong with the birds, and that observation led to his discovery of perspective. In a little copybook bound in marbled pressboard, he painted landscapes—sunsets, woods, mountains—that got better and better. He made some butterflies with long tails that Mopsy thought a real artistic achievement. A portrait of Mozart was almost satisfactory except for one eye that was out of control. A few marquis of the eighteenth century followed, painted under the influence of similar subjects that his mother was doing in oils on pale blue satin pillows, which were in fashion. Uncle had been born acutely near-sighted, but for close work his myopia was actually an advantage. He could immediately distinguish the most minute details of a butterfly's anatomy, while landscapes appeared in a blurred suffusion of pattern and color. Visitors were enchanted by his precocious conversation, his long golden curls, and features so delicate that his mother dressed him as a girl until he was five. Alexandra Vladimirovna was an accomplished pianist, and not long after she died, on January 2, 1888 (she was only fifty-two), Uncle astounded everyone by sitting at the piano and playing from memory his grandmother's favorite piece, "Si oiseau j'etais." "He was very quick in mind and body," Mopsy remembered, "a great tease and a real pest at times for Nika and me. Sometimes with Nika it would end in a fight." Nika had a violent temper, and once beat up Uncle so badly he couldn't sit for days. The brothers were complete opposites, as if early on they had divided the spectrum of behavior, and each was committed to defending his part of it. If Uncle was socially brilliant and uninhibited, Nika was silent and serious. Nika seemed to have inherited the Panayev piety. He had been Alexandra Vladimirovna's first grandchild, and she had doted on him. Instead of giving him conventional toys, she dressed him in priest's robes and recited to him, instead of nursery rhymes, the lives of the saints. Nika would wander solemnly through the rooms of Shideyevo, swinging his censer and casting incense. When he was seven his mother found him in the pantry with the butler's daughter. He had her laid out on a table and was giving her last rites.

During his teens Nika gravitated to responsible subjects like politics, economics, and agronomy, while all Uncle cared about were his butterflies—"the painted toys of an aristocrat," as his tutor called them. Nika was very restrained and Mopsy, eight years his junior, was always a little afraid of him. In his teens Nika started getting into photography. His pictures at Shideyevo document an existence that Uncle would describe years later as "a patriarchal state—lyrical, mellow, and nostalgic. It was like an extension of the time of Turgenev. Nothing was rocking under the earth."

Alexandra couldn't take the heat of Tashkent. After a year she returned to Shideyevo and waited there for her husband to finish his tour. She brought Mopsy and Uncle with her. Nika stayed with his father. Shideyevo was Alexandra's personal domain; she had lived there more than any place in the world. The peasants called her "Generalsha," the General's wife. She wore about her waist a set of big keys that was always getting lost, and rode around the estate in a wicker cart drawn by two Anglichane—Shetland ponies with bells in their ears. She was six feet tall, "an unusually tall and handsome woman," we learn from a novel

based on the Avinoffs at Shideyevo, "her face . . . quivering
with nervous quickness and kindness; her whole frame full
of life and energy. If she had not been so tall, she might
have been called stout, but now she seemed in perfect pro-
portion. Her eyes were brown; her forehead was white; her
hair and eyebrows were black, and her profile was beautiful."

The novel is *Rolling-Flax, or Summer Days in Little Russia*,
by Sinclair Ayden, published in London in 1902. *Rolling-
Flax* is a Ukrainian variety of tumbleweed. In his poem "Do-
omki," Taras Shevschenko compares the footloose plant to
our lives. We are driven about by fate, as balls of rolling-
flax are buffeted across the steppe. The wind drives one to
our feet. We stoop to pick it up, but the wind catches it and
carries it beyond our reach. "Such is fate," Shevschenko
concludes. Sinclair Ayden was the pseudonym of the children's English governess, Frances B. Whishaw. The daughter
of a Dover banker, she came to Russia when she was twenty-
seven to learn the language. A cousin in Moscow, married
to a Count Putiatin, suggested she apply for a position with
Mrs. Avinoff, who had just returned from Tashkent with
two of her children. Miss Whishaw was hired in 1894, and
stayed with the family for five years. Mopsy's childhood was
filled with a succession of nurses and governesses. The first
was Fraulein Rose, a German girl. Then the Frenchwoman,
Madame Khermuth, who died in the house in Kharkov. In
Tashkent there was another French girl, Mademoiselle
Marie. Miss Whishaw taught Mopsy, between the ages of
four and nine, and from nine to sixteen she had a hefty
mädchen from Switzerland, Fraulein Alice Brandt, plus Miss
Lister, an English girl, for one summer. The most influential
of these was Miss Whishaw. It happened that Miss Whishaw
was extremely cultured. She soon had Mopsy reading *Chat-*

terbox from cover to cover, and speaking English without the extravagantly thick accent that would later compound the pathos of many émigrés. At seven Mopsy wrote her first poem in English. She had just been punished.

> *I do not care what people say.*
> *I know they always lie.*
> *I only wish I was away*
> *Somewhere where I could die.*

Miss Whishaw's father was a collector of geometrid moths, so she understood Uncle's obsession, and being herself a gifted watercolorist, she could give him and Mopsy tips on technique. Miss Whishaw was a plain, spunky product of Victorian England. Once she joined several dozen peasants who were making a pilgrimage to the catacombs in Kiev, where several saints were buried. On foot it took three days. Her nemesis was the boys' tutor, Nicolai Ivanovitch. He had been thrown out of the University of Kharkov for subversive ideas and membership in a secret group of radicals. Mopsy recalls him as a "typical future Bolshevik." Alexandra Nicolaevna had engaged him. Her husband would not have approved of the choice. He had a low opinion of university students. "Education makes . . . a Russian noisy," the general in *Rolling-Flax* says. "If I had my way, I would close the universities for good now—abolish them altogether. They are yearly turning out a mob of hungry, lawless discontents, who will not work."

Squared off around the samovar, Nicolai Ivanovitch and Miss Whishaw would sit on the balcony and argue endlessly about such topics as Home Rule in Ireland. Mopsy remembered thinking it strange that they kept calling each other "my dear" when they were supposed to be quarreling. Nika, when he came back, took a photograph of the two of them against some foliage with his mother. Nicolai Ivanovitch, leaning on the palings of a fence behind them, is quite handsome, *type* Lenin, with peculiarly brilliant, narrowed eyes, a pointed beard, and a double row of brass buttons on his white collarless jacket. Miss Whishaw is vigilant under heavy lids. She looks like someone who is probably never going to marry, and in fact she never did. Mopsy visited her after she had gone back to Dover. She was working on the book then, but wouldn't let Mopsy see it. Years later, her sister sent it to them. "You might be interested in this book," the covering note said. "I think your lovely house is described in it." Everyone read it and agreed that it contained a lot of truth and a lot of nonsense.

Alexandra Nicolaevna, who is about thirty-five in the photograph, conforms closely to her description in *Rolling-Flax*. She busied herself with planning the meals; there were seldom fewer than twenty people at her table. She tried to interest the peasants in learning to read and write, with little success. They seemed determined to remain illiterate, perhaps out of spite, and only reluctantly went to her school. She also ran a dispensary for the peasants, administering turpentine, iodine, boric acid, and quinine, the last for the "swamp fever," possibly malaria, with which they sometimes came down. One of her patients was old Pindy, who had helped build the house in 1826. His age was estimated to be one hundred and ten. Pindy lived ten miles away and came once a week for his medicine. Getting off his wagon, he would walk his old horse up the final rise to the house. He seemed to have forgotten that serfdom had been over for thirty years. "And how much did they pay for you?" he would ask, slapping the backside of a pretty girl in the kitchen. Nika photographed him sitting on a stone wall with his white beard and perfect bowl of white hair coming down almost to his eyebrows, and his gnarled hands folded humbly in his lap. Like most of Alexandra's patients, Pindy thought that if he drank off the whole bottle of medicine at once, he would feel better that much faster, and he had to be convinced to take it in daily doses.

When the peasants felt really sick, they went to old Karakutsa, who looked after the sheep and was said to be able to stop bleeding with whispered incantations. Karakutsa's remedies, which relied heavily on the local flora and fauna, had been practiced since the days when Perun was still god of the steppe, and the fact that he himself had lived to such an old age (he, too, was said to be a centenarian) was a good advertisement for them. Reviling modern medicine, Karakutsa would seize the arm of his patient and locate precisely between the wrist and elbow a second, fainter throbbing, which he called the "brain pulse." The brain pulse, he said, was an infallible index of the condition of your body. "Your brain pulse is dead," he would tell his patient. Holding the arm tightly and swaying back and forth with his eyes closed, he would murmur his incantation so quickly—three times in one breath—that his patient couldn't make out the words. For payment he accepted hens, shoes, vodka, whatever he was offered.

There were three thousand dessiatines of prodigiously fertile land on the estate (a dessiatine is 2.7 acres), of which two thousand were kept up. Sometimes the crops ripened so quickly that dessiatines of rye and oats, and even of wheat, were left to rot because nobody had time to get them in. The wheat harvest of 1906 was exceptional. To help them celebrate their good fortune, the Avinoffs invited forty people. Tassels of wheat were placed in vases around the house among the flowers. After a sumptuous banquet everyone toasted His Excellency the Harvest with champagne and danced until dawn. With some of the profits from the harvest Alexandra had a set of jewelry made up by Fabergé. The necklace, bracelets, rings, earrings, and brooch were made of golden spikes of wheat, with tiny diamonds as kernels. Mopsy wore the jewels when she was presented at court the following year.

At the emancipation in 1861, each serf had received four acres. But the peasants still needed cash, and the easiest way to get it was to work for the Avinoffs. They got three meals and wages—about fifty cents—a day. In summer the *muzhiks* worked six days a week. In the winter there was little to do, and they stayed home and made articles to sell in the markets of Poltava and Ekaterinoslav: wooden snow shovels, twig brooms, felt boots, unglazed milk-pots, crafts of carved wood, bark, and silver. (Ekaterinoslav, the present Dnepropetrovsk, was about forty miles away.) The busiest month was August. With every horse, wagon, and driver in use, it was a bad time to travel. Everyone, even mothers with newborn babies at their breasts, took to the fields, and with thrilling songs and flashing sickles hacked down the wheat and corn. The work began at dawn and ended after dark. Sometimes the *muzhiks* would make a bonfire on the open steppe, and while one told stories, the rest would sit and finally fall asleep in its glow.

There were two villages below the house, Novoselovka and Homohivka, joined by a road and separated by the lower garden. Their combined population was about three hundred. The cottages, nestled together in the shade of wil-

lows and poplars, had bright white sides, and their roofs were
thatched with tall reeds from the marsh. The walls were
made of clay basted on a willow frame. Inside was a stove
built up in tiers called *lezhankas*, on which members of the
family slept. Strings of shriveled mushrooms and bundles of
dried herbs hung from the ceiling. The *krasny ugol*, or "pretty
corner," where icons glimmered behind a perpetual flame,
was in the east. On Saturday, their day off, the peasants
went up to church. The lively little tune the bells played at
four-thirty to summon them—Mopsy reproduced it instantly
though she hadn't heard it in more than half a century—
went like this:

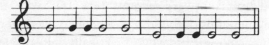

The bells tolled across the valley on Saturday afternoon, at
ten on Sunday morning, for the special service on each of
the thirty saints' days, and during blizzards, when they were
rung, on Alexandra Nicolaevna's orders, to help travelers
keep their bearings. The Saturday vespers lasted an hour.
The peasants came in through the main entrance and stood
at the rear of the church, dropping to their knees and crossing
themselves at a signal from Anton Mihailovitch, the prayer
reader. For many years the services were performed by the
old *batyushka*, Father John. Another bearded hundred-year-
old, he had been in residence since the time of Andrei
Fyodorovitch, but he was so timid that he hardly dared address the Avinoffs, unless it was to compliment Mopsy on
her painting. "The brush of Raphael," he would say. Once
at Easter the *batyushka* and his aide went down to the villages
to bless the peasants' eggs. At each cottage they were offered
a glass of vodka, and when they had made their rounds they

returned, reeling, through the lilac allée in the lower garden. The lilacs had been trained to grow together, forming a canopy. For some reason the *batyushka* and his aide decided to climb into the lilacs, where they passed out, and Mopsy found them asleep there the next morning. Father John died soon into the new century. After his death a monk named Father Neon, from a monastery in Poltava, conducted the services except when the archbishop of Poltava visited while making his rounds of the district, as he often did, with his friend the chief of police and a retinue of bearded, black-robed *batyushki.*

Besides the field hands from the villages, around a hundred *dvorniki* or yard servants were attached to the house and the numerous outbuildings, where a variety of activities went on, making Shideyevo practically self-sufficient. The *dvorniki* were landless. Not all of them had been recruited locally. By the end of the century a significant number of *dvorniki* were leaving estates and drifting into the cities, where they got work in factories, lived in slums, and became ripe for the teachings of Karl Marx. The outbuildings formed a courtyard with one side of the house. Mopsy made me a sketch to explain the layout. The first outbuilding on the south side, linked to the house by a connective bridge, contained the kitchen, the laundry, quarters for the cooks and the two coachmen, Jacob and Terrence. Then came the ice house. Ice was brought up from the *liman* by oxen, covered with straw, and kept there over the summer. Then the carriage house. It had a number of now-extinct conveyances. The landau was an open wagon with two seats facing each other and a capacity of eight. Nika took a picture of everyone heading off for a picnic in the landau. Uncle is wearing a white cap with a big visor and holding upright, like a slack air sock, a long-handled butterfly net. Then two *lineikas*, used for bathing expeditions and as back-up transport for larger picnics. The bathers swam nude in the river, one sex at a time. Nicholas Nabokov, the composer, has described the *lineika* as "a Russian cross-breed between an English brake and an American covered wagon." Then two sizes of coach, a *kareta* and a *kolyaska*. Then a *chetvyorka*, which was like a *troika* except that it was drawn by four horses instead of three. With a top speed of forty miles per hour, it was the fastest rig at the Avinoffs' disposal. And finally, Alexandra's wicker *karzinka*.

After the carriage house came the stables, with about thirty horses. Then the piggery. The pigs were looked after by a Cossack who through long association had come to look like a pig himself. Then the barn, where more than fifty oxen were kept. They were for ploughing and bringing up the water, and they always traveled in a double yoke. Then the sheep shed. Karakutsa's vicious sheepdogs had a standing feud with the hunting pack, which occupied the house end of the courtyard. There was an imaginary line in the middle of the yard, and terrible fights broke out whenever a dog went over his side of it. Then the black bakery, where dark bread was made and the field hands got their meals. Then the dairy. Then the white bakery, where *bubliki* (bagels), *bublichki* (smaller bagels), buns, and loaves of bread were made. The baker Pyotr Ivanovitch lived there with his wife and their masses of children. Then the blacksmith's shop. Then the shop of the shoemaker, who was also the tanner, harnessmaker, and bookbinder. Then the machine shop, where engines were fixed and flour was ground. The next building was rented to Yavorovsky, the Honest Jew. He was a rabbi and attended to the commercial needs of the community. In his store you could buy cloth, sweets, needles, kerosene, and other basic items. As they were the only Jews around, the Yavorovskys missed the pogroms, though other Jews as nearby as Ekaterinoslav were persecuted.

The last house in the courtyard was the Winter Wing, or the Flesgel, as it was called, a large brick building with four apartments where the butler Roman Vasilievitch, Father John the *batyushka*, and the cabinetmaker Vasily Bartole-mevitch (who also made frames for Mopsy's paintings) lived, where guests were put up, where the Avinoffs stayed in the winter, when the house was closed, and where the estate manager, Frederic Augustovitch Brauns, had his office. "So you see we were fully equipped," Mopsy sighed. "We didn't depend on anything."

Miss Whishaw suggests, and Mopsy confirms, that while the General was still in Tashkent, Alexandra was paid an unusual number of calls by a general practitioner in Poltava named Dr. Wolkenstein. He was a Tolstoyist and like Tolstoy wore a *roubashka*, or peasant shirt. His wife had been deported to Siberia as a revolutionary. He was bald and not particularly handsome but "a great charmer," Mopsy recalls, who spoke with feeling and had dark, searching eyes. Alexandra, we are told in *Rolling-Flax*, "enjoyed a gentle flirtation, and vibrated sensitively to the opinions of others." The four of them—Alexandra, Dr. Wolkenstein, Nicolai Ivanovitch, and Miss Whishaw—spent hours on the balcony, arguing about the fate of Russia. According to the novel, there was a hectograph in the basement of the house, on which Al-exandra and the doctor ran off seditious pamphlets. If this was true, Mopsy knew nothing about it.

Alexandra's liberal episode ended, in any case, when her husband came back from Tashkent. Life returned to normal with the General at the head of the table. (He had been promoted to lieutenant general in Tashkent.) In a passage that Mopsy dismissed as "complete nonsense," Miss Whishaw describes mealtime at Shideyevo, with the family reunited:

Dinner was usually a very long, and a very trying meal. Everyone was placed according to rank; the women sitting near Alexandra Nicolaevna, and the men near the General. Conversation flagged, because half the people were admitted to the table as a favour, and were not supposed to speak. Amongst those who were below the salt was the Kharkov dressmaker; she had especially stipulated in her contract that she was to dine with the family. Fraulein Alice was expected to be seen, not heard; and the General thought it was quite unnecessary for Nicolai Ivanovitch to make a remark. He disapproved of students and universities, and thought the education of the masses was quite a mistake.

Occasionally Father John, the *batyushka*, dined with the family; owing to the excessive respect he felt for Alexandra Nicolaevna, he used to rise like a little boy in school whenever she spoke to him—frequently spilling his soup as he did so. As a rule she did not attempt to keep up a conversation with him. Lastly, out of politeness, and for the sake of the children, the conversation was carried on in English, and a bored look settled upon the faces of those who were destined to sit for more than an hour, listening to what they could not possibly understand.

Nicolai Alexandrovitch had always had a beard. In a photograph from around this time, it is shorter and more scraggly than it was in his Preobrazhensky days, and comes to two points, which were probably trained by thoughtful stroking. He is massive, in his fifties now, leaning forward in his chair as if short of breath, and staring with a wild, hard look. Nicholas was a collector, of old coins, old buttons, old silver, old firearms, old lace, Persian rugs, fine porcelain, and all sorts of stuff that he had picked up on his tours of duty. He was especially proud of the carpets he had bought in Bukhara in 1878, during one of the wars between Russia and Turkey. He had gory tales of that campaign, of arriving at the only waterhole in a day's ride and finding an Arab with a knife in his back floating in it. Most of his collection was gathering dust in a huge room in the basement called the *korovaya*. It was like a museum and perfect ghost habitat. The children knew there was a ghost down there. Some of the choicer items cluttered his office. Mopsy remembered a trunk that was filled with old lawsuits, all of which seemed to have been instigated by a lawyer named Trischov. A generation back, his mother's ancestors had feuded bitterly. Another trunk was filled with seeds, future dessiatines of rye, barley, and melon. From his desk Nicholas made a show of running the estate, though most of the details—the book-keeping and the daily assignments of work—were left to a full-time estate manager. He had a big letter A, with a crown over it, tacked up on the front and back of the house, over the pillars. After he retired, in 1904, he continued to wear his uniform, including his medals and his visored cap, and took several newspapers with which he kept track of comrades-in-arms' promotions, retirements, and deaths. He told funny stories to his children. One was about a fire at the Ecole des Pages, which he had attended. The Ecole des Pages was the most exclusive boys' school in St. Petersburg. The students wore smashing red-and-gold tunics and white pants, and were trained to be pages in the imperial court. The fire was started by a magnifying glass that had been left on a windowsill. After it had been put out, the director of the school, who was not a very bright man, called the students together and lectured them sternly. "How grateful we all must be that it didn't start at night," he said.

The children adored their father. Uncle acquired his passion for collecting, his subtle brand of humor, his lavish attention to guests. Uncle lived in the church wing, in what was called the Archbishop's Room. There, in spurts of nervous energy, he darted from project to project, littering his chaos with husks of the sunflower seeds he was constantly eating. His collection of Little Russian butterflies was representative by 1896. He had all the blues, cabbages, sulphurs, woodnymphs, checkerspots, and fritillaries. He had the European tiger swallowtail, which is smaller and chunkier than ours. He had four species in the genus *Vanessa*: the red admiral, the peacock, the tortoiseshell, and the painted lady. Their resemblance to New World *Vanessas* is very close. He had the festoon, a small, intricately mottled Old World species with deeply scalloped brown lunules along the edges of its wings. He had several kinds of *Parnassius*, which Vladimir Nabokov has described as "strange butterflies of ancient lineage, with rustling, glazed, semi-transparent wings, and catkin-like flossy abdomens." The ramifications of the genus *Parnassius* would consume Uncle's attention until he died. For his birthday that summer his father gave him *The Butterfly Book*, by William J. Holland. Holland was a world-renowned lepidopterist and the director of the Carnegie Museum in Pittsburgh. Uncle was delighted with the book, and had no idea, of course, that one day, as Holland's successor, he would occupy the office in which it had been written.

Mopsy remembers the General as a wonderful father who

taught her to embroider and cross-stitch, who encouraged her painting with little prizes, and supported everything she got interested in. Some of her earliest artistic efforts were the menus he asked her to paint for his dinner guests. Before that, she remembers, when she was two or three, drawing something, maybe a bird, and being taken bawling to her crib before she could finish it. She went through a period of drawing only noses. Then she discovered mouths. Her first full portrait was of a Chinese doll with beady black eyes. Uncle, who became a skillful draftsman when he was still a boy, was her main teacher. Miss Whishaw was a great help, too, and the house was filled with dozens of fine oils, which Vladimir Panayev had picked up when he was collecting art for the Hermitage. Crowding the walls in the sumptuous, close-packed décor that was typical of the period, they were silent inspiration. A place of honor in the largest room, the blue drawing room, was given to Catherine the Great by Levitsky; she was, after all, the donor of Shideyevo. In the same row was a portrait of Empress Anna by Caravaz. Then, in three tiers, the family. The wall was lined with high-backed chairs with massive mahogany arms. A chandelier of Venetian glass morning glories hung down. On other walls were landscapes by the Flemish masters, Teniers and Jordaens, a madonna by Memling, a flower painting by Mignon, a Venetian scene by Guardi. Among these works Mopsy dreamed of becoming another Madame Vigée-Lebrun, who had painted the aristocracies of Europe and Russia the century before.

In the winter of 1905 she made a snow statue of Marie Antoinette in the garden, while Uncle made one of Voltaire beside it. They were so lifelike, down to the buttons on the philosopher's frock coat, that the night watchman was terrified when he happened on them, and knocked them down when he realized they were only snow. But Nika, to our lasting gratitude, managed to photograph them. No one makes such elegant snowmen anymore. The Avinoffs did not go to St. Petersburg that winter, because there was trouble in the capital, a small revolution that was like a dress rehearsal for the big one that would come in twelve years. It was quickly crushed, but the ripples of discontent spread into the countryside. Several estates in Little Russia were burned, and their owners killed. A detachment of Cossacks was stationed at Shideyevo, and the winter passed quietly.

Mopsy painted little portraits of her friends, and they received them as presents for their patience. Her best friend was Tanya Makcheeff, who lived on an estate twenty versts away. In a picnic photograph Tanya is a pretty, self-possessed fourteen-year-old in a sailor suit. Mopsy would pick her up in the *karzinka*, and she would visit for several days. Once, in the red drawing room, they saw the ghost of a young woman that fit the description of the friend of Lyuba Lukianovitch who had stolen the cross from the altar. They baked pastries, and took them to Schekuchin's house. It was a beautiful walk, for almost a mile along the marsh. Schekuchin was a cultivated man living in seclusion. His cottage was in a grove of old mulberry trees that were the size of oaks. He would serve them tea and jam in his faded dressing gown. His parents had owned a big estate not far away, but they had disowned him years ago after he fell in love with his mother's chambermaid and took her to Paris. Now he lived with his homely daughter and a large library, most of whose volumes were about homeopathic medicine. He was always persuading his daughter that she had some ailment so he could try one of his cures on her.

Tanya moved to France in 1912, and after the Revolution she and Mopsy lost touch. For sixty years neither knew what had happened to the other. Tanya married a man named Vladimir Smirnoff, who had gotten out of Russia with little more than a document showing that he once had owned a famous vodka firm. He sold the rights to his name, and they lived on the proceeds until his death in 1934. One day a few years ago Tanya spotted a review of Masha's memoirs in an émigré newspaper published in Paris. She ordered the book, and learned from it that Masha was living with Mopsy in America. They had a joyous reunion by letter. Tanya lives in Marseilles. On her bed table, she wrote me, is her portrait by Mopsy, done when they were seventeen.

In 1898 General Avinoff received a brigade in Helsinki (Finland had been annexed by Russia in 1809). After three winters there he took his last command, a division near Kiev. Uncle entered a gymnasium in Kiev, and Mopsy took lessons from a young art student who would only let her use two colors, burnt ochre and black. She worked hard at oil-painting, though she was happier with watercolors, because Madame Vigée-Lebrun had painted in oils. In 1904 the General retired, and they went for the winter to St. Petersburg, where they had an apartment on the Liteiny Prospekt. Mopsy took lessons from a minor artist named Karpinsky. Several winters later, she went to the Encouragement des Arts and studied with the court painter, Eberling, who was famous for his portrait of the ballerina Karsavina. He told her not to worry about the outline of the face, but to concentrate on the shape of its highlights and shadows. One summer, in Florence, she took lessons in miniature-painting. She learned that in *pointillage* the dots should never be seen, but covered with a wash to blur them.

When she was twenty she fell in love with her cousin, Leo Panayev. They met in St. Petersburg. He was five years older, and like everyone in the Oktirsky Regiment, wore a gold hoop in his left ear. After four days he proposed. Mopsy was ecstatic, but her mother and Uncle, who recognized in him the fanatical piety for which the Panayevs were known, warned her not to be hasty. The romance lasted about a year. Finally Uncle made her write a letter breaking it off. Mopsy was miserable, and Leo volunteered for duty in Mongolia. When war broke out in 1914, he and his two brothers rushed to the front. Fighting from their horses like Knights of the Holy Grail they were all killed in the first two months, and became instant legends. The tsar awarded them each posthumously the Cross of St. George. A book was written about them and distributed to the troops. On page twenty-nine of the copy in Mopsy's house (which belonged to the tsar himself) was a photograph of Gury Panayev, the second brother, with his legendary horse, Vendetta. Vendetta is helping Panayev get into a coat with his teeth.

In 1908 Serge Avinoff died childless, leaving his real estate fortune to his two nephews. Uncle had graduated from the Imperial Law College in 1905 and was working as an assistant secretary-general in the Senate, monitoring correspondence from suspected revolutionaries abroad. One letter he carefully steamed open was from a man in England named David Green, who would later become David Ben-Gurion. Uncle's salary, plus a small allowance from his parents, who were richer in land and works of art than in cash, hadn't enabled him to progress very far with his butterfly collection. But now, with this inheritance, he could move into high gear. That summer, during the long vacation that the government took, he went to the Pamir Mountains with a young entomologist from St. Petersburg, Alexander Kirichenko, and on its alpine prairies and rockslides they netted several thousand specimens. Several were new to science. The prize catch was a splendid aberration in the genus *Apollonius*, with black ocelli, or eyespots, instead of the usual red ones. Most of the butterflies of European Russia had been classified, but in central Asia there were, and still are, many discoveries to be made. It is not just that the region is so remote and imperfectly explored, but that in its isolated mountain valleys, butterflies develop characteristics of their own; new forms are continually evolving.

Between 1909 and 1914 Uncle sent out forty-two collecting expeditions across the continent. His agents were mostly students at the University of St. Petersburg. They brought him material from the Caucasus, from Armenia, from Persia, from the Hindu Kush, from Tien Shan, from Bhutan and Sikkim. In 1912, with Alexis Jacobson, an experienced entomologist, and Michael Mamayeff, an enthusiastic young sportsman, he traversed the western slopes of the Himalayas from India to Turkestan. He was twenty-eight, and would be pondering the data and impressions from this trip for the rest of his life.

Mamayeff and Uncle arrived by steamer in Ceylon (as he would recount in the *Pittsburgh Record* nineteen years later) and passed through the grand old cities of India—Madras, Agra, Delhi, Benares. They saw the mighty wall of the Himalayas from Darjeeling. Permits were procured from the government of the viceroy for them to collect in the remote parts of Kashmir. In Rawalpindi they met Jacobson and with seventy coolies proceeded in primitive native vehicles called *dongas* to Srinagar. From Srinagar a family took them in their houseboat on the river Jhelum to Ganderbal, where they bought horses and started the ascent into the Himalayas. Foothills smothered with irises gave way to a balmy zone of fir trees. In a high valley where they camped for several days, they met another party of travelers, Mr. and Mrs. Bullock Workman of Philadelphia, who were on their way to explore the glaciers of the Karakoram. Wading through deep snow in the Zoji-la Pass, they entered Ladakh. For several days they rode through a desolate, treeless moonscape. One evening Uncle caught a field mouse and dropped it into a special container that had been given to him by Lord Rothschild. The year before, he had visited Tring Park, Lord Rothschild's private zoo in Hertfordshire. The flea collection there was unrivaled. Many of the specimens were mounted under individual magnifying glasses. Of the thousand or so recognized species, Tring lacked only a few. One was said to parasitize a rare Tibetan field mouse. Hearing that he was going to the Himalayas, Lord Rothschild asked Uncle to try and get it for him. Ascertaining that it was the right mouse, Uncle dropped it into the container, which was filled with kerosene, and waited hopefully for the flea to float to the surface, but none appeared. "I got the carrier," he would report to Lord Rothschild, "but it was clean. I couldn't get you the infestation."

Uncle made many studies of the barren land and the lamaseries that clung to the cliffs like colonies of coral. He used pastel and watercolor, but found pen and ink most effective, because the hills stood sharply in the glaring sun, and the shadows were unusually black and clear. Working quickly, he filled page after page of his sketchbook with meticulous gossamers that represented dark values and were as limpid as the land itself.

They visited Lamayuru, one of the largest and most revered lamaseries in Ladakh. It seemed to Uncle like an enchanted city of hobgoblins, a bizarre fairyland that had sprung from the mind of an Arthur Rackham. The monks lived in cells that honeycombed the cliffs, and scurried along winding passageways whose walls were decorated with mantras. Gaudy prayer flags fluttered everywhere, and there were monuments called *chortens* that symbolized the five elements of nature, and looked somewhat like the cupolas of a Russian church. All paths converged upon a central temple in which a huge statue of Chenrezig, the Bodhisattva of Compassion, gestured with a thousand hands. The monks were invariably humble, round-faced, and beaming. With contagious merriment they showed the gruesome paraphernalia of the devil dance—the frightening masks, the skulls and beads of human bone. Uncle wondered how, with so much of the male population in lamaseries, there were still enough men at large to make possible the widespread practice of polyandry. Many of the women in Ladakh seemed to have several husbands.

In Leh, the capital, a Moravian missionary took them to meet the ex-king of Ladakh, who had recently been deposed by the Maharajah of Kashmir and was living as a private citizen in the city where his ancestors had ruled for centuries. The king gave him a beautiful jade cup, and Uncle reciprocated with his flashlight, which the king accepted as something bordering on the miraculous. Leaving Leh before the batteries gave out, the explorers trekked into Rupshu, a high tableland southeast of Ladakh and on the frontier with Tibet. Rupshu proved to be an El Dorado for butterflies. Uncle netted several new species and subspecies, including a *Parnassius* that no one has seen or caught again. He named it *Parnassius maharaja*. They saw *kiangs*, wild asses. About the only people they met were shepherds. The sheep carried

specially constructed bags of salt, which had come from several highly saline lakes in the vicinity, and were headed for
Tibet, where salt was like money. From Rupshu they headed
north on yaks, which they traded for twenty-two horses, and
they rode the horses through a succession of passes into
Chinese Turkestan. As they neared the top of the Karakoram
Pass, at 18,600 feet, they passed many horse and camel
skeletons, and stopped often to save their mounts from a
similar fate. Even at that high elevation there were butterflies, and though their lungs were ready to burst, Uncle and
Jacobson ran down a few that were extremely desirable. Mamayeff shot a few representatives of the genus *Ovis*, first
cousins of the sheep of Marco Polo, which inhabit the Pamir.
He bagged some ibexes, antelopes, and a number of unusual
birds. "The big game hunting of Mamayeff throughout the
trip was on the level of all expectations," Uncle wrote rather
dryly.

There was an awkward moment at the border when the
Chinese authorities asked to see the stamp in their passports
that was required to enter the country. By showing them all
sorts of irrelevant documents, Uncle managed to convince
them that they were on a mission of such importance that
it would have been undignified for them to even show their
passports. His performance was so impressive that when they
got to Kashgar, the governor of the province was waiting for
them with a sixty-course dinner. Most of the branches on
the tree of life were represented at this banquet. There were
even some wormlike invertebrates dipped in a bright indigo
sauce. When it was over Uncle asked the governor if he
could take his picture. "I am afraid I am so ugly the lens of
your camera will crack," the man replied. "On the contrary,"
Uncle assured him. "I shall make a thousand copies and paste

them all over my room." The governor blushed and asked Uncle how old he was. Uncle knew how age is revered in the Orient. "A sparrow like myself is in his teens," he said, "but you must be well over a hundred." The governor searched for a self-effacing comeback. "My head may be bald," he stammered, "but it is completely empty." "Nothing of the sort," Uncle protested with a brilliant smile. "It is only transparent, like a beautiful crystal." Thoroughly charmed, the governor made Uncle a mandarin, third class, on the spot. This title enabled them to pass safely through the torrid plains of Tarim, where strangers were regarded with suspicion, and to reach the eastern edge of the Pamir, where they entered Russian Turkestan. From Osh the intrepid explorers caught a train to Tashkent, where years before, when he was a boy, Uncle's association with central Asia had begun.

While Uncle was diverting himself on the Roof of the World, Nika had joined what was often called the "conscience-stricken nobility." Already in Tashkent he had gotten mixed up with a radical element that included Sasha Kerensky and was led by an older student in his early twenties, named Kolashnikov. When he returned to Shideyevo Mopsy noticed that he was even quieter and more serious than before. He refused to take part in frivolous gatherings with the adolescents on neighboring estates, and even stranger, he and his father, after spending nearly a year together, seemed to have little to say to each other. But before she could make out what was going on, Nika went off to the University of St. Petersburg, where he did brilliantly in economics and grew a beard, which made him seem even more remote to her.

In 1901, there were riots at the university. Kolashnikov

surfaced briefly to incite the students, then mysteriously disappeared. Nika's best friend, Volyansky, who had done something terrible, committed suicide. Nika himself, when he came to Shideyevo, was worried that Okhrana, the secret police, was on his heels. He worked outside all summer with the peasants, and refused to talk about it. That fall he transferred to the University of Moscow, and fell in with the Moscow liberals: Prince Serge Troubetzkoy, the dean; Paul Milyukov and Fyodor Kokoshkin, both history professors; Dmitri Shipov, chairman of the City Council; Vladimir Dmitrievitch Nabokov, a jurist whose son would become the last great voice from that culture, and who would himself be killed in 1922 by a bullet intended for Milyukov at an émigré political rally in Berlin. These men would found the Constitutional Democratic Party in 1905, and confront the tsar with a manifesto for a Parliament. The best hope for Russia, they felt, was to make it a constitutional monarchy like England.

There had already existed, since the reforms of 1864, a democratic institution called the *zemstvo*. It operated on a local level, building hospitals, schools, and lunatic asylums, keeping roads and bridges in repair, providing transport for the police, watching the crops, and taking appropriate steps in years of famine. The *zemstvos* had begun to do great things, but after 1881, in the wave of reaction that followed the assassination of Alexander II, their power was sharply cut back. Nika became deeply involved in the movement to bring them back to life. Between 1904 and 1912 he wrote five monographs: "Count Korff and the Zemstvo Reform of 1864," "On the Senate Inquest into the Impediment of Democratic Government in the Province of Saratov," "On the Question of Mutual Relations Between Provincial and

District Zemstvos," "Local Self-Government," and "An Attempt to Systematize the Literature on Zemstvo Self-Government."

Nika became good friends with a fellow student, Igor Demidov. There is a photograph of them both in front of some trees at Shideyevo, looking very thick and conspiratorial in their beards and long coats. Demidov has a walking stick and a hip flask. A pamphlet, no doubt subversive, is tucked under Nika's arm. Demidov had married a woman named Katya Novossiltsev, whose mother was a Scherbatov. The Scherbatovs were one of the great Russian families. They were the Scherbatskys in *Anna Karenina*; on the steps of their palace in Moscow, where Katya's grandfather lived, Kitty stops to adjust the black velvet ribbon around her neck. Tolstoy himself was a friend of the old prince and came sometimes to the house in his dirty *roubashka*. Masha told me how the man who stood at the door with a golden staff came in once to announce Count Leo Tolstoy, then asked, with a sneer of disgust, "Shall I let him in?" Masha was Katya's older sister, more spirited than beautiful, and so well educated that her conversation was almost intimidating. The old prince was a liberal, and the Moscow dissidents would often meet at his home. His dance hall became a weekly political lecture hall, and the speakers often railed against the tsar and his policies; after the pogrom at Kishinev in 1903, for instance, Nabokov advertised in the newspaper that his court uniform was for sale. After the Kadet party formed, it met frequently at the Scherbatov palace. Katya and Masha would type minutes of the meetings.

One evening Demidov brought Nika to a meeting and introduced his sister-in-law. Masha was captivated by this "intelligent, benevolent panther with the kindest eyes on earth," as she would later describe him. He seemed to like her, too, and returned often, but was so shy that Masha began to wonder if he was ever going to propose. The match was finally arranged by their respective governesses, who got together and practically forced Nika to ask for her hand. After honeymooning on Lake Como, they came to Shideyevo in August 1906. The newlyweds were met by a welcoming committee from the village who all shouted "Long live Nicolai Nicolaevitch and his bride!" The family was waiting on the balcony. "My father-in-law, in general's uniform, held a silver icon," Masha wrote. "My mother-in-law, tall and stout, carried the traditional Russian plate of bread and salt used in welcoming a bridal couple. Nearby were my young brother-in-law, Andrey, whose pale face showed great sensitivity and intelligence, and my eighteen-year-old sister-in-law Ellie, with large dark eyes like Nika's." In fact, Alexandra was filled with foreboding about her son's marriage, and refused to give it her blessing for a year. Not that it wasn't a brilliant match socially, but Masha's family was so liberal. "You'll both end up being hanged in prison," Alexandra predicted, which wasn't far from the truth.

Masha noticed how much gayer and more self-assured the peasants of Shideyevo seemed than the ones on her family's estate in central Russia. They seemed to look up to Nika, who had brought them the latest labor-saving machinery, threshers and harrows from England, and taught them to improve their breed of cattle. "Prosperity was evident from the moment we entered the village," Masha noted. She was impressed by the collection of Old Masters, and by Mopsy's portraits. Mopsy was still painting in oils. She had been slaving over a portrait of a peasant girl holding some lilacs, and it wasn't working. She asked Mopsy to make her a copy of Largillière's oil of Madame de Maintenon, in the long hall. The result was so close that when Masha later showed it to the critic Grabar, he exclaimed, "But this young lady is a genius! For the life of me I couldn't tell her copy from the original." In the evenings they would play cards on the balcony. Mopsy would bring out her pet finches for some air. The smell of jasmine and acacia from the garden was overpowering. Uncle would set up his telescope and show Masha flies on the backs of cows grazing in the marsh, and cupolas of churches in distant villages that weren't visible to the naked eye. She and Nika stayed at Shideyevo through the fall. "One golden day followed another," she wrote, "like amber beads upon a string."

One evening in St. Petersburg, Uncle brought to dinner a colleague in the Senate, convivial, blue-eyed Leo Schumacher—my grandfather. Leo was a bright young Baltic German. At twenty-five he had already reached the rank of collegiate assessor, which was equal to an army major. He was a solid man about Mopsy's height, and had a fund of amusing stories. His family had lived in Russia from the time of Peter the Great. One of Leo's ancestors, Johann D. Schumacher, had been director of the Academy of Sciences in St. Petersburg during the early eighteenth century, when Michael Lomonosov, the Russian da Vinci, was making astounding discoveries. Leo's grandfather, Alexander Danilovitch, had served on Alexander II's commission to liberate the serfs, and his father Arkady had recently been appointed president of the commission for liquidating the government's debts. "After paying his own debts, Arkady Alexandrovitch now pays the debts of the government," Nika would joke. There were about two million Balts in Russia who held high positions in the government and controlled the banks and large businesses. The indigenous nobility, among whom it was widely considered bad form to work for a living, had little aptitude for commerce.

Leo told the Avinoffs how, a few weeks before, he had met Gregory Rasputin on a train to Yalta. After blessing a huge crowd, Rasputin got on the train and entered Leo's compartment. He was wearing his usual black velvet kaftan with a red silk shirt. His hair was long and straggly, his beard was filthy, there was dirt under his fingernails, and he smelled. His eyes—pale blue, almost white—were unsettling. Women had fainted just from looking into them. Leo, on the other hand, was fastidious in the extreme about the way he looked. If there was a spot on his suit, he wouldn't wear it; he had a special little brush for his moustache.

"May I join you?" Rasputin asked.

"Why certainly," Leo said, and with a shudder of disgust he kept reading his paper. Rasputin was slightly miffed at the lack of interest Leo was showing in him. "Don't you know who I am?" he asked. "Of course I do," Leo said, still reading. Perhaps egged on by Leo's coolness, Rasputin started to launch into his life story. He was on his way to Livadia to join the imperial family. "I'm always with them," he boasted, "wherever they go."

"How is it that you, a simple peasant, got into this entourage?" Leo asked.

"I lived in Siberia and was the worst sinner," Rasputin said. "But one day, in a field, I realized the beauty of nature, and fell to my knees and repented. After a long pilgrimage I came to St. Petersburg. The empress heard of my healing powers and summoned me. I've been with her ever since."

"How is it, if you're so holy, that I hear of all these scandals in night clubs?"

"Well, I repented, and I can sin again, and repent again," Rasputin said. He proceeded to analyze shrewdly the important people at court, and predicted that with his death the imperial family would be in danger. "I am their protector," he told Leo.

What a capital fellow, this Leo Schumacher, Uncle kept telling his little sister. But Mopsy was still sick about her cousin. "I didn't care who I married after that," she told me.

In November 1913 she and Lyova Schumacher (he was known from then on by the affectionate diminutive) were married. It wasn't an *affaire de coeur*. Marriage in that world often wasn't. When they returned from their honeymoon in Italy, Mopsy was pregnant. On August first, the world war started. Their first child was born in St. Petersburg on October 2. They named her Sophie, but her nanny called her Zoric, which means "Morning Star" in Ukrainian, because she kept waking everyone up before daybreak with her crying. The nickname stuck. Soon afterward Lyova was stationed in Starokonstantinoff, a town a hundred miles from the front. They were there two years, in constant earshot of exploding shells. As the *maréchal de noblesse*, Lyova was in charge of recording the noble births in the district, and as chief of the local *zemstvo*, he was in charge of local administration, caring for the wounded, and keeping the soldiers supplied with guns and bullets.

In the beginning, morale was high. The tsar's popularity was greater than it had been in years. Russians forgot their discontent and concentrated on hating the Germans. In 1915 there was a thirty-day pogrom of the Germans in St. Petersburg. People with German names were hunted down, and some were lynched. St. Petersburg itself was Russified to Petrograd. It was a bad time to have a name like Schumacher.

On January 18, 1916, Collegiate Assessor Leo Arkadievitch Schumacher and all his descendants were permitted by imperial decree to use the name Shoumatoff. According to family legend, the tsar, looking over the document, which is now in my father's safe, exclaimed, "Shoumatoff—how well it sounds!" There is a princely line called Shakhmatoff, and in Leningrad I heard on the radio that a heart transplant had been successfully performed by a surgeon named Shoumakoff; but as far as I know we are the only Shoumatoffs in the world: my parents, my brother and I, my wife and our two children.

Lyova's parents stayed Schumacher. They were too old to change, they said. They lived in a large apartment belonging to the government on an intimate square whose buildings had lilac or cadmium washes and lacy white trim. Arkady Schumacher was a small, energetic man. Unlike most of the Baltic bureaucrats, he was not stuffy or hidebound in reaction, he did not shave his head or wear a monocle. One of their daughters, Olga, lived there with her husband, Thomas de Hartmann, a young composer of such promise that the tsar, after attending one of his ballets, had personally exempted him from military service. The de Hartmanns would become disciples of the Georgian mystic, G. I. Gurdjieff, and would escape with him to the Caucasus.

Lyova's mother, Olga Konstantinovna, was, on her mother's side, a great-granddaughter of Josephine Emilie-Louise de Beauharnais, the story of whose helping her husband escape from prison by changing clothes with him is familiar to most French schoolchildren. She was Empress Josephine's niece and her *dame d'atours*, the lady-in-waiting in charge of her wardrobe. She helped bring the rose to the attention of the French people, and was disfigured by smallpox while her husband, Antoine-Marie Chamance de Lavalette, fought in Egypt. Napoleon rewarded him for his loyal service by making him postmaster-general. On July 18, 1815, during the Bourbon restoration, he was arrested and condemned to the guillotine. His wife went to him and, removing her clothes, hid behind a screen while he, dressed as she, was escorted to the entrance of the prison, where a horse was waiting. By the time the trick was discovered, de Lavalette had a good start to Luxembourg. The soldiers gave chase but lost him in a thick fog. Respecting valor and women, they let her go. Not long afterward, she went insane. Her daughter, also Josephine, married a governor of Warsaw named Phillipeus (first name lost). *Their* daughter married a man named Wolfert, who by a Polish woman named Labounsky, was said to be a morganatic son of Kaiser Wilhelm the First. *Their* daughter was Olga Konstantinovna, who told Mopsy the story.

There was a small, exquisite portrait of Josephine Phillipeus in the apartment. She had been a great beauty. Her hair was in an enormous chignon, interwoven with strands of pearls. Diamonds sparkled at her ears, and her bare shoulders were draped with a filmy stole. Mopsy recognized the artist, Peter Sokoloff. He had painted the prominent families of Russia during the reign of Nicholas I. His portraits were enlarged miniatures in watercolor, on paper rather than the alabaster, porcelain, or ivory which most miniaturists preferred. Since Masha had asked her to copy a Sokoloff portrait of her Scherbatov grandmother, Mopsy had come to admire his work more than anyone's. Sokoloff showed her that watercolor didn't have to be runny, blotchy, or thin; it could be controlled, and vibrant, like the complexion of a young woman.

Mopsy copied the portrait of Josephine Phillipeus; they seemed to be done by the same hand. She painted an enlarged miniature of her mother, who had to sit still for seventy hours. Every hair of her sable and ermine wrap stood out. It was a wonderful likeness. The style of Mopsy's early portraits was evolving. It was derived from Sokoloff, but soon her colors were richer and closer to real skin tones than his, her figures more proportional, and not as stiff.

When Uncle returned from Tashkent, he had ninety percent of the known species in central Asia—eighty thousand butterflies in all. Twenty thousand were in just two genera, *Parnassius* and *Colias*, and there were some twenty new forms to describe. He kept them in cabinets that lined his St. Petersburg apartment. After the Revolution his butterflies were impounded, like all private property. They were taken to the Zoological Museum, where I arranged to see them one morning. I was met at the turnstile by the curator of beetles, a robust man of about sixty named Dr. Kryzhanovsky, who wore in the lapel of his loose-fitting suit the Order of the Patriotic War. He showed me two beetles named for Uncle by the celebrated Russian evolutionist, Andrei Semënov Tian-Shansky. *Carabis avinovi Sem.*, with a coppery red thorax and iridescent green-and-black forewings, lives in the mountains of Sakhalin Island, north of Japan, Dr. Kryzhanovsky told me. *Colpostoma avinovi Sem.*, a nondescript black one not more than a quarter-inch long, inhabits the upper soil surface of forests east of Tashkent that are between two and three thousand meters above sea level. Uncle and Semënov Tian-Shansky had often collected together before the Revolution. Uncle had caught the butterflies, Semënov Tian-Shansky the beetles. "He was the teacher of my teacher, and died at the age of seventy-five during the seige of Leningrad, from starvation," Dr. Kryzhanovsky told me sadly. We looked at tray after tray of Uncle's *Parnassius*, but could not find the unique specimen of *Parnassius autocrator*, well-known in entomological circles, which Uncle had named for the tsar four years before he abdicated. A German had caught it for him in northeastern Afghanistan. Many of the specimens in the museum had Uncle's labels or those of another pre-revolutionary collector, Prince Nicolai Mihailovitch Romanoff. I got the feeling not too many butterflies had been caught after 1917, or at least had not been mounted.

Speaking in admirable English at the February 5, 1913, meeting of the Entomological Society of London, Uncle described his Himalayan expedition and passed around a box that contained his rarest trophies, which brought gasps from the assembled company. In Rennes, France, he called on the celebrated lepidopterist Charles Oberthür, and saw the fantastic collection of Roger Verity in a villa north of Florence. I remember being taken by my father when I was four to see Dr. Verity, the retired doctor of the English-speaking colony, in the dappled light of his wooded hilltop gaping at his trays of *Parnassius*.

Back in Russia Uncle wrote a series of monographs on the biogeography of central Asian butterflies. The Imperial Geographical Society gave him its gold medal, and he was acclaimed a great traveler. At the same time, he was experimenting with certain techniques in his painting to replicate insect wings and luminous shafts of light. There were two exhibitions in Moscow of his entomological studies and his mystical landscapes, which were strongly evocative of Tibet. He met other painters—Benois, Serov, Vrubel—and in one gallery his rainbows, strange clouds, and sketches of the Pamir were hung beside the tumultuous abstracts of Kazimir Malevich and Vasili Kandinski. But his philosophy of art had little in common with that of the two avant-gardists:

his "phantasmagorias," as he called them, celebrated the beauty and intricacy of nature. His people and objects were still recognizable, while Kandinski and Malevich had virtually rejected the external world except for line and color. Uncle attended solemn meetings of the Geographical Society, and with other dabblers in the occult, dimly-lit seances of a clairvoyant named Gusik, a frail Pole who spoke incoherently and was always in a somnolent state. He played delicate improvisations on the piano for the composer Scriabin. He watched the empire's final, extraordinary cultural flowering, and gave himself to it.

In 1911 (the year his father died) Uncle had resigned from the Senate to become a *kammerjunker*, or gentleman-in-waiting, to the tsar. Nika was mortified by his decision to become involved with the court, but his little brother's politics, for all the wildness of his imagination, had always been deeply conservative. The court position was unsalaried, and called for three thousand dollars' worth of uniforms, including a cape with a sea-otter collar, a gold-embroidered tunic, and a tricorn hat cockaded with ostrich feathers. Mopsy remembered seeing him in full regalia on April 1, 1913, at a huge reception in the Winter Palace to celebrate the three hundredth anniversary of the Romanoff dynasty. Every lady had to carry the train of the lady ahead. Mopsy held her mother's. Behind her was the widow of Admiral Makharov, who had died in 1905 at Tsushima, when in a few hours the Japanese sank most of the Russian fleet. She refused to hold Mopsy's train. "But madame, it is etiquette," Mopsy said. At last, with majestic disdain, the woman picked it up. "I looked back, and all I saw were her nostrils," Mopsy recalled. "Uncle was in the gallery with all his gold and feathers, looking like a rare butterfly." When it was her turn, she approached the emperor and curtsied deeply. She thought his eyes were beautiful, his face appealing, and his Russian excellent, but she could not help regretting that a tsar as weak as the last Louis had come at such a bad time.

Uncle was installed at the court on the same day as Prince Felix Yusupov, who would murder Rasputin six years later. The list of gentlemen-in-waiting in the Court Calendar for that year—a little red book the size of a psalter—reads like a roster of the famous names of the empire: Gagarin, Troubetzkoy, Davidov, Tolstoy, Volkonsky, Dolgoruky, Tatishchev, Sheremetyev, Pouschine, Lamsdorff, Berg, Kantakuzin, Scherbatov. Because of his attentiveness and his fluency in several languages, Uncle was put in charge of receiving foreign guests. Late in July 1914 he took part in the presentation to the tsar of an envoy from one of his cousins, the new duke of Mecklenburg-Schwerin. The ceremonies were followed by a lunch with the tsar, his four daughters, the envoy, and the *Oberhofmeister*, or Grand Marshal of the Court, Count Paul Benckendorff. "We had *botvinia*," Uncle recalled much later, "a complicated cold soup into which you are supposed to slip a side dish of sturgeon, crayfish, eggs, and chopped greens—a sort of iced bouillabaisse. The envoy had some difficulty with the dish, and the emperor showed him how to handle it. Conversation was animated and general." After lunch, Count Benckendorff took Uncle aside and told him to get the envoy out of the country. "Russia is about to declare war on Germany," the count whispered. "Nicholas signs the mobilization order tomorrow." The envoy knew nothing of these plans, and the tsar, who hated unpleasantness, wouldn't have dreamed of telling him directly. On the way to the railroad station, where a special train was waiting, Uncle explained the situation.

"The envoy thanked me profusely for having saved him from internment as an enemy alien. He said he would send me a star of the Griffin of Mecklenburg, making me a knight commander, but of course, he didn't." On the way home, all Uncle could think about was that the trip he had planned for the fall to southeastern Tibet, from Sadiga to Ta Tsienlu, was probably off.

Because of his bad eyesight, Uncle was excused from military service (it would have been hard to imagine him in the trenches, anyway) and worked for the Zemsky Union, an organization that began as a sort of Red Cross, and gradually took on, rather schizophrenically, the supplying of ammunition to the front. At one point, in Lodz, Poland, he and a railroad station full of casualties were completely surrounded by the Germans, but they managed to break through on a hospital train. The Zemsky Union sent him twice to America to buy arms. He entered New York City the first time on March 15, 1915. He had expected to find the New World in blossoming springtime, but instead New York was having one of the worst blizzards he had ever seen. Some American munitions representatives met him at the dock and took him to his hotel. They had tickets for the Ziegfeld Follies that night, they said. Uncle had already noticed in the *Times* that the New York Entomological Society was having a meeting that evening at the American Museum of Natural History. Of course it took priority. "On the very first day I set foot on American soil," he would recall, "I found myself in the familiar and congenial company of fellow entomologists, on the premises of an institution of which I myself was to be a trustee many years later." He was called upon to give an impromptu talk on the relationship between the butterflies of central Asia and North America. When he got to his hotel there was still time for him to see the Follies. Will Rogers delighted him immensely. A cowboy with a lasso fitted perfectly the picture of American life that he had gotten as a boy from the novels of Fenimore Cooper and Captain Mayne Reid.

A latecomer arrived and settled himself with two showgirls at a neighboring table in the front circle. "But to my amusement," Uncle wrote in a passage that is a good specimen of the rococo prose of his later years, "it was the portly old gentleman who outshone his feminine companions in bejeweled splendor. He had perfectly tremendous studs scintillating with gems, and cuff links that were solitaires of prodigious caratage. It was Diamond Jim Brady in person. I admit an unexpected revelation of an America I had heard of but never thought was credible." Uncle made a sketch of "this grotesque personage" on his menu card and gave it to a woman who thought it was very amusing.

The great dancer, Vaslav Nijinsky, was in town, and on another night Uncle watched him perform at the Century Theater. Nijinsky was at the peak of his career. He had not yet leapt, in his quest for the fourth dimension, into catatonic madness. When he performed the *entrechat-dix*, which only he could do, and covered fifteen or twenty feet in a single *grand jeté*, he seemed to stop in midair for half a second. *Le Spectre de la Rose* lasted just twelve minutes, but the curtain fell to thunderous applause. *Scheherazade* was so powerful that it left the audience drained and clapping weakly. Uncle went backstage—he had met Serge Diaghilev in St. Petersburg—and made a portrait of Nijinsky, still in costume and glistening with sweat. Then he went back to his hotel and painted a macabre watercolor of his "Reminiscences of the Ballet." Nijinsky, in a costume of curled petals, is slowly, like someone stretching awake, bursting into blossom. A horrible caricature of Kaiser Wilhelm threatens the audience, which consists of Diaghilev in his beaver hat, a poodle, and a matron peering through opera glasses. Behind them a hansom cab is going down a street in a strange pastel light.

When Uncle returned to Russia, the mood of the country had changed. With the number of dead in the millions, there was no longer any enthusiasm for prosecuting the war. People were openly speaking against the tsar and his German wife; revolution was in the air. Three days before the imperial family was arrested, Uncle left Petrograd and went to Shideyevo, where he served, during the brief existence of the Provisional Government, as the last marshal of nobility for the district of Kobelyaki. One evening in July he was examining the reeds below with his telescope and discovered a small flock of gray cranes wading stealthily after frogs. There was a distant rumbling of thunder. The cranes, frightened, took to the air and flew low over the house. At that moment he had an intuition that the old Russia was about to disappear forever, and that on his next trip to America—the Zemsky Union was sending him again in September—he would be going to stay. He went into the house and wandered from room to room, touching objects whose grace and beauty had informed his sensibility. He went into the library and wondered which of his seven thousand entomological titles he should take. Hübner's monumental work, with its large engraved plates, was tempting, but it was much too heavy to carry on the trans-Siberian express. The situation had so deteriorated by then that there was no way for anything to be shipped. Whatever he took with him he would have to carry himself, and be unobtrusive about it. At last he settled on just one volume, the original one hundred plates for a work contemplated, but never published, by the eighteenth-century British lepidopterist John Abbott. He had paid a small fortune for it at an auction in London, but it was really priceless. It would be the nucleus of his new library.

Before he left Shideyevo, he tried to get it all into one painting, ten inches by fourteen, and nearly succeeded. In it is the blue drawing room, or rather its reflection in a large oval mirror originally from the Winter Palace, which had been given to Vladimir Panayev. There are the portraits, the white marble columns at the door, the row of mahogany chairs, whose seats are upholstered in shiny white chintz with blue bachelor buttons (a detail that can only be verified with the help of a magnifying glass). Through an open window, the *liman* with its whimsical crook can be seen beyond the line of Lombardy poplars in the lower garden, whose tips are illuminated by the end of a rainbow. A porcelain man in eighteenth-century dress is playing a flute and standing on one of the General's Bukhara rugs. In the center of the picture is a swirling vortex made up of flowers—delphinium, peony, iris—and leafy vegetables, topped with a spiraling green ear of corn. In the upper right the chandelier of Venetian glass morning glories hangs down. There are glimpses of an ornate doorway, a blue Venetian glass vase, an arching white ceiling painted with octagonal frescoes, a peacock feather from the estate of neighbors named Eius. Forty-five opalescent soap bubbles are rising in the picture, which seems like an unobtainably opulent dream on the verge of dissolving.

Alika, who has known five generations of us and taken care of three, enters the story now. She was born Olga Romanova Alekseevna on a farm in Lithuania, a month after Mopsy, in January 1889. "Alika" is simply an affectionate diminutive of Olga. Though she has lived in America for more than sixty years, her English is still fractured, her accent thick

Eastern European. "During war I work for nice people in Petrograd, Dolgenovs. Friends of Schumachers. Big apartment.
Sixth floor on street corner. One day in February I take Dol-
genov boys in park. Student says, 'Take children home. Revolution starting.' I see through window Cossacks riding.
General is shooting from fourth floor. Bullet from street
comes through window, sticks in my pillow. Drunk soldiers
break in, looking for guns. Then Cossacks come in, say tsar's
brother is coming to stop revolution. Dolgenovs want to go to
Finland. I don't want. Schumacher's son married to rich lady
in south. They have girl. In south it is quiet. I go."

Mopsy and Lyova were on an estate near Starokonstantinoff when they were called to the local church for important
news. As the priest read a statement in which the tsar announced that he was abdicating, everyone in the church
wept. The Shoumatoffs returned quickly to Petrograd. At
the Schumachers' apartment they met Alika, a handsome
woman of twenty-seven, with jutting cheekbones and an air
of dependability, and decided to take her to Shideyevo. "We
was three days on the train," Alika continues, "then horses
brought us twenty miles from Poltava. Big house. So many
halls, halls. I used to get lost. So many help." Alika's job
was to take care of two-year-old Zoric. She was a wild child
and wouldn't let Alika comb or dress her. Picking berries in
the garden, Alika was amazed at the fertility of the soil.
Having been worked to the bone from childhood, she was
amazed, too, at the carefreeness of the peasants. After putting
Zoric to bed, she would go down to the village and listen to
the women singing Ukrainian songs. The air was so clean it
made you want to sing. For ten years Alika had worked in
a dress factory in Riga, and had almost died of tuberculosis.
There were thirty Austrian prisoners of war working on the

estate. They were just as glad not to be fighting. They would join in the songs and dance gallantly with Alika and the peasant women.

Uncle kept saying how wonderful America was, and after he left, in the beginning of September, he started sending cables urging them to join him. Early in October, Alexandra Nicolaevna came to Alika and told her they were going to visit her son in America. Alika wondered what to do. Lithuania had been overrun by the Germans. She didn't even know what had happened to her family. What else could she do but go with these people? In the hurried days before their departure, Alika helped pack the trunks and baskets. Mopsy made a pilgrimage to the Kozhelschina monastery about forty miles away, and bought a small traveling icon of the Virgin, painted on mother-of-pearl, to protect them on their journey. A generation before Mopsy's time, a miraculous healing had happened there. One day the crippled daughter of Countess Kapnist was polishing icons with her nurse when she heard her mother, a vain, ambitious woman, say to a visitor in the next room, "Isn't it terrible, I have to bear this cross—a crippled child?" The girl prayed to the icon of the Holy Virgin for strength and struggled to her feet, completely cured. There was a tremendous furor in the district. The countess built a monastery and wanted her daughter to be the Mother Superior, but the girl ruined her plans by getting married.

They left Shideyevo in three carriages and a wagon: Mopsy, Alexandra, Zoric, Leo, his secretary Stepanov, Alika, and a maid named Mila, who would turn Bolshevik during the trip and be deported as a communist soon after they reached America. The leavetaking was not as emotional as it might have been because they thought they were going only for eight months. The estate was left in charge of Brauns, the manager. He was to take the paintings for safekeeping to their house in Poltava. Years later, in the postwar forties, a black Cadillac pulled into my parents' driveway in Westchester County. They were raking leaves. My father had just gotten out of the navy and was working in New York. He had bought a small frame house that had quartered the servants of the turreted mansion on the corner. I had just been born. The man in the Cadillac introduced himself as the son of Frederic Augustovitch Brauns, the manager of Shideyevo. A mystery for many years, what had happened to the paintings, was suddenly clear: Brauns had sold them and come to America.

In 1912, Nika had spent an hour alone with the tsar, showing him around a *zemstvo* exhibition, and found him shy but engaging. The emperor had been equally taken with Nika. "Your brother is a brilliant man," he had told Uncle at a function the next day. "He has such a charming manner, too. Very natural and simple. I felt quite at ease with him." Whether Nika, in his longing to see Russia a democracy, supported the deposing of Nicholas in February 1917 is not known. He did serve as Undersecretary of the Interior in the government that took over, first under Prince G. E. Lvov, then under his old schoolmate, Sasha Kerensky. Bruce Lockhart, the British agent in Russia, knew Nika then. "I was in almost daily contact with the men who, sorely against their will, formed the first provisional government after the abdication of the tsar: Prince Lvoff, Chelnokoff, Manuiloff, Avinoff, Maklakoff, Novikoff, Kokoshkin," Lockhart wrote. "From intimate personal intercourse I knew that they were appalled by the problem that confronted them as Russian patriots. The problem itself was very succinctly put by Maklakoff . . . in one of those parables in which, owing to the censor, Russians were experts. A motor-car is going down a steep hill. At the bottom there is a precipice. Your mother is in the front seat next to the driver. You yourself are in the back seat. Suddenly you realize that the driver has lost control. What are you to do?"

Nika kept an extensive diary through 1917, but during a raid of his Moscow flat in the thirties, the Soviet secret police found it hidden in the samovar. Other accounts of the rise and fall of the Provisional Government survived: there is Trotsky's, and Kerensky's own, but perhaps the most objective is that of Vladimir Nabokov senior.

The Provisional Government became, as Masha put it, like one of Uncle's soap bubbles, reflecting every color of the spectrum, and eventually bursting. Kerensky was a masterful speaker, who could modulate his voice from a boom to a whisper, but as events quickly showed, he was unequal to the task of uniting the country in a democracy. His big mistake was to underestimate the determination and the ruthlessness of the Bolsheviks. In Mopsy's judgment, he was a "pompous actor who did more harm than anything." Once, in the Russian cathedral in New York, Kerensky ran up to Mopsy and kissed her hand. My brother met him, too, in the early sixties, when a freshman at Stanford University. A forgotten old man by then, Kerensky was reading a book in the Hoover Library. Nick introduced himself as the great-nephew of Nicholas and Andrey Avinoff. Kerensky's eyes started to glisten. "Nika was a beautiful man," he said. "A saint. But Adya was a snob."

Early in March Nika was made chairman of a commission to draw up the procedures for electing the long-awaited Constituent Assembly. The assembly was to decide Russia's future form of government. It was to be a real parliament, with representatives from every part of the country and every segment of its population. Russians had been waiting for such an assembly for over forty years. But when it finally convened, early the following year, the Bolsheviks were firmly in power, and it never had a chance. Between the seventh and sixteenth of November, Lenin directed his successful coup d'etat from headquarters at the Smol'ny Institute. But Nika's commission continued preparing for the elections, which were to begin on the twenty-fifth. On November twenty-third, a Bolshevik ensign entered the Tauride Palace and in the name of the Executive Committee of the Congress of Soviets ordered the electoral commission to disband. Lenin by then had no interest in the Constituent Assembly, though a few months before he had been one of its loudest supporters; he had no desire to work with the Kadets, the Mensheviks, or anyone. "N. N. Avinoff was in the chair," Nabokov wrote in his memoirs, "and his answer, in behalf of the whole commission, was a categorical refusal. The officer left, went to Smol'ny for instructions, and came back with a document signed by Lenin and containing an order—very badly worded—to arrest the Kadet electoral commission and send its members to Smol'ny Prison."

The commission was kept in a cramped little room with a low ceiling for five days. "There were from twelve to fifteen of us," Nabokov continued. " 'Among those present' I remember Avinoff, Branson, Baron Nol'de, Vishnyak, Gronsky. . . ." While they were in prison, the elections took place. Of the 41.7 million votes cast, only 9.8 million were for the Bolsheviks. On January 19, the day after the Constituent Assembly finally convened, Lettish soldiers were sent by Lenin to break it up with fixed bayonets. Some of the deputies fled south and joined the White Army, others left Russia for good.

So Nika had no less than the last hope for democracy in Russia on his mind when the Shoumatoff party arrived in Petrograd in October. It was Nika who had arranged for Leo to go to America as a representative of the Ministry of Supplies. The United States had entered the war and had been sending arms to Russia through Vladivostok since May 29. Contracts worth a hundred million dollars were being negotiated. Nika knew that it was no good for his mother and sister to stay in Russia any longer; he also knew that he was staying. Masha and he had already fought about it. She had demanded that Nika think of her and take her away before the country fell to Bolshevism. She was not about to be a martyr. From what she had already seen of the masses in action, she was beginning to agree with Flaubert that universal suffrage was the curse of mankind. Nika had only looked at her sadly. Mopsy had begged him to leave with them, too, but with no better luck. "He was stubborn and impossible," she remembers.

The bitter northern winter had already fallen. It was dark from three in the afternoon to ten in the morning. There were shortages of candles and kerosene, and the use of lights was discouraged for fear of attracting Zeppelins. In the darkness all civilized order was falling apart. Looting and mugging were widespread. The American ambassador, an elderly plutocrat from Missouri named David R. Frances, had to give up his nightly constitutional on the Furshtatskaya, which he was in the habit of taking with a cigar in one hand and a portable bronze cuspidor in the other.

The Shoumatoff party left Petrograd on the night of October fourteenth, on the last trans-Siberian express. It was a big holiday—the Feast of the Protection of the Virgin. At the station Nika, with Zoric in his arms, led the way through the crowd. This was the last they would ever see of him. Stopping only at major stations like Baikal and Irkutsk, the train took three weeks to reach Vladivostok. Its corridors were packed with soldiers and civilians. Another train, with its windows smashed, and full of mutinous soldiers, chased them into Manchuria. Mopsy, who was five months pregnant with my father, suffered throughout the crossing. The woods of Siberia seemed endless. They were already filled with snow. Sometimes for the whole day there was not even a house. Zoric became very sick. An army doctor aboard diagnosed it as pneumonia, and wired ahead for medicine. Alika soaked towels in turpentine and hung them in their compartment. In Manchuria they lost the Bolshevik train by pulling off on a siding. Farther on the track was demolished and they stopped for two days while it was repaired. Zoric's fever broke, and by the time they reached Vladivostok, she was much better. In the station they napped on their baggage until the steamer was ready to take them to Japan, where they were transferred by rickshaw to an overnight train to Yokohama. Alika recalls that the Japanese women on the train scratched their heads with long sticks so as not to spoil their coiffures. In Yokohama they were taken again by rickshaw to the *Tanya Maru*, a steamer bound for Honolulu. On Hawaii Alika saw her first banana tree, and was shocked to discover that pineapples grow on the ground. Lyova bought a paper and read that Russia had fallen. That meant that the several hundred thousand imperial roubles he had with him were worthless and that his sponsor, the Ministry of Supplies, no longer existed. Their total assets were now what they had with them: some dresses, linen, silverware, diamonds, around fifty thousand dollars in American currency, five pale blue satin pillows painted on by Alexandra Nicolaevna, about a hundred glass negatives of Nika's photographs, and six icons, including a copy of the family icon.

The suddenly stateless, missionless diplomats continued to San Francisco, where they discovered they had gained a day. After two days of sightseeing they took a train east. Mopsy saw that America was not just a land of gangsters and skyscrapers, as she had imagined, but a vast, open country like Russia. On December first they arrived at Pennsylvania Station. Uncle was there to meet them. His enthusiasm about America was heartening.

✥ ✥ ✥

Since the beginning of October 1917 no one in the family had been back to Shideyevo. Mopsy had heard a rumor from a neighbor who had got out of Russia in the early twenties that the house had been destroyed in the civil war. Sixty-two years later, I didn't know what I'd find or if I'd even be allowed to drive out there. It would depend on whether the local Intourist officials in Poltava would permit an excursion beyond the city limits. Leaving Kharkov, my wife and I and our baby son headed west toward Poltava in the beginning of October. The steppe at least could not have changed much. It stretched in every direction like a dusty black sea, and so flat we could see the earth curving. It already had languorous and idyllic connotations for me. I had read Aksakov, exulting in its "immeasurable, immense solitude," as he fished in a river "so clear that a coin dropped to a depth of fourteen feet could easily be distinguished lying on its sandy bed"; or waded through the "long succulent grass, dotted with countless flowering shrubs, fragrant clover, scarlet gilliflowers, Turk's cap lilies, and valerian."

I had read Gogol's early stories. "How intoxicating, how

magnificent is a summer day in Little Russia!" he wrote in one. "How luxuriously warm the hour when midday glitters in stillness and sultry heat. . . . Everything might be dead; only . . . from time to time the cry of a gull or the ringing note of a quail sounds in the steppe and . . . the insects . . . flit like sparks of emerald, topaz, and ruby." I had read the journal of John Rickman, a British Quaker who served as a country doctor in Little Russia during the First World War and through the Revolution. "There are few things pleasanter than a sledge drive across the steppe on a Sunday morning," he wrote. "There is a stir in the air, the snow under the runners squeaks crisply, and the muffled thumping of the horse's feet and the rocking of the sledge over the undulating ground produce a peaceful contentment."

In the government of Poltava, seventy percent of the steppe is used for agriculture: corn, sunflower, and white sugar beets, mostly. Seven percent is wooded—mostly along the rivers—and the remaining twenty-three percent is clay or sand and is used to make bricks, tile, glass, and ceramics. By now the crops were all in, and there was already a white icing of frost until mid-morning. We passed people walking in recently harvested cornfields and collecting missed ears in burlap bags. Some of the fields were chartreuse with mustard that had already flowered in them since the last harvest. But most of them lay in strips of bare black earth—the famous *chernozem* that lies up to five feet deep and is one of the world's most fertile mediums. We felt dust in our nostrils, even though the windows of the car were up. In Mopsy's day, everyone had shielded the lower half of their faces with dust protectors, called *pylniki*, when out on the steppe. Occasionally a flatbed truck loaded with greens would roar past us, with bits of its cargo flying off. We saw groups of men and women

lying on the roadbank or on piles of straw and roasting potatoes. They wore drab quilted clothing and hats with ear flaps
pulled down. Those who had potatoes for sale had one displayed on the end of a stick, and sat eating them while waiting for business. They were like latter-day Potato-eaters.

The villages of the open steppe are different from those
in the north. Because of the scarcity of wood, the *izbahs* give
way to *hatas*, whose roofs are thatch or corrugated tin, and
whose walls are brick or whitewashed stucco. In one village
we stopped at a tearoom whose patrons were mostly truckers,
and had *galoushki*, pieces of dough in a fatty bouillon. The
Avinoffs had served *galoushki* to their hands at the day's end.
After lunch I bought and smoked a fine Cuban cigar. In front
of the cottages of another village, kerchiefed *baboushki* were
sitting behind buckets of apples. We stopped and asked one
for half a dozen. She said she was only selling them by the
bucket. I asked how much she wanted. "Pay whatever you
want," she said.

In Poltava, I went to the Intourist office. They were very
friendly, not full of protocol like their Moscow counterparts.
The excursion to Shideyevo was arranged on the spot. That
morning I set out in the car with a picnic basket and a
handsome young woman named Tanya, whose round face
and narrow eyes were perhaps a sign of Tatar blood. Tanya
and I would spend much of the next few days together in
the archives of libraries and museums. She was a natural,
friendly person and would touch me on the arm when she
got excited about something.

We headed south, toward the Dneiper, through little
villages that were just as Gogol had described them more
than a century before, each with its central mud puddle that
never dried, and blinding white geese waddling in it but

never seeming to get dirty. Tanya asked to stop in one, where her father-in-law was living in retirement, and ran off to say hello. In a little while she returned with some gefilte fish, wrapped in newspaper; it is a Ukrainian dish, as well as a Jewish one.

Although I'd never seen them before, I felt as if I'd been born with a sense of these surroundings within me. The feeling of déjà vu started to get really strong when we reached Nekvorosche, where Mopsy had gotten her mail. Nekvorosche was a particularly cozy hamlet. Its main street was cobbled and lined with whitewashed *hatas* that stood in the shade of old oaks and poplars. We went into the one official-looking building and shook hands with the secretary of the village soviet. He knew who the Avinoffs were. "My great-great-grandmother, Anna Sobuta, worked for them," he said. "One winter, when they were in St. Petersburg, she found a bundle of money they had left in one of the rooms. When they returned in the spring she turned it over to them. The General peeled off a twenty-five-rouble note and gave it to her for her honesty. It was more money than she'd ever had." I asked how to get to Shideyevo, and what was there. He said it was a *kolkhoz*, a collective farm, now, the Maxim Gorky Collective Farm. The big house and its outbuildings were long gone, except for one of the barns, which had been a school for many years, and was now the central office of the *kolkhoz*.

Not far from Nekvorosche, we came to a high bluff that plunged into a marsh in which a gleaming band of water—the river Orel—twisted. We took the road that went along its crest, the same road that Catherine the Great had used during her tour through Little Russia. I was starting to get very excited at the thought of finally coming face to face

with this nineteenth-century novel from which I had somehow emerged, and which had always been more appealing
to me than any of the scenarios I'd been able to conjure for
myself a hundred years later.

After several miles we met a man driving a cart with
wooden wheels. The harness, whose tugs were connected to
a thick wooden hoop that arched over the horse's neck, was
typical of rural Russia. I asked the driver what kind of wood
the hoop was made of. "Willow," he said, taking a pipe from
his mouth. "You soak it in hot water until it bends." When
I said that I was an Avinoff, his jaw dropped. "*Seriozno?*"
he asked. "Are you kidding?"

I recognized from Nika's photographs the broad, straight
approach to the house, but the cherry orchard on either side
of it was gone, and instead of a six-pillared portico at the
end, there was a small post office. We parked and went in.
A woman of about fifty, with an orange scarf about her head
and shoulders and a mouth brimming with silver, was gos-
siping with the postmistress. When I explained who I was,
she got very excited. We practically hugged each other. She
led me outside to the edge of the ramparts. I recognized the
liman in the distance and could tell from the alignment of
its two pools that we were standing exactly where the house
had been. But there was no trace of it, no rubble, or even
a depression in the ground. Except for an area that had been
cleared for a playground, the site was smothered with tall
grass and wildflowers: campanula, clover, and yarrow,
mostly. The village below looked clean and prosperous, but
much smaller: there were only a few *hatas* at the road junc-
tion, where dozens had been before. "Come," said the
woman with the orange scarf and the silver smile, skipping
down the ramparts like a child and beckoning. "The vineyard

was there. This was the nobles' garden. I heard from Mama that it was beautiful, but *ooo*, a lot of work." I waded after her through the overgrowth, flushing a nettle wren. A smell of burning straw and dung came from the houses below. We entered a yard, which an old woman was sweeping with a twig broom. Huge sweet potatoes and calabashes of assorted shapes and colors, a wooden pitchfork, and other homemade implements stood against the house. The small barn was full to the roof with hay, and there was a good supply of straw-and-dung bricks, called *kiziaki*, the main fuel of the steppe, piled against its wall. "You're old enough to know, Auntie," said the woman who had brought us there. "This is the grandson of Elizaveta Nicolaevna Avinova. He has come from America." The old woman looked scared, uncertain how to respond to such an unusual event. "No, I wouldn't know," she said, shaking her head emphatically. "I didn't come from here." Then her husband came out in his bare feet—he had been taking a nap—and stared at me through a milky veil of cataracts. He asked us in and sat us at a table covered with a checkered cloth. The interior—the shriveled herbs and strings of dried apple slices hanging from the rafters, the stove with its *lezhankas*, the icon in the corner— was right out of *Rolling-Flax*. Tanya translated his patois into Russian and squeamishly refused a glass of milk from their cow. It was still warm. "I don't think I ever spoke with Elizaveta Nicolaevna," he began, "but I used to watch her drive by in her *karzinka*. She married a stout man. Her brother Nika was good to us. He brought us plows and winnowing machines that made our work easier. Andrey never did a thing for us. I can still see him running down the brick path in the garden after butterflies. What more can I say? I was only fifteen when they left. I took care of the pigs, then the cows. There were many herds. They asked Masha, the servant girl, to go with them to America, but she didn't want to. She still lives in the district, but not in this village."

"My grandmother is still alive, too," I said (she still had a year to live), and showed him a postcard of her portrait of Roosevelt.

"She must be a hundred," he said.

"No. Almost ninety-one."

"You don't say. And what of her brothers?"

"Andrey died in America in 1949. Nika stayed in Russia. He was arrested in 1937. We don't know for sure, but he was probably shot in prison."

"After they left," the old man went on, "the manager, Frederic Augustovitch, took most of what was in the house to Poltava and sold it. The villagers took some. My father got one of the General's old flintlocks, but that got sold long ago. The books were taken to Kobelyaki in fifteen carts. One of them weighed three *puds*, my uncle Afanasy told me. [A *pud* is thirty-six pounds avoirdupois.] A few months later, the Germans came."

Between 1918 and 1920 the Ukraine, as Little Russia had just renamed itself, was a turbulent limbo. The estates there, as in all of Russia, had been nationalized on November 8, 1917, but on the following January 28 the Ukraine, taking advantage of the chaos after the Revolution to break away from Russia, declared itself a republic. Its independence was short-lived, however: the Bolsheviks took Kiev on February 8, and were themselves driven out by the Germans within the month. In the Treaty of Brest-Litovsk on March 3, the Ukraine received a second independence that was in effect a German occupation and lasted until the Central Powers were defeated in the West and the armistice was signed on November 11. By the end of 1918 five separate armies were fighting on the Ukrainian steppe. The old man remembered a brief period in 1919 when anarchic peasant bands under the semi-legendary guerrilla leader, Nestor Makhno, took over the big house. This was after the Germans had come and gone twice. Ukrainian nationalists, with yellow-and-blue flags, also passed through that year. Then, during 1920, there was a savage civil war in which the Bolsheviks, helped by Makhno's bands and the Ukrainian industrial working class, crushed both the nationalist government of Petlyura in Kiev and the White Army of General Anton Denikin. The territory became the Ukrainian Soviet Socialist Republic, which it still is, although the yearning for independence, both at home and among exiles, is as strong as ever. That summer, the old man said, he and the other villagers watched Red *partizani* put the big house to flame. "They burned it so the Germans wouldn't come back and shoot us," he explained.

Word of my arrival had reached the president of the *kolkhoz*, a man of about forty-five named Boris, who was waiting for me on the ramparts. He took me into a building that Mopsy would later recognize from my photographs as the old machine shop. In his office he told me that after three years and nine months, the current five-year plan for the Maxim Gorky Collective Farm was one hundred and two percent on schedule. There was a knock on the door. A boy came in with a brick that had the letter A stamped on it. It was from the old brick factory near Schekuchin's house. Boris wrapped the brick in a copy of the *Komsomol Pravda* and gave it to me. "I understand Avinoff was a retired general from St. Petersburg," he said. I gave him some photocopies of Nika's photographs. He had never seen what it looked like in the nineteenth century. We went to his house—I had asked to visit the home of a typical *kolkhoznik*—and he showed me the modern wall system in his living room. It was made of Formica that looked like laminated oak, and had a drop-leaf bar and a television-audio section. There were about six hundred television sets on the *kolkhoz*, he told me. We went to see the monument commemorating the two hundred and twenty men from the village who had been killed in the last war. Fresh flowers were strewn beneath it. Whole clans—the important peasant families in Mopsy's day—had been wiped out. I counted ten men in the Oleshko family, eight Kalnechenkos, fifteen Moshuras. An old man with a bad leg, who had been leaning against a wall of the nearby House of Culture, which was a sort of recreation hall, hobbled over and shook his fist at me. "You go back to your country and tell them we want peace," he said. "I was wounded in that war. Look how many died from our village. We don't want that ever to happen again."

Tanya was getting anxious to return to Poltava. I took a final walk to the edge of the ramparts and decided that I had probably learned all that I was going to learn. As we were getting into the car, the woman with the silver smile ran up and gave me a watermelon. I was very grateful for it. In Leningrad I'd stood for half an hour in a watermelon line.

I threw the brick out the car window on the way back to Poltava—something I now deeply regret. It seemed at the time a perfect example of useless baggage from the past. But I had taken a lot of pictures, to show Mopsy when we returned to America. She was distressed as we looked at my slides. "It's so sad," she said. "Everything is a kind of wilderness." She couldn't understand how they could have destroyed the house so thoroughly. The walls had been four feet thick. They must not have only burned it; they must have blown it up. It had not just been destroyed; it had been destroyed with a vengeance. I wondered if partisans who were just passing through would have gone to all that trouble. Certainly the people there now had seemed to share none of my nostalgia. "Before, we didn't have the right to walk in the forest and the fields," an old woman I had met on the ramparts, carrying a bundle of reeds on her back, had said to me. "It was the nobles' land. Now it belongs to us." I thought of a passage in Rickman's journal in which he describes how, after the tsar had been forced to abdicate, the peasants came to him complaining of new symptoms:

Presbyopia had not previously affected the daily life of the peasant as he did no near work; when he cut logs to build his house or sawed wood to make the window frames he did not measure closer than an inch. But now old men came to me with aching eyes: for they were learning to read now that they could do so without incurring the suspicion that they wanted to revolt. They borrowed schoolbooks and took instruction from their grandchildren. Of their land hunger there had been much talk before the Revolution came, but I never guessed that the craving would be so strong.

For the rest of that evening, Mopsy was unusually quiet. But gradually she recovered her spirits, and we heard again her resonant, resilient laughter. "It is as it says in the psalms," she said at last. "Man is like grass. It was there, and nothing remains."

Mopsy's last Easter.

UNCLE'S COPY OF
THE OVINOVSKAYA
ICON.

GENERAL ALEXANDER AVINOFF AND FAMILY. THE BOY IN VELVET
AND RUFFLES IS NICHOLAS.

SHIDEYEVO, FRONT
VIEW.

SHIDEYEVO, BACK VIEW.

Mopsy (right) and governess in the entrance hall with trompe l'oeil in the background.

The church wing at Shideyevo.

CHURCH INTERIOR.

THE HALLWAY AT SHIDEYEVO.

SHIDEYEVO INTERIOR WITH ALEXANDRA NICOLAEVNA.

A drawing room, Shideyevo.

UNCLE AND MOPSY PLAYING BINTZ WITH TWO OF THEIR GOVERNESSES.

ALEXANDRA LUKIANOVITCH
NÉE PANEYEV, MOPSY'S
GRANDMOTHER.

THE VENEZIANOFF
PORTRAIT OF
VLADIMIR
PANEYEV'S
CHILDREN.

MOPSY (LEFT),
FRAULEIN BRANDT,
AND ALEXANDRA
NICOLAEVNA IN
CRIMEAN
HATS WITH
"THUMBSTICKS"
(THE THUMB IS
INSERTED IN THE
FORK WHILE
WALKING).

Nicholas Avinoff.

Frances Beatrice Whishaw.

ONE OF MOPSY'S
GOVERNESSES.

TEA ON THE BALCONY AT SHIDEYEVO (LEFT TO RIGHT): ALEXANDRA
AND NICHOLAS AVINOFF; MOPSY; THE GENERAL'S AIDE-DE-CAMP,
"BOOTS"; MISS WHISHAW; UNCLE, HOLDING AN INSECT; THE RADICAL
TUTOR IVAN IVANOVITCH.

ALEXANDRA NICOLAEVNA (LEFT) WITH IVAN IVANOVITCH AND
MISS WHISHAW.

PINDY, THE OLD SERF.

ALEXANDRA NICOLAEVNA
AVINOFF IN COURT DRESS.

ALEXANDRA NICOLAEVNA RECEIVING THE ARCHBISHOP OF POLTAVA
AND THE CHIEF OF POLICE.

GOING ON A PICNIC IN THE LANDAU. UNCLE IS HOLDING A
LONG-HANDLED BUTTERFLY NET.

A PICNIC WITH FRIENDS AND NEIGHBORS. MOPSY IS SECOND LEFT,
UNCLE FIFTH, AND NIKA SEVENTH.

HAYING AT SHIDEYEVO.

TENNIS AT SHIDEYEVO.

GRAPE TASTING AT SHIDEYEVO (LEFT TO RIGHT): FRAULEIN
BRANDT; MASHA; ALEXANDRA NICOLAEVNA; MAKRAUSOV,
THE ESTATE MANAGER BEFORE BRAUNS; MOPSY.

THE COURTYARD AND OUTBUILDINGS.

THE FLESGEL, WHERE THE FAMILY STAYED DURING THE WINTER WHEN THEY WERE AT SHIDEYEVO.

THE POND AT SHIDEYEVO.

ON THE BALCONY (LEFT TO RIGHT): A NEIGHBOR, TWO UNIVERSITY FRIENDS OF NIKA'S, MISS WHISHAW, UNCLE, ALEXANDRA NICOLAEVNA, MOPSY.

THE AVINOFF FAMILY, 1899 (LEFT TO RIGHT): NICHOLAS, UNCLE, ALEXANDRA, NIKA, MOPSY.

MOPSY.

MOPSY IN UKRAINIAN
PEASANT DRESS.

MOPSY'S SNOW STATUE OF
MARIE ANTOINETTE.

UNCLE'S VOLTAIRE.

UNCLE WITH HIS
BICYCLE.

PORTRAIT WALL IN THE BLUE DRAWING ROOM. CATHERINE THE GREAT
IS SECOND RIGHT; PETER IS TO HER LEFT; NICHOLAS I IS FAR RIGHT.

Igor Demidov (left) and Nika, the two
young revolutionaries.

Lyova in uniform.

Mopsy and Lyova as newlyweds.

Olga Konstantinovna Schumacher.

Arkady Alexandrovitch
Schumacher.

MOPSY'S COPY OF PETER
SOKOLOFF'S PORTRAIT OF
JOSEPHINE PHILLIPEUS.

ONE OF MOPSY'S EARLY
MINIATURES OF HER
MOTHER.

UNCLE IN COURT DRESS.

SHIDEYEVO. ONE OF THE VILLAGES BELOW THE HOUSE WITH THE
LIMAN IN THE BACKGROUND.

THE SAME VIEW TODAY.

Part Three

George
Vashington
Bridge

It was a new world. Most of the former Russian nobility, suddenly out in the cold, with their life support system unceremoniously pulled out from under them, hadn't the first idea of how to make a living. Outside of card-playing, horse-riding, and a fluency in French, they had no skills to speak of. Since the time of Catherine the Great the Russian noble had been a Voltairian aristocrat. His function had been ornamental, to cut an elegant figure. He had not been expected to make a contribution, or to sully himself with mundane matters, as he had during the time of Peter the Great. In the unpublished memoirs of a noblewoman named Irina Ta- tischev, Kerensky's soldiers burst into her Petrograd palace and ask where the kitchen is. She realizes that she doesn't even know. She'd only seen the food come up on the dumb- waiter. To many nobles like Irina, whose devotion to the tsar was unquestioning, almost childlike, the Revolution came as a complete surprise. They couldn't understand why anyone would have wanted, in Irina's words, to "cut the branch he was sitting on." They'd always loved the peasants, and thought the peasants loved them. Now, in exile, they expected any day to return to a "remorseful, hospitable, racemosa-filled Russia," as Vladimir Nabokov put it.

The easiest way to stay afloat was to marry money. There was a market in America and on the continent for Russians of noble rank, especially titled ones, and a good many cashed in on it. The Shoumatoff party, however, had other re- sources. Mopsy could paint exquisite likenesses of people. Uncle had many well-developed sides. He could have had a career in any number of fields—law, diplomacy, piano, art, art history, entomology. He spoke seven languages, read another ten, and exuded erudition. Thanks to Miss Whi- shaw, he and Mopsy spoke perfect English. From their child- hood in Tashkent, they had gotten a taste for adventure and strange places that would help them respond to their new situation with gaiety and interest. Uncle was thirty-three, Mopsy twenty-nine. Their best years were ahead of them. Lyova was thirty. His English wasn't bad. Like many Baltic Russians, he had a background of business administration.

He was a doer, not a brooder. People who knew him describe his personality as "sparkling."

They took a suite at the Savoy—Mopsy, Lyova, Uncle, Alexandra Nicolaevna, Zoric, Alika, Leo's secretary Stepanov, and the maid Mila, who had been Bolshevized on the boat to Honolulu. Uncle and Leo went to Washington and liquidated their commissions. Uncle had already deposited in a New York bank several million dollars of Zemsky Union funds with which he had been entrusted. When the Bolsheviks heard about this money, they demanded that Uncle sign it over. Of course he refused. The funds are supposed to be still gathering interest somewhere. Only the restoration of the Romanoffs could free them.

After a month at the Savoy they hadn't come up with a game plan, but one thing was certain: at fifty dollars a day, they couldn't stay there much longer. They rented an apartment on West End Avenue, and waited for my father to be born. He arrived on February nineteenth. They named him Nicholas. It wasn't a surprising choice. The family is saturated with Nicholases. Both his grandfather and great-grandfather had been Nicholas. So was his uncle, who was still in Russia. My father would name his first son Nicholas, and when my second boy was born two weeks early, by sheer coincidence on Pa's birthday, there was no question that there would have to be a Nicholas in the sixth generation.

With the money that was left, they bought a dairy farm in the Catskills, a dilapidated house with a turret, a veranda, a barn, and a hundred acres near the town of Pine Bush. Norman Armour, the first secretary at the American embassy in Petrograd, had recommended Ulster County. As a commercial venture, the Pine Bush farm was not a success. They sold their milk to Borden's. On its first run to the milk train, Uncle was delegated to drive the wagon. He wasn't sure of the route, and at an intersection the horse pulled one way, and Uncle the other, the wagon capsized, and all the milk spilled into a ditch. The only one who took the farm seriously was Alexandra Nicolaevna, who was already being called by her new American name, Grandmother, which she would have for the rest of her life. Grandmother wore a set of jangling keys about her waist, as she had at Shideyevo, and threw herself into making preserves, wine, and black currant *kvas* with her new friend, the local Dutch Reformed minister, Dr. Sciple. Zoric remembers the sound of corks popping merrily in the basement, and that the *kvas* was awfully good. If it was hard for Grandmother to have been exposed to so much change so late in her life, she never let on. There was a photograph of her in her velvet and ermine court gown on one of the walls, but even in a plain calico house dress, she was still regal. To one American visitor, she seemed "lost in a dream of the past" as she went silently from room to room; but that may have been because she didn't speak English. With anyone who knew Russian, she was perfectly voluble. The visitor also noticed the deep reverence that her children showed her. Little Zoric, however, was already full of mischief like her father. Once she overturned all the chairs in the dining room and ran to Grandmother, screaming "The Bolsheviks are coming! The Bolsheviks are coming!" and the poor woman went into a panic.

The farm became a port of call for newly arrived émigrés. A room downstairs, with four beds, was practically a dormitory. Some came for the weekend. Some bought places nearby. Nichvalodov, who had gone to kindergarten with Uncle, was there a lot. Uncle's cunning miniature of him in the turban of a Persian emir survives. Philopov had been an admiral. His eventual postrevolutionary career is unknown. Toyazholov was a heavy drinker. Uncle did an ingenious Cubist caricature of him as a wine bottle. Deruzhinsky was a noted sculptor. Lodizhensky, once a general, started a restaurant on Manhattan called the Double Eagle. Golokhvastov wrote a long symbolist poem about the fall of Atlantis that Uncle would illustrate in the forties. Brazol was a literary critic and a criminologist, whose books were edited by Maxwell Perkins, a secret agent for both the tsarist and American governments, and a notorious anti-Semite. I have read two books that mention Brazol in half a dozen professions. Each list is different. Iliaschenko was a *porte-malheur*. He was always associated with calamity. He acted on your pocketbook, health, and transportation. If you were in a car with him, you'd have a flat. If you were trying to make a train with him, you'd miss it. If he wandered into the kitchen, your soufflé would stop rising. At the very mention of his name, you were liable to trip. He had been a neighbor in Poltava, and was more or less a permanent fixture.

During the day the émigrés would roll up their sleeves, undo their collars, and work in the vegetable garden. Parties would comb the woods for mushrooms and berries. Once everyone practically died from some mushrooms Uncle had picked. He was positive he'd identified them correctly—they were orange chanterelles and not their toxic mimic, *Clitocybe illudens*—yet everyone felt done in, and was dictating his will. They all recovered, though, and Uncle later discovered that the fungi had been growing near some poison hemlock.

In the evening they would all sit on the porch and rehash the Revolution, or talk about job openings. A lot of Russians were working at the Lion Match Company in Long Island City, which had been started by Kerensky's ambassador to the United States, Boris Bakhmetyev, but none of the Pine Bush crew was quite ready for factory work. After dark—and it got really dark in that Catskill valley—they would stay on the porch and tell ghost stories, a favorite Russian pastime. Grandmother told one about her grandmother, Praskovia Panayeva, which was so well-known that it was in most of the Russian anthologies. Praskovia Alexandrovna had been despondent, and was being guarded continuously so she wouldn't kill herself. One night the dogs began to bark, the door opened, and in walked her father, who had been dead for several years. "Will you please pull yourself together, for the sake of your children, and stop having these thoughts about suicide?" he said, and then went out again. All four attendants saw and heard him clearly, and Praskovia Alexandrovna snapped out of her depression immediately.

Another one was told by Pouschine, a frequent guest at Pine Bush, who, as the last governor of Petrograd, had been in charge of the burial of Rasputin. During the Turkish war of 1878, his grandfather and another young officer had made a pact that the first one of them to die would appear on the day of the other's death. The young officer was killed soon afterward, but Pouschine lived for years longer. One morning, when he was an old man and had all but forgotten the past, as he was gazing down the lilac allée in his garden, he saw a young officer standing at the end of it and beckoning to him. Though in perfect health, he summoned his priest and his lawyer, and sat in his armchair, waiting for the end. The day passed, the sun began to set, there were smells from the kitchen. Everyone was becoming skeptical about his presentiment. Suddenly, there were shrieks in the hall, and the kitchen maid burst in, followed by the chef, who was waving a long knife. She threw herself at the grandfather's feet, and by mistake the cook stabbed and killed him.

Lyova told an even stranger one. When he was in the Senate, he was invited by a colleague, Count Komarovsky, to the count's hunting preserve in the government of Vilna. The count went there once a year to shoot the *gluhar*, or black grouse. The first night they all went to bed very early. The *gluhar* sings before daybreak, and that is the best time to shoot it, because when it sings, it becomes deaf. You can walk right up to it, if you stay out of sight. Soon after Lyova had turned out the lights, a cat jumped on his bed. Lyova petted it. It seemed friendly. After a while another cat jumped on, and Lyova petted it, too. A third jumped on, and then they began to come in great numbers. They all seemed friendly, but Lyova was getting smothered, and shouted for help. The gamekeeper came in and turned on the lights, and all the cats disappeared. The keeper said it was best to leave the lights on. "Why?" Lyova asked. "I'll explain in the morning," the keeper said. Lyova confronted the man at breakfast. Reluctantly, he confessed that he had been making money on the side by raising cats and selling' their skins. The fur was at its best, he said, when the cat was skinned alive. He took Lyova and the count to a pit where he had thrown dozens of skinned cats. "You mean those cats last night were ghosts?" Lyova gasped. The keeper nodded. He had been visited by them at night, too. Back in St. Petersburg Lyova took the count to a friend of his, a mathematics professor who dabbled in exorcism. The professor said to let two or three live cats loose in the house, and the ghosts would go away. It worked. A few years later, Lyova related his experience to Ben Ames Williams, a well-

known short story writer, who, without asking or crediting
him, wrote it up for the *Saturday Evening Post* as "Creatures
of the Night."

One of the former notables who touched base at Pine
Bush in 1919 was an old friend of Uncle and Nika's, Prince
George Lvov. He had been the first prime minister of the
Provisional Government that took over after the tsar's overthrow, and was in America to plead its cause. Those who
had not abandoned it after the Bolshevik coup had regrouped
in Omsk and were desperate for help. Lvov had just arrived
in the country, and expressed to Uncle his astonishment at
the presence of policemen in a democracy. As prime minister
he had done away with the police and released not only all
the political prisoners, but everyone in jail. He was on his
way to the White House to see President Wilson—it was a
week before the Versailles peace conference—and asked Uncle to come with him as his interpreter. "The views on
government that he expressed to Nika were rather fuzzy,"
Uncle would recall. "Many years later, I asked Mrs. Wilson
what impression he had made on her husband, and she replied that the only thing he had said to her about the talk
was, 'What a magnificent beard Lvov has!' " Uncle's inter-
preting was so helpful to Lvov that he asked him to go on
with him to Versailles. They were there three months. Since
Russia was in a state of civil war and had no stable government, it was not formally represented at the conference. Lvov
was the chairman of a subsidiary conference between the
various White Russian splinter groups. At his main mission,
to persuade the Allies to help them fight the Bolsheviks, he
failed. The Allies decided not to interfere directly against
Bolshevism, but to contain it with a *cordon sanitaire* of small
states, which they would guarantee against any aggression.

The tall, bearded figure of Lvov, standing in front of the house at Pine Bush in a fedora and a Chesterfield coat, is unmistakable in one of the photographs. "He spoke in rather jerky little monotones," wrote Bruce Lockhart, the British agent who saw a lot of Lvov between the February and October revolutions. "He was a shy man, and although he bore an aristocratic name, more like a country doctor than an aristocrat. He was an ideal President of the Zemstvo Union, but he was not the stuff of which revolutionary Prime Ministers are made. And yet I doubt if at this period any member of his class could have 'held down' his post. Nature brooks no interference with her processes, and the time for dictators had not yet come or had already passed."

While Uncle was at Versailles, news of interesting Russians over the hill reached the landscape painter, George Inness, Jr., and one afternoon he had them to tea. His house, Chetolah, was filled with paintings by him and his father, who belonged to the Hudson River school. They both painted tremendous vistas with smoke rising from distant cottages and rain misting down. Inness *père*, an epileptic and a Swedenborgian, was a colossal, aberrant figure in the history of American art. His landscapes were more abstract—fuzzy, softened envelopes of space—than his son's, whose iconography was more conventional and specific. The similarity of their styles and subject matter was for the younger Inness a serious psychological problem. Once, in despair, he had burned all his materials and sworn he would never paint again. A few days after meeting the family, Inness came to Pine Bush, and was so taken with Mopsy's small, minutely detailed portrait of Grandmother that he asked Mopsy to do his profile on ivory, as a surprise for his wife. This kind gesture came at just the right moment: Mopsy had been praying to her icons, especially to St. Spiridonius, the money-bringer, for a living other than farming to present itself. Inness liked his portrait so much that he wrote out a check for two hundred and fifty dollars, double the agreed amount. We still have his thank you note, with a small, verdant landscape he whipped off in oils at the top of the page. This was the first money Mopsy made from her art. Grandmother didn't like the idea of it at all. In Russia, a young lady painted watercolors for her own amusement. To be a professional artist was like being an actor or a clown. Your money was supposed to come from a mysterious source, never from the labor of your own hand. But this was a new world.

One afternoon Inness came over with some friends, Frank Seaman and Olive Sarre. Seaman was an advertising tycoon, and had fallen in love with vivacious Mrs. Sarre. Neither of their spouses would give them a divorce, so they were living in sin in the Catskills. Seaman built a many-storied log house in which to entertain his New York friends and clients, and called it "the Hut." Other buildings were added, and he got the idea of running the place as a business. If Mrs. Sarre couldn't be seen with him in society, he would bring society to her. The first hundred guests invited to Yama Farms, as the resort was called, included the "Famous Four," Thomas Edison, Henry Ford, Harvey Firestone, and the long-bearded naturalist, John Burroughs; and they returned often to camp in its woods. Words of Burroughs were engraved over the Hut's immense stone fireplace: "It is so easy to get lost in this world. I come here to find myself." Yama Farms became a haven for harried industrialists, a place where they could enjoy the company of the outstanding intellects of the day without being fussed over. The "first hundred" proposed a second, and soon a distinguished clientele was coming from all over the hemisphere. "If you were introduced to Mr. Waterman," Mopsy recalled, "it would be the fountain pen; Mr. Colgate, the soap; Mr. Eastman, the Kodak." It was understood that no mention would be made of money. The guests got whopping bills long after their visit. No expenses were spared for their comfort. Trout were kept alive in vats of seething water. There was a tricky nine-hole golf course, and the rooms were filled with antiques chosen by Mrs. Sarre. Seaman ran the place at a large deficit, which he made up by signing new advertising accounts with his guests.

Mrs. Sarre saw that the Russians Inness had brought were having a rough time and being noble about it. Certainly they were not cut out for cows, chickens, and the farming routine. She asked if Mopsy would come to Yama Farms and do a miniature of her. "What does a woman of your age want with a portrait?" Seaman asked when they were back in the car. She said that it was a "war contribution." In time Seaman saw that Mopsy's work was something it wouldn't hurt to be associated with, and he invited her to be a sort of portraitist-in-residence at Yama Farms.

Sometime in 1920, the family sold the Pine Bush farm and moved to the village of Napanoch, twenty miles deeper in the mountains, and next to Yama Farms, where Seaman installed them in a colonial mansion called Southwick. It was a rambling country house that had gone on growing. High ceilings gave the rooms a sense of openness, and a portico of white columns reminded the family of Shideyevo. For the first time they began to feel at home in America. At Yama Farms they met a lot of people. Uncle was actually proposed to by Evangeline Johnson, a Johnson and Johnson Johnson, but gently let her know he wasn't interested. There is a picture of him, taken during a picnic with the pharmaceutical heiress, sitting cross-legged in his bowtie on a slab of speckled granite that projects vertiginously over the cliffs behind Lake Minnewaska. Miss Johnson ended up marrying Leopold Stokowski, the conductor, and when she complained after a year, Uncle told her, "Well, now you must face the music." He became friends with Carl Akeley, a big-game hunter who had shot the stuffed elephants at the American Museum of Natural History. Akeley gave Zoric a book called *Tales of Nature's Wonderland*, and helped set up in the basement of Southwick a child's museum of butterflies and rock crystals. When they were introduced to Poultney Bigelow, he was wearing an old corduroy suit and introduced himself as Poultney Bigelsky. Bigelow had recently sailed around the world in a small boat. He had been thrown out of Russia in 1910 for saying offensive things about the tsar. When they returned to Southwick, he was sitting at the piano in a tuxedo, playing the Russian national anthem. He would become a good friend, as would Edwin Bechtel, who had roomed at Harvard with the poet Wallace Stevens and had cultivated in Bedford, New York, an extraordinary rose garden where, at the end of boyhood, I used to go for inspiration. Once they watched a tree-chopping contest between Edison, Ford, Firestone, and Burroughs. Seaman gave each man an ax, and they started swinging at trees of similar girth. Burroughs won, as expected. "Only God can make a tree," he exclaimed when his was down. Edison was supposed to be deaf, but when Uncle said that ninety percent of Russians had heard of Thomas Edison, he heard it quite well. Mopsy painted Ford's son Edsel and Edsel's family, but it was tiny Harvey Firestone whose family, over the years, would give her more business than any other. There must be sixty of her portraits in Firestone homes and boardrooms.

Famous writers, scientists, explorers, musicians—people who fit the category of "Lion of the Hour"—were invited by Seaman to entertain his guests. Ethel Newcomb came and played the piano. Rose O'Neill, who had invented the kewpie doll, came and painted murals of the fat pink cherubs with tiny wings in a room that became known as the Rose O'Neill room. Even the Hindu poet, Rabindranath Tagore, who had won the Nobel prize in 1913, spent a few days at Yama Farms. He came walking down the snowy road to Southwick one morning with Baron Rosen, who had been Russia's ambassador to the United States in 1905, at the time of the humiliating Portsmouth peace with Japan. "I'm not responsible for bringing this Indian," Rosen said to Grandmother, who was drinking tea in the kitchen. "I was walking down the hill to see you, and he joined me." Mopsy and Uncle were fascinated with Tagore, and both asked if they could do his portrait. He agreed, took off his top hat, and sat in an armchair in the middle of the living room. As sister and brother sketched from different angles his dark, steady eyes and his flowing white beard, Tagore compared the human condition to that of an unhatched chick, pecking away at its shell and not knowing what is in store until the egg breaks, and real life begins. At one point, as the poet was pulling a handkerchief out of his pocket, a dime spilled out onto the carpet. "Isn't it odd," he said in excellent Oxford English. "An old gentleman gave me this as he was waiting for his car. Do I look like a tramp?" That evening, Seaman identified the donor of the dime as John D. Rockefeller. Before leaving, Rockefeller had mentioned giving ten cents to an "old Negro."

Mopsy did a big likeness of Seaman for the reception room. She painted Rudolf Wurlitzer, the music publisher, tuning a Stradivarius. In three years at Yama Farms, she painted about fifty portraits. By then she was established. Without entirely breaking her connection with Yama Farms, she moved her studio to the Plaza Hotel, where she had more work than she could do, and from then on it was always that way. After that brief, disagreeable taste of poverty at Pine Bush, she would never have to see it again.

A few years ago, driving through the heart of what is now the borscht belt, I stopped at Napanoch. Southwick had burned to the ground not long before, and on its foundation stood a cinderblock Elks' Club. The Hut had met the same fate several decades earlier, and had been replaced by sprout hardwoods and a terminal trailer park, run by a man from the Bronx who could tell me nothing about Yama Farms.

In 1926, the family moved to Merrick, on the south shore of Long Island. Lyova had become a partner of Igor Sikorsky, who had started the Sikorsky Aero-Engineering Corporation and was trying to build a viable four-engine plane. While the family still had the farm, Lyova pitched in; there is a snapshot of him in his fedora, sitting at the wheel of a tractor, and another of him standing in overalls and looking convincingly like a hayseed. Bald on top, five-eight, two hundred pounds, he put on weight in exile. In business situations, an old associate told me, he let you do the talking, and didn't waste words; but in company he became an inspired raconteur. When they moved to Napanoch, Lyova rented an apartment in New York, near Gramercy Park, and just came out on weekends. He worked briefly for the Hershey Chocolate Company. Then he was on the entrepreneurial side of radio, which was just taking off—who would have imagined, ten years earlier, they'd be plucking sounds out of the air? He was an usher at the Russian Orthodox church in Manhattan

and drove a Studebaker. His children doted on him. He told
them marvelous stories in installments. One, whose main
characters were named Longfellow and Shortfellow, went on
for several years. My father remembers visiting his office in
the Flatiron Building, then a prestigious address; the company he was working for made siphons for seltzer bottles. He
met Sikorsky at the Orthodox church in 1923. Sikorsky
seemed more like a poet than a manufacturer: he was a self-
effacing, deeply religious man, with moustaches that drooped
over his lips, giving him a slightly Tatar appearance. His
name was not yet synonymous with the helicopter; after that
remarkable breakthrough, whenever he had to introduce
himself to people, he would say "I am Sikorsky," and sheep-
ishly twirl a finger above his head. His second love, after
flight, was music. At work, he hummed the symphonies of
his friend Rachmaninoff. In Russia during the war, he had
built seventy-five large, four-engine bombers of advanced
design. But he was at heart a pacifist. He meant the helicopter
to be an angel of mercy, not a gunship. Now, in America,
he dreamed of building palatial passenger planes, with state-
rooms and grand pianos. He would undoubtedly be dismayed
at how we pack them in today. Sikorsky had no shortage of
energy or ideas. The problem was money. He had gotten out
of Russia with the equivalent of several hundred dollars, and
was supporting himself by giving lectures on astronomy. His
first backer was Rachmaninoff. The composer gave Sikorsky
five thousand dollars, and that was enough to start a company.

It was, in the beginning, a strictly émigré operation.
Rachmaninoff was the vice-president; Lyova managed the
money end. Sikorsky wasn't a businessman, he just wanted
to build planes, and reluctantly agreed to be the president.

The personnel manager was a dashing former officer in the White Army named George Meyrer, who had been wounded during the civil war while charging a hilltop installation of Bolsheviks. The hill was so steep that the bullet entered his shoulder and went out through his lower back, just missing his heart. "The reason it bypassed my heart," Meyrer told his beautiful wife Tanya (from whom I heard the story), "is that I was so scared my heart was in my boots."

Construction of the S-29, Sikorsky's first metal, twin-engine, passenger transport plane, began in Lieutenant Utgof's backyard in Old Westbury, then moved to a rented hangar on Roosevelt Field. There were twenty or twenty-five mechanics, "calling each other Baron, Count, or General, like inmates of an asylum, and making tools of anything handy," the *New Yorker* reported on August 8, 1926, for "Sikorsky recruited his workmen from unfortunate and educated fellow-countrymen. All wear overalls and speak several languages."

My father remembers Sikorsky visiting Napanoch in 1925 and helping him build a toy airplane whose fuselage was a spool of thread. Mopsy happened that weekend to be painting a man named Arnold C. Dickinson, who owned a flourishing paper mill in Fitchburg, Massachusetts. Dickinson got talking with Sikorsky, and decided to invest a hundred thousand dollars in his company. Sikorsky was so grateful that he made Dickinson the president, and stepped down to vice-president in charge of engineering. Now they could go full steam with the S-35, Sikorsky's latest design, which he hoped would be the first plane to fly from New York to Paris. Lyova and Mopsy were among the hundreds of spectators who lined Roosevelt Field with their cars and watched the S-35 start down the runway at 5:00 A.M. on September 21, 1926. The pilot was the famous French World War ace, René Fonck. The engine was British, and had cost fifteen thousand dollars. The plane was loaded with gas and supplies. Halfway down the runway, the auxiliary landing gear released and dragged on the ground, tearing off part of the rudder. The plane rose to about fifty feet, then plunged into the ravine at the end of the runway and burst into flame. Fonck and the navigator escaped without injury, but the assistant navigator—Islamov, a good friend—and the radio operator were incinerated in the wreck.

The company was set back by the disaster, and lost the transatlantic race to Lindbergh, who reached Paris the following year. But in 1928 Sikorsky signed a lucrative contract with Juan Tripp, who had started Pan American Airways. Zoric would go on the first flight of the Sikorsky clipper S-38, which later flew to Rio. Wall Street took an interest in the company, and that year it graduated from its makeshift émigré phase. Nineteen twenty-eight was also the year the family became American citizens. Having boned up on American history, they trooped down to the immigration hall in Manhattan. Uncle was asked by the examining officer to explain the third amendment. "I don't know," he stammered nervously. "And actually," he continued with a brilliant smile, "I don't want to know, because I consider the Constitution of the United States such a perfect document that it needs no amendments." Alika was examined at the same time and remembers the ordeal vividly. In ten years, she had learned almost no English. "I was reading a little book I had, and the Avinoffs, they help me. They ask questions like 'What flies over the courthouse?' Supposed to say 'flag.' One Russian say 'pigeons.' 'When the president dies who takes his job?' One Russian say 'the undertaker.' Or

'How many stars in the flag, and what for those stars standing?' In those days it was forty-eight." Alika was asked to name the first president. After some thought, she answered, "George Vashington Bridge." The family, who had primed her with names and dates, groaned. Somehow, though, they were all admitted. Nineteen twenty-eight was also the year Lyova drowned.

The family's social life in Merrick was lively. Lyova was a *bon vivant*, and entertained constantly. Grandmother took charge of the cooking. Prohibition was in effect, but Gordon's gin was available in bottles that said "For Medicinal Use Only." The family saw a lot of the Sikorskys. Uncle designed the company's Winged-S logotype, and argued with Sikorsky over interpretations of the Scriptures. Sikorsky played the violin. Mopsy had a beautiful voice. Uncle would sit at the piano and play Viennese waltzes and Ukrainian folksongs in cascading arpeggios all over the keyboard. Sometimes Rachmaninoff would join them. He and Uncle had already become friends in St. Petersburg. We still have a fine sketch Uncle made of Rachmaninoff's head in red crayon: bald, thick-lipped, his long, gaunt, brooding face looking down, a thick vein pulsing at his temple, he seems a massive intelligence.

The family moved in two circles: aviation people, who were mostly Russians, and Merrick people, who were Americans of long standing. In those days, Merrick was the summer resort of thirty-five families, all of whom had considerable property and most of whom were related at least by marriage. Today, on one of the old estates, there are thirteen hundred houses. One of the families was that of Henry van Rensselaer Schuyler Fairfax, a round-faced, round-bellied man who had all the good New York names. His children were cousins and playmates of Henry and Albert Lanier. The Lanier boys, who were there when my grandfather drowned, were grandsons of the Georgia poet, Sidney Lanier. They were in their late teens. "Like everyone in Merrick, we were interested in tennis," Henry told me. He is now in his seventies and lives not far from me in Westchester County. "There were three grass courts at the Merrick Club, which also had a creek-side beach. If you were a man, you played in white flannels. Only sissies wore shorts. You shot ducks and dug clams in the Great South Bay. The causeway to Jones Beach had not yet been built, and there were miles of virgin seashore. Nature still predominated, and the hunting and fishing were still good. In the evening you could drive to Lynbrook and dance to Meyer Davis's orchestra. Sometimes the music was so soft you'd be dancing and not even notice it, but still be keeping time. Afterwards—it had been such a grand evening you didn't want it to end yet—you went for a joyride on the motor-parkway. Six was about all the car would hold. If you got up to forty, that was fast."

Every Fourth of July the members of the Merrick Club hired a motor launch and went seven miles across the Great South Bay to picnic in the wild dunes of Jones Beach. That year there were about thirty-five in the party, including Lyova, Mopsy, Zoric, and my father. Everyone went for a swim when the boat landed at eleven o'clock. The men were already in dark trunks that went halfway to their knees, and, as modesty required, separate tops. The women had on knee-length skirts and bathing caps. After the swim, Henry and Albert Lanier and the other young men went off to gather driftwood for a clambake. Everyone ate and drank heartily, then went in for a second swim. The water deepened gradually. At two hundred and fifty feet out you were still only up to your waist. The surf was gentle, but there was a terrific undertow. Lyova went out over his head, far from the others. Suddenly he was calling for help. Albert Lanier and Hugh Cotton swam for him, but in the excitement Hugh swallowed some water, and Albert had to bring him in. Henry Schwabb, the president of the Merrick Club, swam out to Lyova with his mountain-climbing rope. A great explorer, he was also president of the American Alpine Club, and always carried a rope. My father swam out, too, but he was only ten, and there was little he could do. Lyova was a heavy man. Two others—David and Lawrence Wright—reached him first. They brought him in and laid him on the sand. He was a ghastly purple, and showed no sign of life. Henry Sturgess, who had learned first aid in the war, started artificial respiration. Henry Lanier and Missy Chamberlain jumped in the launch and dashed across the bay. They were back in forty-five minutes with a doctor, but it was no good. Shortly after three, the doctor pronounced him dead. The cause of death was given as drowning, but the five witnesses I have talked to all believe he had a heart attack. His insurance man was a friend of the family, and was instrumental in getting the double indemnity for accidental death. Mopsy was left with three children; their third child, Elizabeth (Baby), had been born in 1922. With Sikorsky's aircraft doing so well, she'd been on the verge of taking an early retirement from professional portrait painting.

There was a full Russian funeral for Lyova, who was laid out in an open coffin, and when it was over, Mopsy sold the house in Merrick and all her Sikorsky stock. That was regrettable, because the people who kept theirs through the crash of 1929 doubled their investment, and if she'd stuck with Sikorsky, we'd all be millionaires. But Mopsy wanted to make a clean start. After a period of mourning, she bought a Cadillac and a big house on the North Shore (Hidden Hollow, it was called) and started to paint in earnest. Much of the time she was on the road, painting the notables. She was in Philadelphia, painting Drexels and Biddles and Dukes. She was in Wilmington, doing Du Ponts. She was in Chicago, immortalizing Marshall Fields. She was in Newport and Palm Beach, in San Antonio and Atlanta, on the eastern shore of Maryland and the north shore of Boston, and especially in Pittsburgh.

One afternoon, she showed me a scrapbook that contained color photographs, in no special order, of some of her portraits. They were "nothing interesting," she insisted. "Like painting flowers. Just like painting flowers." Most of her subjects had belonged to old American families, but there was a smattering of self-made millionaires. The first man was a son-in-law of Richard K. Mellon. Then came Harvey Firestone, done for the World's Fair in heroic size, though he was practically a midget. Then John W. Thomas, the first president of the Firestone Rubber Company; Walter Hoving, the president of Tiffany's; Thomas Ewing, a typical-looking specimen of the American gentry, at the tiller of his yacht, with a can of Budweiser in one hand. "He was later caught in a storm and drowned," Mopsy told me, "and a clubhouse was built in Newport in his memory for young people interested in boating. This is Brinkley Smithers," she said of the next one. "He was an alcoholic and started a big house like the A.A. This is John Thouron, an Englishman who married one of the Du Pont girls. This is one of the many Phippses— Ogden—who ended his life as a young man by overtaking some pills." On to Harvey and Raymond Firestone—sons of the old man. To Leonard McCullen, president of Conoco.

To a spastic boy of four, in velvet and ruffles, who couldn't hold his head up. To Robert Woodruff, the tsar of Coca-Cola. To George Humphrey, Eisenhower's Secretary of the Treasury, for a room at the Harvard Business School. To Reverend John Andrew, with a cross. "He was the chaplain of the archbishop of Canterbury and is now rector of St. Thomas' Church on Fifth Avenue." To Major Hoffman Nickerson, an artillery historian with marvelous white moustaches. To Howard Peabody of Lake Forest, on his plantation in Natchez, Mississippi. To Charles Robertson, "a man of great wealth through being married to an A&P girl." To Governor Carl Sanders of Georgia, two terms before Carter. Behind him the dome of the capitol, made of "all the gold they could find in Georgia." To Arthur Krim, "who bought the movie rights to The Hobbit." To various belles from Atlanta, San Antonio, Pittsburgh, and Houston. To Fifi Fell, "a great beauty, now married to John Schiff." To Svea Svenson, a laundress who won the chance Mopsy donated to a fundraiser for Operation Democracy. To the young Henry Fords of Detroit, the Libby Owens Fords of Toledo, and other Fords—"alkali" as opposed to "motorcar." To Redmond Stuart, a famous foxhunter from Baltimore. To the "Listerine" Lamberts of Los Angeles. To the "polo people": the Winston Guests and the Raymond Guests. "Neither of us made a dent on each other," Mopsy recalled. To Ethel Derby, a daughter of Theodore Roosevelt. To Mrs. Thomas "IBM" Watson. To Mrs. Blossom, a benefactress in Cleveland. To Mrs. Frothingham, a teetotaling dowager from Boston.

"I certainly covered the upper crust," Mopsy sighed, closing the scrapbook. "They're terribly nice if you approach them the right way. To classify them in general, I would say that they are proud of their ancestors." Some she just painted.

Many became lasting friends. She never left a portrait, in any case, that wasn't satisfactory.

Mopsy was doing some work in Aiken, South Carolina, in 1937 when she met a tall, serenely beautiful woman named Lucy Rutherford, who had been Eleanor Roosevelt's private secretary years before. (Most of what follows has been distilled from *Presidential Memoirs*, Mopsy's memoir.) The liaison between Mrs. Rutherford and Franklin Roosevelt dated from 1914, but it wasn't made public in their lifetimes. Lucy provided a warmth and a femininity that Eleanor couldn't. She and Roosevelt met as often as they could without arousing suspicion. Lucy invited Mopsy to Allamuchy, the Rutherford estate in New Jersey, to do portraits of her and her ailing husband, Winthrop. Mopsy painted her in a turquoise chiffon tea gown, and Rutherford surrounded by his fox terriers. Lucy dressed as if to diminish the thirty years between them. Like those of Catherine the Great and Marie Antoinette, her complexion was *fort animé*. The only word for it was brilliant. It was so transparent it had no shading. Cuzzy (Nicholas Robbins), Mopsy's photographer, fell in love with Lucy as he was taking snaps of her and began to write deeply respectful poems about her. She had that effect on men. With his chiseled features, sharp eyes, and a sarcastic expression around his mouth, Rutherford (the mysterious Mr. R. with whom Consuelo Vanderbilt was going to elope the night before she married the Duke of Marlborough) looked like an English peer. He was known for his bluntness. Mopsy and he talked about their fox terriers. Mopsy had had one named Bobick in Russia. Rutherford's favorite terrier was named Brass Tacks. Mopsy and Lucy became good friends, and, as often happened, she ended up painting all the children. One evening in 1943, as the two women were driving through the woods of Allamuchy, shining up deer in the headlights, Lucy brought up Roosevelt. Mopsy realized from the adoring way Lucy spoke about him that the rumors she'd been hearing were true. "None of his portraits come close to capturing him," Lucy said. "Would you paint him if it could be arranged?"

Two weeks later, Mopsy was invited to the White House. As she was shown into the President's office, he was all smiles. His hand seemed, as someone had observed, to stretch across the room. She finished a small head and shoulders, twelve by ten, in three mornings, and chose for it an antique mirror frame. The portrait shows him in his black navy cape, with a few gray clouds. Roosevelt was delighted with it. Color reproductions were soon hanging in Churchill's home at Chatsworth, Stalin's office in the Kremlin, and homes around the country. That July he invited Mopsy and Uncle for lunch at Hyde Park. Roosevelt showed them an icon he had acquired and chatted with Uncle about the occult. Both men were interested in phenomena for which science had no explanation. Then two attendants carried the President out to a Ford convertible with hand controls, and he took them on what Mopsy remembered as "one of the giddiest rides I've ever had." She sat in back, giggling nervously with Grace Tully, his devoted private secretary. The President drove with speed and assurance on the narrow, winding roads, talking away and returning the salutes of his guards. Once he pointed to a butterfly and asked Uncle what it was. "A viceroy, Mr. President," Uncle said.

It was agreed that Mopsy would do another, life-size portrait for the White House, but she heard nothing more about it until an evening in the middle of March 1945, when Lucy called. Roosevelt had just returned from the meeting at Yalta and had gone to rest at Warm Springs. "He's frail and thin, but having lost so much weight his face looks the way it did when he was younger," Lucy said. "If this portrait is painted, it shouldn't be postponed." So Lucy, Mopsy, and Cuzzy pooled their gasoline coupons and set out for Georgia in Mopsy's Cadillac convertible. The President was waiting for them in an open car before the drugstore of Greenville. He was wearing his navy cape and drinking a Coca-Cola, and a small crowd had gathered around him. When he saw Lucy his face lit up, but Mopsy could see that he was a sick man. In the snaps Cuzzy took the next morning his face was ashen. He looked like Woodrow Wilson in his last year. A second set had to be taken.

When Mopsy started the portrait, on the morning of April twelfth, the President was full of pep. She was struck by how good his color was (this was, a doctor told her later, the sign of an imminent stroke). There were all kinds of documents spread around the room, with Roosevelt's signature drying on them. "My laundry," he joked, and laughed heartily. While Lucy and his cousin Margaret Suckley were chatting on a sofa, she placed the eyes. Another cousin, Laura Delano, came in briefly with her dog. The President was absorbed in some papers, looking up at Mopsy's request. She went over the shadows with Windsor blue, and the face came to life. Then the Filipino butler came in and started setting the table. "We have fifteen more minutes to work," Roosevelt said. Mopsy was painting the upper part of the face, near the hairline, when the President suddenly raised his hand and passed it over his head several times in a strange, jerky way. Then, without a sound, he slumped forward in his armchair. Lucy and Margaret Suckley were still talking, unaware that anything had happened. "Lucy, Lucy, something is wrong,"

Mopsy said. Then she ran out, calling for Dr. Bruen, who was away having lunch. Lucy, completely shaken, caught up with her and said they'd better leave. They went to their rooms and started to pack. As they were walking to the car Mopsy heard Dr. Bruen talking hurriedly on the phone to his superior in Washington, Dr. MacIntyre. "He was quite well when I left him this morning. Complained of a slight pain in the neck, but now something very acute has happened, sir." Miss Tully, in tears, saw them off. In Macon a flag was at half mast. They stopped at a hotel and tried to call Warm Springs. The woman at the switchboard was sobbing. "The President is dead."

When Mopsy got home, the house was already surrounded by reporters. They jotted hasty descriptions of her as she rushed inside. In the morning she held a brief press conference, keeping Lucy's name out of it. Almost every major publication bid for the rights to reproduce the portrait. "Like Schubert's unfinished symphony, it will remain forever unfinished," the Philadelphia *Enquirer* wrote, "the picture of a man thinned by illness, pitifully aged by world care, spiritualized by high purpose." Left as it was, half done, the portrait has a great sadness, as if the man were almost fading away before you. Only the head is colored in. Dark circles subtend the eyes. The mouth is set in a straight, dead-solemn line. The cape is only started on. Just the collar is blackened. Half of the crimson Harvard tie is painted, and there is some loose gray wash behind the head.

Years later, I met by chance a man who had waited for a week outside Mopsy's house, trying to buy the rights to the portrait for *Life* magazine. But it was the *Daily News* that finally got them, for twenty-five thousand dollars. The portrait and a feature about Mopsy ran in the Sunday *Coloroto*

Magazine on May 27. "Mrs. Shoumatoff's one evidence of Bohemianism seems to be a certain absent-mindedness where materials are concerned," the inventive reporter wrote. "She often has a glass of something to drink at hand while she is painting, and if the drink happens to be the same color as the paint she needs at the moment, the chances are fifty-fifty that she will mistakenly dip her brush into the drink instead of the paint. Mrs. Shoumatoff has absentmindedly painted in champagne, tomato juice, and martini cocktail." The books that later appeared about Roosevelt's death were no more accurate about her, and deepened her loathing of publicity.

For several years after Roosevelt's death, Mopsy was a celebrity. If she started taking dancing lessons, it was noted in the society columns. "Tall, graceful, Russian-born Elizabeth Shoumatoff, who's as much at home behind an easel as the average housewife is behind the kitchen stove, has sold her Mill Neck studio," Cholly Knickerbocker wrote in 1947. "Liz, who won more recognition for her unfinished portrait of FDR (she was working on it at the time of his death) than for any of her completed jobs, hated to sell the place. But she's been out of town so often fulfilling artistic commitments that she never had time to enjoy it." An increasing number of commissions were crowned heads and presidents of countries. She'd already had several brushes (pun not intended) with royalty. During the twenties she painted two Romanoffs in exile. The first, in 1924, was Princess Irene Yusupov, the daughter of Grand Duchess Xenia, the tsar's sister, and the wife of Prince Felix Yusupov, who killed Rasputin. The Yusupovs had come to America to sell a black pearl necklace that Catherine the Great had given to Prince Potemkin, and to try to buy back from Joseph

Widener two Rembrandts that Yusupov had sold to raise cash when they had first got out of Russia. They had taken a suite at the Plaza Annex. Princess Irene was a classic beauty, with strangely lifeless, gray-green eyes. She showed Mopsy some of her own paintings, of grotesque female heads with bloody tears and cut throats, which she did from time to time when the spirit moved her. They were like French *illuminures*, three inches by five, with fine gold borderwork. She had begun to produce these "Arnolfs," as she whimsically called them, in the spring of 1917. She painted them in a trance, and often left them unfinished. Prince Felix, whose cheeks were rouged, was divinely handsome. He was still haunted by Rasputin. "Not to be outdone," Mopsy recalled, "Prince Felix brought out his own creations, and they were even more peculiar than his wife's—large charcoal drawings of horrible men with beards and hair sticking out of their nostrils."

Grand Duchess Marie, another of the tsar's cousins, appeared in New York later in the twenties and wrote a best-selling autobiography, *The Education of the Princess*. Mopsy's portrait of her was used for the frontispiece. Her eyes were cold and the same color as Princess Irene's. "Born in 1890," her book begins, "I have stepped through the ages. My earliest memories are of surroundings so remote and unlike the world of swirling traffic and shining towers that I see from these windows, as to be, by comparison, medieval. When I try to think back to that time, I am persuaded that in calendars there is no reality, and that the early events of my life are hardly anything more than a fairy tale."

Mopsy shared the Grand Duchess's sense of unreality, and for a while they saw a lot of each other. There is a photograph of them together on a review stand at a reunion in Fort

Ontario, Canada, leaning into a strong wind, with two rows
of the emperor's bemedaled former officers. Alone among
friends, Grand Duchess Marie couldn't have been less formal.
But then she would suddenly try to pull rank. Mopsy eventually got tired of being asked to drive her to her appoint-
ments. "She had a talent for getting mixed up with
undesirable people," Mopsy recalled. "To me she was still a
symbol of the imperial house of the Romanoffs, but it was
rather pathetic the way she tried to carry out that prestige."

Early in 1956, Mopsy painted her second president, William Viscount Shadrock Tubman of Liberia. The son of an
Atlanta preacher, Tubman had just been elected to a third
term. He was Mopsy's first black. She was worried whether
she could pull it off, and did some research at the Frick Art
Reference Library in New York before flying to Monrovia.
"I looked at the famous portrait of Henri Christophe, the
emperor of Haiti, and one by Reynolds of a handsome Negro
in a powdered wig and silk coat with an unfinished background of clouds." Tubman decided against the top hat and
tails that he usually wore on state occasions and posed in a
light tan suit, with a cigar in his left hand, the Capitol behind
him, and a sky full of puffy white equatorial clouds. He had
such a ready smile that Mopsy had trouble getting him to
hold a serious expression. The portrait was a present from
the Firestone Rubber Company, which has vast holdings in
Liberia. President Tubman made Mopsy a Knight of the
Humane Order of African Redemption, and after he pinned
the red-and-white order on her, they marched between two
rows of chieftains from the Liberian hinterland, with whom
he was unable to communicate except through interpreters.
She returned with all sorts of presents for her grandchildren—
drums, ceremonial swords, glossy publications—that made

Liberia seem like a wonderland. I did a report on the country for my fifth-grade geography class and got an A+, and I've been writing about the tropics ever since.

In 1968, after Lyndon Johnson called Peter Hurd's portrait of him "the ugliest thing I ever saw," Mopsy was called in. On the day the sittings began, President Johnson was in a black mood, as he was at the unveiling of her portrait a few months later, at a small party at the White House that I attended. He had been getting a lot of bad press. The Vietnam War had made him unpopular and he had decided not to run for reelection. For most of the evening he sat in a hallway, holding his head in his hands. As I was discussing with Justice Douglas salt-water intrusion along the Florida coast, Johnson's daughter Luci Baines appeared in a dress that was so low-cut that her sister Lynda Bird ordered her to change it. Johnson liked the portrait and invited Mopsy to the LBJ Ranch, where she painted him leaning on a stone wall with the Pedernales River in the background, in a cowboy jacket with the presidential seal on it. This portrait was reproduced on a postage stamp. Others ran like measles through the Johnson family: three of Lady Bird, Luci Baines in a Scarlett O'Hara gown, Lynda Bird in the Oval Room, with long false eyelashes. One of her last projects was a Nugent grandson. In her last months she painted the wife of her plumber, who had saved for several years and refused the discount she offered him. She painted my brother. She painted Bert Lance. "He absolutely conquered me," she told me over the phone. "He's as tall as they come and huge, with the nicest face." She painted a rich friend of Lance's who flew up from Georgia in his Lear jet. A few weeks before she went to the hospital, she was driven into town to discuss a portrait with Madame Chiang Kai-shek.

Now and then I would meet marvelous old Russians at Mopsy's. They would usually pat me on the head and say *molodyets*, clever boy. One was Vladimir Storozhev, a polyglot who translated at the U.N. for many years (quite a number of émigrés got work there). Storozhev grew up in Manchuria and with his narrow eyes and inscrutable expression could easily pass for an Oriental. His father, Ivan, was the district attorney of Ekaterinburg, the Siberian city where the imperial family was shot. "Father was such a brilliant prosecutor that he never lost a trial," Storozhev told me one evening at Mopsy's. "They promoted him to district attorney of Kazan, the state capital. But then he began to think, 'How many times has my eloquence sent an innocent man to jail?' The thought so disturbed him that he quit his job and became a simple defender. On his first case the court appointed him to defend a *zhulik*, a petty crook accused of stealing some galoshes. Father looked at his record and saw that he had already been convicted of several thefts. 'This man is guilty no doubt,' he thought to himself. He called in the rogue and said, 'Tell me the truth and I will defend you to the best of my ability. Did you or didn't you?' The thief starts to sob, seizes an icon, and swears his innocence. Father thinks, 'What better proof could there be of the correctness of my decision to be a defender? If I was on the other side, this man would be in jail.'

"I remember sitting in the gallery at the trial. I was about four, and just beginning to realize what was going on around me. Father's speech had the jury in tears, and the thief was acquitted. A few weeks later Father ran into him on the street. He fell down on his knees and wept with gratitude. 'Thanks,' he said. 'You're a great man. But now I can tell you. We cheated them.'

"Father was so disillusioned that he gave up the law completely, and became a priest. After finishing seminary, he moved back to Ekaterinburg. The imperial family had been arrested and they were being held in the house of a rich merchant named Upatiev. When I flew my kite from the roof of our house, I could see the tsar's children playing in Upatiev's yard, and the tsar himself would come out once a day and split wood for an hour or so. The night before they were shot the family celebrated mass in Father's church. The deacon started singing, then they all started in. They weren't supposed to, but looking back, it wasn't a mistake. Two mornings later I was on the roof flying my kite when Father called me down and told me they had been shot. It was July seventeenth, I remember, and very hot.

"After they were murdered there was a disturbance in Ekaterinburg, and the Cheka rounded up *zhalozniki*, hostages, as they usually did after a disturbance. The *zhalozniki* were innocent civilians. Their names were posted at the Cheka's headquarters in the American hotel. They were arrested and usually shot. We lost many friends that way. This time my father was on the list, but his deacon's brother worked for the Cheka and warned him to stay away from home that night. So he and a few others dug a hole in the cellar of a convent and walled themselves in with a supply of food. Four days later, Admiral Kolchak marched into Ekaterinburg and freed the city. Father joined the White Army as a chaplain. After the civil war, we escaped to Manchuria."

Another time Mopsy had her dear friends the Troubetzkoys over. Prince Serge was named for his uncle, S. N. Troubetzkoy, the radical dean of Moscow University who tried to get a constitution for Russia in 1910 and became a friend of Nika's. The Troubetzkoys have been princes since

the time of Ivan the Terrible. Prince Serge's wife is an Obolensky, and thus a princess in her own right. "The Obolenskys and the Troubetzkoys have intermarried for five
generations," Princess Lyuba told me. "My mother, a Troubetzkoy, was Serge's first cousin. He teases me that I used to
call him Uncle when I was little." Both left Russia as children. They met in Paris during the thirties.

"The Russian Revolution—I still don't know how it happened," Lyuba reflected. "In Paris my mother kept saying,
'The Bolsheviks will be finished in two or three weeks, and
we will go back.' " Lyuba has never been back, but Serge
returned as a tourist a few years ago. "Three times I entered
the house in Moscow where I was born, I was so disturbed,"
he told me. He is a short, unassuming man with a trim
moustache, court manners, and a great interest in Russian
history.

After dinner we looked at the slides I had taken in the
Soviet Union. There were a few dozen of mushrooms. Lyuba
sang out their names as they came on the screen. "We have
this place in Canada where many Russians live," she said,
"and all they do night and day is hunt mushrooms. Ah, that's
a good one," she said of a fawn-colored *Boletus*. The next
was lilac, with a fine mesh of snow-white gills underneath.
A *Russula*. "We have that in Syosset," Lyuba said. "It won't
kill you but it will make you quite sick." The blurry time
exposures I had taken inside the Bolshoi Theater verged on
abstraction, but Serge was able to recognize his family's box,
in the second tier and several to the right of the tsar's. "Our
box," he said, with a deep sigh that seemed to go back to
the beginning of the century.

One afternoon at Mopsy's I met Princess Vera, the last
titled female Romanoff. A small, well-spoken woman, she

shares an apartment on the Upper East Side with a dozen or so cats. "My father, Grand Duke Konstantin, was a cousin once removed of the late tsar and a well-known poet," she told me. "He translated *Hamlet* under the name KR, for Konstantin Romanoff. My mother was the Princess of Sax-Altebourg. I was born in 1906, on the seventh of April by the old style, the day of Antipus of Pergamo. That's why my teeth are good. He looks after teeth.

"I escaped from Russia when I was twelve. I was too young to feel the loss. Queen Victoria of Sweden, a friend of Mother's, invited us to get out. The communists were still not very firm in the saddle. They were afraid of foreigners. My mother was German, so they let us go.

"Three of my brothers were murdered by the communists, together with Grand Duchess Elizabeth, the empress's sister. They were thrown into an abandoned mine pit in Alapayevsk, thirty versts from Ekaterinburg, and left without food or water, the day after Nicholas and his family were shot. It took three days for them to die. Their bodies were taken by Kolchak to Peking. Grand Duchess Elizabeth's sister, the dowager marchioness of Milford-Haven, had her body taken from Peking to Jerusalem on a British cruiser. She had become a nun.

"I was a year and a half younger than the tsarevitch. I remember meeting him once in the spring when the snow was melting. Alexis was all in white—white fur coat, hat, muff, mittens. We got out of our respective carriages. He put me in his. A few paces from the Tsarskoye Selo railroad station, near a pavilion locally referred to as the Salyony Muzhik, the Salty Peasant, but whose real name was the Salon de Musique, there was a big puddle. We stopped. '*Vera tudá*,' he commanded. 'In with you.' I jumped in without thinking. I knew he was the heir to the throne, and I had to obey. Besides, it was fun."

✤ ✤ ✤

During his first ten years in America, Uncle also made rapid progress. He began by testing the waters for an artistic career, and found them warm and receptive. New York was already appreciative of Russian music. Now a wave of deracinated Russian painters—Bakst, Anisfeld, Roerich—was hitting the city, and making quite a splash. Uncle didn't really have that much in common with them, or with anybody, for that matter, but at least they provided a context in which his work could be examined. Early in 1921, he had a one-man show at the Ainslie Galleries on Fifth Avenue. Among the forty watercolors, pastels, and drawings were six Tibetan scenes, three portraits of Nijinsky, one of Rachmaninoff, one of Tagore, six sunsets, a rainbow, a nightmare, and several mordant miniatures. One was a strange grotesque that he had painted for four-year-old Zoric. In it a sinister witch-like marmoset, with striped fur and white fangs, is slinking with a tasseled parasol across an arid landscape that has only a stylized Persian bush and a faint, towering mirage of the Woolworth Building, or rather a statue of the Woolworth Building that Zoric picked up at a souvenir stand. I grew up with this creature on my bedroom wall. She was called by her Russian name, Nyanya Skunks, and fascinated more than scared me. The more you looked at her, the more you discovered. Each of her toenails, for instance, had an opalescent reflection. The painting was meant to convey some of Uncle's initial feelings about America. Then there were several soft pastels Uncle had done in the Catskills. He seemed to be entering a blue period, but his blueness was more like Maxfield Parrish's than Picasso's. "I want to paint the way the lilac smells," he said one evening after a heavy rain in Napanoch.

The reviews were, on the whole, approving. "A decidedly mixed type is Mr. Avinoff," said the New York *Tribune*. "His drawing may be a trifle mannered, but it is skillful drawing, remarkably skillful." "Some of his 'Sunsets' look as though they were taken from the New Jersey Palisades," said the *Sun*. "All of them have a purity of line that can come from only the most delicate perception." "Like the other Russians who have come here, he loves to use details in wholesome quantities," said the New York *Herald*. "He even applies this penchant to the American landscapes which he has produced since coming here, and as the public itself dearly loves details, and lots of them, Mr. Avinoff ought to have a popular success." Only the Brooklyn *Eagle* spoke of "a certain cloying sophistication," and a "lack of the direct simplicity that characterizes the greatest works of art."

As an artist, Uncle did very well in the early twenties. He painted, for five hundred dollars a shot, portraits of such prominent New Yorkers as Mrs. John Gregory Hope, the former Countess Maud Salm, and through Frank Seaman, embarked on a subsidiary career in commercial art that he would later describe as "lucrative." He illustrated an advertisement for Scranton's Lace Curtains that ran on the inside back cover of *Vogue*. He did a series of paintings, which the Johns-Manville Asbestos Shingles Company used extensively in 1923, of a suburban house whose Colorblende Roof withstands the ravages of the four seasons, while nicely complementing its brick walls. He placed a monumental bottle of Colgate's Florient in a rugged setting of Himalayan snowpeaks. For the Underwood Portable Typewriter Company, he cooked up an explorer typing a letter home by candlelight from the Valley of the Kings. The explorer has taken off his pith helmet, and a host of houris, representing "Wingèd Words," is fluttering up from "the machine you will eventually want to carry." He made exotic drawings for the Graybar Company and for Nunnally's, "the candy of the South," that were unlike anything the advertising community had seen before, or would see again. Some of his renditions of everyday household articles attracted attention as works of art. One was included in an anthology of the best commercial art of the decade. He must have been amused by the seriousness with which his work was taken. The whole industry—that people were racking their brains and ruining their health to promote a bar of soap or a tube of dental cream—must have been puzzling.

While scrambling for a living, he had no time for butterflies. In an article for *Études de Lépidoptérologie Comparée*, written in March 1920, he described how he had started as a boy and gradually built up, at tremendous cost and effort, a collection of eighty thousand palaearctic Rhopalocera (Old World butterflies) that was particularly strong in *Parnassius* and *Colias*, only to have it impounded by the Bolsheviks. "At the moment," he concluded in French, "I have given up almost all hope of getting back this collection, and have neither the courage nor the means to start a new one." His French colleague, Charles Oberthür, wrote a stirring foreword to the *récit*—there was even an encouraging stanza from Horace—urging Uncle to take heart, and suggesting that it was his duty to Science to use his God-given talent and start collecting again.

Uncle had met the Bostonian hawkmoth collector, B. Preston Clark, in 1915. While purchasing arms for the

Zemsky Union, he spent several days at the Parker House. While he was out of his room, a man had appeared at the door and introduced himself to his Russian roommate as a fellow entomologist who had read about Uncle in the Boston papers. "Butterflies. Ve don't vant butterflies. Ve fight var," the Russian said. Uncle returned just after the entomologist had left, got his description, and caught up with Clark on crowded Tremont Street. They hit it off immediately. Uncle was a lepidopterist, and Clark a heterocerist, and they understood each other perfectly. They were both amateurs in the true sense of the word: they loved their subject. Clark was president of the Plymouth Cordage Company and owned thirty thousand hawkmoths. Of the sixteen hundred forms then known to science, Clark lacked but fifty. With the possible exception of Karl Jordan and Walter Rothschild, he knew more about the family than anybody.

Through Clark, Uncle had met the dean of American entomologists, William J. Holland, in 1916. When he was sixteen in Russia, Uncle's father had given him Holland's classic work, *The Butterfly Book*. Its companion volume, *The Moth Book*, is still the standard text. In them, for the first time, Holland gave American butterflies and moths names that people could understand. He called *Nymphalis antiopa* the mourning cloak, and *Vanessa atalanta* the red admiral, and brought them a whole new following. Most of his common names are still in use. Only a few, like "the waiter," a long-tailed tropical nymphalid that occasionally drifts up to south Florida, haven't stuck. Holland was a Presbyterian minister in Pittsburgh whose sermons had almost frightening authority. Natural history was just a hobby. Holland was an intimate of the "dukes of Pittsburgh," Henry Clay Frick and the two Andrews, Mellon and Carnegie. Each had made a fortune, and was looking for ways to spend it. Frick and Mellon chose to collect art, and began to buy Old Masters by the shipload. Carnegie decided to enlarge the horizons of the young people of Pittsburgh. He believed it was a disgrace to die rich. The first half of your life should be devoted to amassing wealth, the second to distributing it. Before he died, Carnegie gave away three hundred million dollars. By 1895 he had already presented Pittsburgh with a library and a concert hall. One day Holland showed him a newspaper story about some fossilized dinosaurs that had just been discovered in Utah. Carnegie volunteered to put up the money for Holland to dig up the bones and bring them to Pittsburgh, and Carnegie wrote on a corner of the newspaper, "Give Holland ten thousand dollars," tore off the note, which was good at any bank, and handed it to Holland. That was the beginning of the Carnegie Museum.

With Holland as its first director, the museum grew quickly. He got Carnegie to buy the invertebrate fossil collection of Baron Baillet, which, added to the dinosaur bones from Utah, put the museum at the forefront of paleontology. The entomology section was also superbly stocked. Holland got over a million insects, spiders, centipedes, and scorpions for it. He bought H. H. Smith's beetles from the Amazon, and got missionaries to send him fabulous material from the Congo and the Cameroons (his parents had been Moravian missionaries on Jamaica, so he had good contacts). The specimens were carefully mounted on pins by an octogenarian preparator named Krautworm, and stuck in cork-lined cases. The cases were kept in rows of mahogany-and-glass cabinets on the third floor of the museum. As the collection grew, a steel mezzanine was built for a second story of cabinets. The natural history museum—its exhibits, its collections (most of which are kept from public view)—shares a massive brown-stone building with a library, a concert hall, and an art museum. The brownstone takes up a block of Forbes Avenue in the East End of Pittsburgh and is known as the Carnegie Institute. It was finished in 1912 and rapidly blackened by coal soot. Until after the war particulate pollution in Pittsburgh was so heavy that the street lights were left on until ten in the morning. If you had an important meeting in the afternoon, you had to change your shirt at lunchtime. Most of the pollution was from private homes, from people burning soft coal in their furnaces. But no one seemed to mind it; most Pittsburghers regarded a smoking chimney as a sign of prosperity.

Holland was impressed by Uncle and invited him to join the museum as an associate curator of entomology. Uncle was getting bored with commercial art and missed working with butterflies, so he accepted. He came to Pittsburgh in 1923, and as he started sorting the museum's rich collection, he saw that there were years of taxonomic work just to figure out what had already been acquired. Before long he had picked out twenty-three new species or varities. It was up to him to describe and christen the new finds. He named Colombian and Philippine pierids for Holland and B. Preston Clark, and a Bolivian swallowtail for Douglas Stewart, a geologist who in 1924 succeeded Holland as director of the museum. Holland retired at seventy-seven and devoted his remaining years to revising his monumental butterfly book. Uncle helped him with the section that explained the evolutionary connection between North American and Old World forms. In gratitude, Holland named a wood nymph *Erebia avinoffi* after him, and a small new skipper *Thanaos avinoffi*, after his grandfather, who had skippered the *Dis-*

covery. Uncle was thrilled with these nomenclatural tributes, and for Holland's eightieth birthday he painted on the borders of a testimonial scroll from the staff all the species that bore Holland's name. They were not just butterflies, but a tree, a stingray, a hummingbird, a hawkmoth, and several fish. Holland was by then too old to swing a net, and he was delighted with the dark new variety of Harris's checkerspot that Uncle caught in some woods outside Pittsburgh during the summer of 1927. A few years later, in the White Mountains of New Hampshire, Uncle discovered another, even darker subspecies of the small, intricately mottled brown-and-orange nymphalid. When I was eleven, my father, who was continuing Uncle's work on the highly variable species, paid me a buck for every Harris's checkerspot I brought him. "You can't find them anywhere," he explained. He took me to a brushy wet meadow and showed me their "indicator plant," a wild iris called blue flag. Where there was blue flag, he said, there was likely to be the certain white aster on which the larvae of Harris's checkerspot feed. After their emergence, the butterflies seldom stray more than a hundred yards from their food plant. I must have caught half a dozen of them in northern Westchester that summer, holding the thorax between my thumb and forefinger and sacrificing them with a quick pinch for science and pocket money.

Though Pittsburgh was booming industrially, it was culturally unsure of itself. It had a painter, John Kane, who was doing fine primitives of its steel mills and smoke-filled hollows, but the rich would not have him on their walls. The rich lived in grand Edwardian houses on Fifth Avenue. They were mostly Scotch-Presbyterian executives in steel. Their stratum began to coalesce in the 1880s and lasted two gen-

erations. During the Depression it collapsed completely. Today, many of their big houses are boarded up or broken up
into condominiums, their offspring having moved out to
Sewickley, or left western Pennsylvania long ago. The men
were self-made. They played golf at the Rolling Rock Club,
and sowed their oats in New York. The women, who had
made the grand tour and gone through the art museums of
Europe, were the receptacles of culture. To them the arts
were no laughing matter.

Culture had to come from the Old World, and when
Uncle appeared in their midst, he seemed like the very em-
bodiment of it. "He descended on our city like a fabulous
creature from another planet," a man who would take his
courses in fine arts at the University of Pittsburgh remembers.
"He was the idol of my youth. Like a twirling Christmas
ornament in a department store window, he reflected in
muted brilliance all the facets of the world around him."

Uncle didn't talk about his past, but the women of Pittsburgh found it out. Soon they were vying for the chance to
have a gentleman-in-waiting to the late tsar at their dinner
table. Stories about his omniscience began to get around,
and one wealthy East End woman, determined to trip him
up on a point of esoteric knowledge, went to the Carnegie
Library and consulted a rare volume on Persian rugs. That
evening he was sitting on her living room floor—it was rumored he had learned the virtue of that posture during a
long residence in Asia—when she asked him about an obscure rug she had read up on. He told her all about it—the
town in which it had been woven, the symbolic meaning of
its design, and a couple of other things that weren't in the
book. "I saw a certain amount of Dr. Avinoff at parties and
so on," remembers John Walker, who grew up in Pittsburgh

and later became the director of the National Gallery. "I must say I was deeply impressed by him; and it's hard to impress a bumptious young man who thinks he's rather intellectual himself. I've never known anyone with the universal knowledge he had. I thought it must have been fake— I thought he was a phony—so I probed and probed when I would see him at parties. I wanted to show him up, but never could, because it was all sound, he was all there, he really *did* know. And whenever he came out with an extraordinary erudite fact or something that you wouldn't expect him to know, and certainly no one in Pittsburgh knew, he always did it deferentially, as though he were apologizing for his brilliance. It was very curious. Maybe it's a Russian characteristic. It went beyond modesty. There was something almost obsequious about his attitude toward his gifts, and it irritated me madly."

At one dinner, Uncle was heard to mutter, apropos of nothing, the word "*Porphyrogenitus.*" At another, not long after he had come to Pittsburgh, he was seated next to Mrs. Richard K. Mellon. She kept calling him Mr. Ivanoff. To him that was like being called Jones or Smith. At last he said, "I beg your pardon, Mrs. Mellon, but my name is Avinoff."

"Ivanoff, Avinoff, what's the difference?" she asked.

"Well, what would you say if I called you Mrs. Lemon?" he said tartly. Mrs. Mellon was impressed. It was the beginning of a friendship.

Late in 1924, Uncle resigned his curatorship and, while remaining a research associate of the museum, returned to New York and resumed his art career. He gave "family reasons," but the truth was probably more related to the terrible pay. He left a good impression, and when Douglas Stewart died suddenly in 1925 and the directorship fell vacant, he was called back to Pittsburgh. At a luncheon with the trustees he was asked how, as a scientist, he could justify belief in God, and how he thought the war had affected the quality of modern art. He fielded the questions with his usual dexterity ("True science is not opposed to true religion"; "A lot of inferior art has been produced in the last few years, but I don't think as a result of the war"), and was offered the job. In 1926 he moved back to Pittsburgh, and during the next twenty years he was a familiar sight on Forbes Avenue—an elegant, sparrow-boned man, with pince-nez and natty bowtie, reading as he walked.

Often my father (who went to Kent and then to M.I.T.) would go to Pittsburgh and stay with Uncle for summer vacation or travel with him. When he was thirteen, he mounted eight hundred Amazonian butterflies at a table in the insect lab across from Dr. Holland, who was in his eighties. Holland would entertain him with stories about the great naturalists of the century before, with whom he had been widely acquainted. Periodically, when an antenna or a wing snapped off an insect that Holland was working on, he would roar for the glue with the voice that had made him famous in the pulpit, and old Krautworm, the preparator, would come running with the repair kit, two steps at a time. It was said that some of the spots on Holland's specimens were tobacco juice, and some of the antennae were hair pulled from his own head.

Between 1925 and 1940, Uncle made six collecting trips to Jamaica. My father went with him on five. For Uncle, Jamaica had been "a dream land of tropical splendor" since, as a boy in Russia, he had come across Captain Mayne Reid's book, *The Planters in Jamaica*. He remembered vainly scrutinizing the illustrations for butterflies with a magnifying glass. Years later, when he got there, Jamaica proved to be the lepidopterous promised land he had imagined. Avinoff and Shoumatoff caught over fourteen thousand "bots," as butterflies and moths are called on the island, doubling the number of species described on Jamaica to more than a thousand. Dashing around the island with their tulle nets, pith helmets wrapped in white pongee, pockets bulging with cyanide jars, and canvas leggings to keep off chiggers and ticks, they must have looked like outré creatures themselves. At night, when they were out in the bush, they slept on cots, under bell-shaped canopies of mosquito netting. Once a week or so they would put in at one of the better hotels, shave, shower, slip on a clean white linen suit, and join the vacationing British for dinner. The guests ate in silence in groups of two to four, unless they were excitedly recapping the day's round of golf with such expostulations as "dashed good time" and "rotten luck." In one dining room, with a deft *presto*, my father snagged a noctuid moth that had been dive-bombing a bald, bullet-headed old blighter, and everyone in the room applauded. The *presto* was my father's term for catching a butterfly in midair. It was opposed to an *adagio*, in which you snuck up to where the quarry was sitting.

By car, on foot, or on horseback, the two of them covered most of the island. My father did the driving. Uncle bought a Chevrolet in Pittsburgh, but never learned to drive. In Cuna Cuna Pass, in the remote Johncrow Mountains, they caught the giant *Papilio homerus*, the largest swallowtail in the New World, which is found only on Jamaica and is a famous rarity. When he saw his first *homerus*—broad-winged, five inches from tip to tip, black with yellow discal bands and spatulate tails—sailing in a gully, Uncle called my father, who was a few hundred yards away. He shouted his boyhood name, "Goula," which means "Little Dove" in Russian, and was fairly common in Old Russia. Grand Duke Dmitri, for instance, a cousin of the tsar, was known as Goula in the family. The guides thought Uncle was referring to the bot, and the word Goula entered Jamaican patois. To this day, in parts of the interior, large swallowtails are known as Goulas. Uncle and my father spent hours observing the *Papilio homerus*, and even filmed it in flight with a movie camera. It has no close relative, and Uncle thought it must be the last survivor of some ancient tribe that had evolved before the Lesser Antilles rose up from the sea.

They walked into the Cockpit Country, on the western half, with some trepidation. This region of jumbled knobs and hollows choked with rain forest was the domain of the Maroons, whose slave ancestors fled there in the eighteenth century and were never captured. The Jamaicans themselves stayed out of the District of Look Behind, as the Maroons' territory was called, because of the likelihood of being ambushed. Few whites had been there, and no butterfly collectors. The Maroons were said to have preserved their African ways. They still practiced Obeah, black magic, and some were even rumored to be cannibals. The entomologists entered Accompong, the Maroons' capital, and presented a letter of introduction from the governor-general of the island to the head man, Colonel Robertson. The colonel produced a bottle of rum and began to talk about Hitler, whose rise he had been following on his short-wave radio. "Dat man is a bad man," he said. He arranged a hut for them, with a woman to cook and wash their clothes. They stayed a week, and found the Maroons to be a warm, proud, and contented people.

In a banana garden near a tiny settlement called Wilson's Run, they stumbled on the russet-and-black *Atlantea pantoni*. Fifty years earlier, a planter named Panton had caught several of the insects on the edges of his woodland, and they were named for him. Since then only one other collector had succeeded in catching a *pantoni*, an English spinster named Miss Fountaine. "She was an intrepid woman," my father explains in *Two in the Bush*, his droll, unpublished account of their Jamaican butterfly safaris, "who spent her time traveling in exotic places of the world and more or less casually catching butterflies. She had a fabulous record for picking up the rarest species at every place she visited. It was almost as a matter of course that, when she came to Jamaica in 1911, she captured a *pantoni*. She found it near the obscure village of Troy, on the eastern edge of the Cockpit Country." Twenty-six years later, he and Uncle were able to assemble a fine series of the species, including a dozen of the female, which not even Panton had ever seen. She is almost twice as big, with yellow submarginal spots instead of reddish-brown ones.

It was largely because of their work on Jamaica that my own initiation to the tropics took place there. I landed in Montego Bay early in 1972 with an innocent and pure-hearted animal behaviorist, a whale and sea-turtle girl, with whom I was in love. I still have the notes I made during our ecstatic three-week assault of the island, in a schoolboy's copybook with the Jamaican "Doctor Bird," a swallow-tailed hummingbird, on the cover. In those days I had eyes mainly for birds, and every day brought a new species for my life list: common stilt in salt flat, jacana stealing across lily pads, bananaquit, yellow-backed grassquit, Blue Mountain booby, little tomfool (a flycatcher), saffron finch, frigatebird circling at great height. Near Bluefields, Jane spotted a black-and-yellow sea snake tossing in the surf. A highly venomous but unaggressive Pacific relative of cobras and coral snakes, it must have come through the Panama Canal. We snorkeled the reefs at Negril, on the western tip, and watched brilliantly colored and highly territorial little fish—sprat, chub, parrotfish—chasing each other through antlers of coral, waving strands of seagrass, and cascading shafts of light. We asked after Dr. Drew, a house physician at Oxford who had withdrawn from the world and lived in Negril for many decades. When my father and Uncle met him, Dr. Drew had cultivated a luxurious lawn on the pitted coral rock around his house, and among his numerous outbuildings was a concrete squash court, open to the sky, that he had built himself. His best friend, and the only other white man in thirty miles, was Brownhill, the lighthouse keeper. He lived four miles away. One evening, after sunset, while the leaves and the rock were still charged with an ultraviolet glow, they drove Dr. Drew to the lighthouse. "It has been four years since you have come to see me," Brownhill complained. Dr. Drew wore a black beret pulled down on his head like a skullcap, a white goatee, a white shirt that was open at the throat, khaki pants tucked into high socks, and sneakers. He invited my father to swim in the lagoon below his house "as you are." My father enthusiastically tore off his clothes and jumped off the cliff. Dr. Drew, fully dressed, executed a swan dive and joined him. Too late, my father realized he had mistook what Dr. Drew meant by "as you are." No one in Negril remembered the recluse, but we stayed in one of the tourist bungalows that had smothered his property.

We went up into the Blue Mountains and spent the night at Whitfield Hall, a small inn at five thousand feet. Mr.

Allgrove, the keeper, remembered the two exceptionally well-mannered butterfly collectors who had stayed there forty years earlier. They had sat in linen suits listening to Mozart on the gramophone with him and his wife, who was now dead. All the books at the inn were Victorian. I chose John Ruskin's letters to Charles Eliot Norton to curl up with. For breakfast we had "tree tomatoes," and afterwards Mr. Allgrove showed us a glade that was "a happy hunting ground for hummingbirds." We walked up toward Portland Gap and started the final climb to Blue Mountain Peak, through an elfin cloud forest. The trees were small and twisted and enveloped in mist. They had reminded Uncle of a Chinese landscape of the Sung period. The Spanish moss that dripped from their branches was characteristic of a higher latitude, as were the wintering bands of Cape May and parula warblers. At Hagley Gap, below the peak, we met a tall young woman walking with extraordinary grace and fluidity and a bundle of wash on her head. She unpinned from her blouse and gave us a button that said "His Imperial Majesty Haile Selassie" and had a picture of the bearded emperor in a visored cap.

When I returned to Jamaica six years later with my wife to look for an underground lake in the Cockpit Country, the flow of tourists and imported goods had dwindled to a trickle, and the whole island seemed ready to blow. Many of the hotels where I had stayed were boarded or standing in ruin. In one town we watched two women in a store fighting over the first carton of milk that had been set out in several days. In another we couldn't get a match. As we were photographing some bats on the ceiling of a cave, a group of young Rastafarians who were collecting guano for their ganja patches came up and ordered us to hand over our money.

"How come white man have money and Rastaman have none?" one of them asked. The colonial idyll which my father described seemed to be over. On neither visit, though I looked hard, did I see the small metallic-blue butterfly that has a black tailspot on the underside of its hindwing and is known as Shoumatoff's hairstreak. My father found the new subspecies in four places, and it was named for him in 1943. It shimmers nervously in the trees around sunny upland clearings, and seldom lands. Its food plant and early life are not known. It was rare when he caught it, and hasn't been reported in recent years. The Jamaicans have more urgent things to worry about than the status of their butterflies. My father deposited several Shoumatoff's hairstreaks at the Jamaica Institute in Kingston. The American Museum of Natural History has the type specimens—the original male and female from which it was described by Comstock and Huntington. The Carnegie Museum has a series of five Shoumatoff's hairstreaks. I was shown them by Johnny Bauer, who succeeded Krautworm as the preparator. We spent an afternoon looking at the collection, which is said to be second only to the British Museum's in size and completeness. "There are supposed to be three million specimens, but I know there are more," Bauer told me. He had mounted many of them, one at a time. As I pulled tray after tray from the glass cabinets, I could see evidence of Uncle's infatuation. Bauer showed me a New Guinean swallowtail whose gentian-colored discal bands Uncle had tried to duplicate with watercolors. He had carefully scraped the scales from part of the insect's forewing, leaving only the clear membrane, which he had started to paint over, but seeing that his gentian wasn't even close, he had given up. Bauer showed me insects named for Uncle, like the moth *Zygaena avinoffi*, and others he had named, like *Lerodea tripuncta jamacense ab. sinepunctus*. *Colobura dirce avinoffi* had a false head on the underside of its hindwing. One summer my father watched a lizard strike at the false head of a resting *dirce avinoffi* and bite it off. The first butterfly I saw when I arrived in the Amazon for an eight-month stay in 1976 was this species, clinging to the side of a tree. The false head was so good I couldn't tell if the insect had landed face up or down.

Johnny Bauer pulled out a tray in the Carnegie Museum that contained rows of spotted, hairy, translucent-white butterflies. "*Parnassius*," I gasped. He nodded. Then he held up one of the insects and showed me how its wings and body were covered with fine hairs to help it conserve moisture. He showed me how you could tell it was a female because the abdomen was coated with a chitinous, horny substance called sphragus. "She secretes the sphragus after copula so other males won't try to mate with her," Johnny said. "She's faster than the male, but a good man can run her down." There was a small printed label under the specimen.

P. STOLICKZKANUS FELDER.
HIGH MTS. OF LAHOUL
COLLECTOR SHABANA SHAGOO

Shagoo had been the cook on Uncle's 1912 expedition. Uncle had gotten back in touch with Shagoo and commissioned him to collect for him in the Kashmir.

Through Shagoo and others, Uncle gradually acquired all but one of the twenty-nine species of *Parnassius* known from central Asia. For four *autocrators*, which, in an earlier existence, he had named for the tsar, he paid well into four figures. He lived simply, budgeting for such important splurges. The only *Parnassius* that continued to elude him was the *przewalskii*, "whose dainty white wings are edged with checkered fringes," he wrote, "speckled with black spots, and bejeweled with ruby-red and sapphire-blue ocelli." It almost seemed that he wasn't meant to have it. In St. Petersburg he had tried to barter with the Academy of Science for one of the eight *przewalskiis* that had been caught in the remote Burkhan-Buddha mountains of Tibet by a general whose name they bore, and his aide-de-camp, Kozlov. "I offered the authorities of the museum anything at my command in exchange for a *przewalskii*. A hundred or more rarities that they did not possess, and could not have had from any other source." But the authorities refused. One of the specimens unaccountably slipped out of the museum and into the hands of the celebrated Russian entomologist, Grum-Grshmailo, who later sold it for a tidy sum to a French collector, Baron Deckert. In the summer of 1912, when Uncle was traveling in the Himalayas and unreachable, a stack of telegrams accumulated at his St. Petersburg apartment. The first contained a proposition from Deckert, who was in financial straits and offered to sell Uncle his collection, including the *przewalskii*. Later communications said that the deal was still open, and the last telegram, dated only a few days before Uncle returned, contained the heart-breaking news that Deckert had sold his collection to Sheliujko, who after Uncle had the second-largest private collection in Russia. In 1928, Uncle managed to commission a German missionary named Koenigswald to go into Burkhan-Buddha after the *przewalskii*, but a few days before he was to set out, the man fell sick and died. During the thirties Uncle's hopes of securing one of the elusive parnassian were raised again and dashed twice. In 1940, Igor Sikorsky offered to put a helicopter at his disposal, to drop him into the heart of *przewalskii* country, but then war broke out.

Uncle's greatest contribution to science was a two-hundred-and-fifty-page monograph on another genus from the steppes and mountainsides of central Asia, the Karanasas. Its posthumous publication in 1951 was an event in entomological circles. "While biologists write precisely of species, subspecies, and similar categories," Thomas C. Emmel explains, "such terms have no fixed meanings. Within the Karanasas, hybridization occurs at all levels, and wing shape, colors, and patterns vary apparently at random between one population and the next. Avinoff and Sweadner [the museum's curator of insects, who finished the paper after Uncle died] proposed the local population as the basic biological unit many years before others interested in evolution began shifting their own emphasis from the importance of the species level to the population level." Like the heliconians of the American tropics, the Karanasas seem to be in a state of ongoing mutation. "The infinite variety nurtured by the isolated factors of high barren mountains and deep eroded valleys, has resulted in the impression that no two specimens are alike, that a chaotic condition exists . . . like the colors of pansies . . . among the cultivated flowers," the investigators wrote. Tentatively, they broke the genus down into seventy-five separate forms. Uncle knew that not everyone would agree with them. "Some of these designations may be merged into greater units," he predicted, "or will have to be thrown overboard altogether into the hospitable waters of the sea of synonymy, where due oblivion comes to things that should better be forgotten, or which should never have been mentioned to begin with."

Uncle wanted to be taken as an American museum director and complained that the exotic image the press insisted on giving him put his work in a distorted light. He was good at his job, and thrived at it for twenty years. There was no ready source of money as there had been when Carnegie was alive (he died in 1919), but during the twenties he managed to get a lot of collecting done cheaply, and during the thirties, a rough time for scientific institutions, he managed to keep everyone on staff.

Museums were starting to evolve from the stuffed specimen to the whole environment. It was the golden age of the diorama, and Uncle worked closely with the museum's temperamental, flamboyant staff artist, Ottmar von Feuhrer, on the backgrounds for the habitat groups. In one diorama they re-created the Pittsburgh of ninety million years before, when it was part of a giant swamp, five thousand miles square, with fantastic ferns and horsetails. Without all that carboniferous plant debris, there wouldn't have been any coal, or anything like the city there was now. Uncle wanted the museum to show these relationships. He wanted to transform it from a "somber, gloomy storage place," as he wrote in the *Carnegie Magazine*, to one that inspired "a sense of wonder before the boundless variety and the supreme unity of life." So he thought a lot about the public exhibits. In them examples of the world's seven hundred and fifty thousand known animal species (the number is closer to a million now)—from "the curious-looking dwellers of a greatly magnified drop of water" to "the gregarious species of the polar regions"—should take "their orderly place as ambassadors of their respective clans." The exhibits should range in space to the farthest corners of the world and in time to periods when horses were the size of dogs and dragonflies had two-foot wingspans. They should show that progress in nature "is not uniform. There are waves and cycles, rising tides and ebbs; old types are discarded, new types ascend, but by these spiral paths increasingly higher destinies are fulfilled." But Uncle also knew that problems sometimes arise when dealing with the public. He knew how tempting it was for a souvenir hunter in the Hall of the Big Bones, so he had plaster caudal sections made up for the tail of the brontosaurus, and kept the real ones locked up.

During the war Uncle visited Childs Frick at his beautiful house on Bermuda. Frick was a dedicated amateur zoologist and paleontologist, and a generous supporter of the museum. He recycled his father's coke millions in much the same way Uncle used his inheritance from Uncle Serge. He donated the animals he had shot in East Africa: hartebeest, topi, gnu, klipspringer, oryx, bushbuck, spotted kudu, eland, ibex, dik-dik, as well as the usual run of big game. Uncle did some pastels of reef fish at the Bermuda Aquarium that Frick had made into postcards. William Beebe, the celebrated field biologist, was there too, living at his research station on Nonsuch Island and taking his bathyscaphe deeper than anyone had ever gone. Uncle and Beebe were helping Fairfield Osborn, the president of the New York Zoological Society, with the Pacific World series, a set of handbooks on the flora and fauna of the region, which the government was putting out for the G.I.s. Archie Roosevelt, Theodore's son, on furlough from New Guinea, was visiting Frick, too. Uncle asked him to keep an eye out for a certain New Guinean moth that was the size of a plate. When he got back Roosevelt caught it and persuaded General MacArthur to have it rushed to the Carnegie Museum with his personal stamp on the package. Uncle did a pen and ink portrait of MacArthur and sent it to him gratefully.

Roosevelt once told my sister he thought Uncle was "one of the greatest men there was. He and his sister arrived in this country without a sou to their name and they became two of its most prominent citizens. I'm proud of America because that happened. And I'm proud of them."

Once Uncle wrote Beebe, who had asked him to send anything that had been written at the museum about fish,

My Dear Beebe,

Gladly I send you the solitary product of our icthyological section in the past few years. The single egg that Henn, our curator, has laid in this period I offer you as ceremoniously as an Easter gift bejeweled by Fabergé for the Russian court. If, by chance, like the fabled "purple emu" of the free translation from the French—he "lays another egg," I shall dispatch it without the slightest delay. I know in advance, however, that this labored oviposition will never burst into a caviar of literary profusion.

Few ever caught this sardonic side of him, but it was there. His secretary saved the wicked caricatures he sometimes drew of people while talking sweetly with them on the phone. He would throw them into the wastebasket after they hung up.

During the flowering seasons of 1941 and 1942, Uncle did two hundred and fifty-three watercolors of western Pennsylvania wildflowers. Otto Jennings, the museum's curator of botany, would bring them to him fresh at the end of the day, and he would fall to work immediately. He painted them as they were. If a leaf was partly nibbled by insects, or some rust or smut had discolored it, he showed it that way. Even the lowly smartweed, throwing off a leaf here and there and tipped with a bright pink spike, took on a special vibrance in his rendering. He used Schminke colors, which he considered the brightest and longest-lasting. "Only transparent pigment and no opaque colors," he explained. "No white paint anywhere, not a single stroke used in the highlights. The white is the paper and all light parts are lighter washes of the pigment—thoroughbred aquarelle has been used throughout." The resulting *Wildflowers of Western Pennsylvania*, in two hefty volumes, one with Uncle's plates, the other with Jennings's text, remains one of the most definitive regional surveys in the annals of American botany.

He illustrated his friend Golokhvastov's poem, "The Fall of Atlantis," with a *suite symphonique* of nineteen paintings that were full of esoteric symbolism. The central image was an angelically pure and innocent nude male figure of Ra, for which Johnny Bauer posed on weekends. Bauer was a gymnast and had a beautiful physique. These projects, on top of a frenetic social life, finally took their toll. Uncle never stopped to recharge. His patience with detail seemed unlimited. "He was always interested in the other person," a colleague told me—saluting the janitors in Italian, making special trips to visit Krautworm's niece, a lonely girl who lived on a farm in Ohio, and taking her through the fields in search of birds, bugs, and butterflies. "He told me stories about palaces and princes and taught me to look forward to everything—spring, rain, new buds," the woman remembers. "He was a very quick-moving person," Zoric told me, "darting across the room to see if there was something you needed. In the speed at which he painted he was like a butterfly

hovering. To look at something else he would take his pince-
nez off. Then he would quickly put it back again. So it was
like a butterfly hovering in his hands." On April 10, 1945,
Uncle had a bad heart attack. He was sixty-one and in the
middle of a hundred things. Mopsy got the news at Warm
Springs, Georgia, where she was painting the President.

After his heart attack, Uncle resigned the directorship
and went to live with Mopsy at Hidden Hollow. She installed
a staircase elevator for him, and he took over the top floor.
My brother remembers going up to see Uncle at Hidden
Hollow when he was five or six years old. The room was a
mess, with books and butterflies and drawings all over the
place. In the middle of the chaos was a delicate and restrained
old man who seemed almost to be made of ivory. He played
some game with the boy that had a didactic thrust, and
was nervous that the boy was going to touch something and
break it.

Uncle spent a quiet year at Hidden Hollow, painting
flowers. He made about a hundred watercolors of orchids—
Cattleyas, Laelias, and related hybrids—that a friend who
lived nearby sent over from his greenhouse. He started a
series of Old World roses with butterflies fluttering and clouds
billowing over a sparsely wooded plain. The butterflies were
species he had caught in his boyhood. The plain recalled the
steppe around Poltava. He was calmly looking back to his
youth. He painted the roses in the tradition of the great
botanical illustrators just after 1800, Redouté and Van Span-
donk. But he was painting in a broader manner now, not
with the fine brush of a miniaturist. He was attentive to the
total organic presentation, to the rhythm and harmony of
the growth form, and to what happened when you got a little

aging. One morning, like a rapturous child, he showed Mopsy a watercolor he had just finished. "The odor of the rose seemed to flow from the end of my brush as I painted," he told her. "I became the rose."

Feeling stronger, he moved into a small apartment at 952 Fifth Avenue. There were one-man shows of his flowers, to rave reviews, at Knoedler's, at the Natural History Museum, at the Audubon Society, at the Botanical Garden. He started to go out again. Miss Helen Clay Frick had him for lunch with Osbert and Edith Sitwell, who had recently published a book of verse. Dropping to one knee before Dame Edith, he said, "O what a wonderful book you have given us. But madame, I have to tell you, in that poem about the learned Russian monks—that's not the way they are at all. Of course they won't see the book, but an old Russian like me will know the difference." Dame Edith said nothing, just pulled her sweater tight around her and glared at him. John Walker chose "The Emergence of the Black Tulip" and two other watercolors by Uncle for the National Gallery. "I thought he was certainly the best flower painter I knew of in our age, and it would be good to have him represented." He was profiled in the *New Yorker* by Geoffrey Hellman, who often wrote about museums and collected butterflies himself. "As an example of successful assimilation, Dr. Andre Avinoff, an elegant, courtly, intense, knowledgeable sixty-four-year-old Russian lepidopterist and painter . . . stands high among the czarist emigres in this country," the piece began. He threw himself into a lecture series which the Metropolitan Museum asked him to give. *Life* magazine was about to run a story on him. A montage of Uncle, bow-tied and surrounded by butterflies, naturally, had been chosen, and the copy was in type. "Keeping up with the art world and different scientific groups, he was living in the last months of his life the way he had always wanted," Mopsy, who rented the apartment next door, wrote in a brief memoir. "He had reached great ability in his art, he had acquired a quality of supreme wisdom and serenity, and, with all his interests in the surrounding world, a growing detachment from everything in general. His energy and concerns, regarding what he believed were his responsibilities, lasted almost to the end. It was only three days before his death when some great transformation took place, that suddenly everything that attached him in a physical way to his life was cut off, and his whole being centered from then on in that forthcoming transition of which he had spoken so often in his discussions on life and death, and which, even before any immediate end was antici pated, he pictured as one great release into a fuller existence with an ever-expanding freedom to develop those God-given talents that were specifically yours since time immemorial." He died on July 16, 1949. Like all great men (and many I spoke to described him as "the greatest man I ever knew") he uttered memorable last words. "The air—how clean it is"; as if he had already progressed from the context of the hospital to a more spacious place. There was an impressive funeral at the Russian Orthodox church three days later. He had asked to be buried in the Prince Albert coat he had worn to the Versailles peace conference, and this was done.

✤ ✤ ✤

Though Uncle had a wide circle of acquaintances, he always remained something of a mystery. Not many Pittsburghers could say that they had ever been to his rooms at the Schenley Hotel. Behind his gregariousness and his optimism there was a great reserve, maybe even a degree of pain. He talked about things, rarely about people. His manners were formal. He rarely put you on a first-name basis, and you certainly wouldn't have dared to ask him a personal question. But his close friends, and of course the family, knew how he took being wrenched from his homeland, and how he worried about his brother still over there. In a letter to Tim and Maud Clapp (Clapp was the director of the Frick Collection in New York) he wrote in 1941:

> According to recent war news some bitter fights are occurring in a marshy region midway between Poltava and Neprovsk. From all indications, this must be very near our old estate. As I think I told you, the old house derives its name, "Shideyevo," from the Tartar word, "shada," meaning fortress. No one can foretell the future development of present events, but I cannot help feeling somehow that this head-on collision of the two totalitarian systems will result with broken cervicals for both sides. It goes without saying that the third totalitarian dictator will have the same fate while his star dwindles to the size of an indescript and practically nameless planetoid. You do not blame me for making a distinction between Russia, which has a long history in the past and, I trust, a fine future to come, and its present government as a passing phase of its existence. The stubborn resistance of the population and the army, I interpret in terms of a natural protection of the country from any invasion and not necessarily as a sign of a steady support of the present political system, which I hope will disappear in due time from the face of the earth.
>
> Meanwhile I do not have any direct news from my

brother, from whom I have not heard for many years; but I realize from the information I receive from time to time from his wife that he is either in prison or in exile somewhere.

After their separation in October 1917, Nika wrote his mother faithfully until she died, but the letters revealed little beyond the nature of his work, and the interest he took in it. Even if it hadn't been dangerous, Nika wouldn't have said what they were really going through. Grandmother lived until 1933. In order not to be a burden on her children, she had become increasingly independent. She made the rounds of the Orthodox churches and émigré communities in the metropolitan area. She traveled on her own. There is a snapshot she had taken of herself in a rain slicker, leaning against a railing beneath Horseshoe Falls. She looks thoroughly invigorated. After Alika married a Cossack and moved to Brooklyn, Grandmother would often take the subway and visit them. She had her own friends. She wore black most of the time, with her hair up. She had a strong, kind character. On her deathbed she made Mopsy promise to break off with a dashing Russian test pilot who worked for Sikorsky. Mopsy had been seeing a lot of him, but she kept her promise. Nika wrote how sad he was to hear that she had died, and that was his last letter.

But still there were indirect bits of news. When Mopsy was painting Cyrus McCormack, he recalled being taken around a tractor exhibit in Moscow by a "saintly" man who turned out to have been Nika. "Saint" is the word that was commonly used to describe him. Mopsy and Uncle read eagerly the fragment that appeared in Bruce Lockhart's memoir, *The British Agent*, in 1933:

. . . the realists were few in number. They included men like Avinoff, the former Assistant Minister of the Interior . . . a man of great intelligence and objectivity . . . whom no one could help liking. The revolution had destroyed everything he held dear in life. But . . . in the course of a brilliant exposé of the revolutionary movement he told me sadly that the Bolsheviks were the only government that had showed the slightest sign of strength, and that the counter-revolution had no chance of success for years to come.

Later in the decade, Mopsy's maid took a strange message from a man who said he was staying at the St. George Hotel in Brooklyn, but wouldn't leave his name. He said that he had been in a prison camp with Nika, and that Nika was still alive. In 1940 Zoric was visiting a woman in Babylon who took in paying guests. One of the guests was a Swede who was recovering from an appendectomy. Zoric started talking with him. He said he represented a Swedish match company, and was going to Pittsburgh as soon as he got better. "You must look up my uncle, Andrey Avinoff, when you get there," she said. The man slapped his forehead and said, "That's the name. I have a package for him. A friend of mine who works in the Foreign Ministry in Stockholm gave it to me. He found it when he was housecleaning some files. It was addressed to someone in America, but the label fell off, and I couldn't remember the name." The package contained some of Uncle's photographs of the Pamir and Karakoram expeditions. Nika had given it to a friend at the Swedish embassy in Moscow to take out of the country a dozen years earlier.

Occasionally they would get a letter from Masha. She

had been exiled to Kazakhstan, near the Chinese border. Then she was living somewhere outside of Moscow. But she hadn't seen Nika since 1937, and didn't even know if he was still alive. A. W. Mellon, who was very fond of Uncle, had offered to help after he became Secretary of the Treasury, but Uncle thought it would only make matters worse. He'd about given up hope until one night in 1944. He came to dinner at the Grays' beside himself (Peter Gray was chairman of the biology department at Pitt). "The most extraordinary thing happened," he told them. "My sister-in-law just wired from Paris. She got out of Russia!"

When the war was over, Masha came to America. She arrived in May 1947 with a Nansen passport (a document devised by Dr. Fridtjof Nansen, the League of Nations' high commissioner for refugees, which enabled stateless persons to travel) and filled them in on the last thirty years. After Lenin broke up the Constituent Assembly in January 1918, it was obvious that they should have left, or at least gone south with Nabokov senior and the others Lenin arrested. But Nika wanted to stay. ("After the Great October Socialist Revolution, Lenin invited the former nobility to stay and work for the common cause, without fear of reprisal," I was told in Moscow by an Intourist girl named Olga. "Lenin was a nobleman himself. Many of them stayed. Of course they lost all their wealth and property.") Nika was put in charge of a fuel cooperative known as Kooperatop, whose purpose was to keep Moscow supplied with coal and firewood. With rail service disrupted by the civil war, the city was in danger of freezing. He did his job well, and the Bolsheviks saw that he was useful. Masha had managed to move most of the valuables—the Aubusson carpets, the family portraits, the silver—from her grandfather's palace before it was nationalized, and they were living in the twenty-room house of friends who had escaped to France. They still had six devoted servants, including old Joseph, her grandfather's butler, who refused to stop wearing his white tie and tails. Joseph opened the door the first time the Cheka, as the secret police was then called, came to arrest Nika. "My friends, what can I do for you?" he asked. The policemen, with leather coats and pistols drawn, stood gaping for a moment. It was just a check-up, and Nika was soon released. He was made president of the K.U.B.A., a society for members of the learned professions. By September 1920 their friends' ballroom had been partitioned, and they shared the house with ninety people. They still ate with Scherbatov silver thin potato gruel and an occasional windfall of horsemeat. Between 1920 and 1933 Nika was arrested five times by the G.P.U., as the Cheka was renamed. There were never any charges, and he was always released within several months and instantly re-employed. He was still useful. While he was in prison, Masha typed his economics papers and translated foreign technical articles into Russian. Through Gosizdat, the government publishing bureau, she worked on an anthology with Henri Malraux, André's communist brother, who had come to the Soviet Union for a fifteen-month visit. In 1933 Nika was arrested again. The G.P.U. was now the N.K.V.D. This time it looked as if someone wanted Nika out of the way. Masha went straight to Nikolai Krylenko, the commissar of justice, and pleaded for Nika's release. Krylenko had done some exploring in the Pamir and was familiar with Uncle's writings. "So he's the brother of that white vermin?" Krylenko asked. But he admired Masha's guts, and a few weeks later Nika came home, minus a front tooth. He had been sentenced to ten years of "Urals"—hard labor in the mines—

for "attempting to sabotage the textile industry of the U.S.S.R." Ten years before, he had bought Masha two pairs of *valenki*, felt-and-leather boots, on the black market. He had already begun serving the sentence.

In 1934, less than a year after his release, Nika was made head of the Economic Planning Department of the Ridder Combine in the Altai Mountains. It was a three-year assignment. The Altai Mountains are in Siberia, and Nika thought it would be best for Masha to stay in Moscow. Soon after he had gone, she was arrested, kept four months without charges in the Butyrka Prison, released, and put to work translating articles about milking machines. Nika did much to improve the plant's efficiency. He was so useful that they refused to let him come back to Moscow when the three years were up. Masha went to the attorney general, Andrei Vyshinsky, and again personally secured his release. They were together until November. But Yezhov had succeeded Beria as head of the N.K.V.D., and a new wave of purges had begun. Surviving members of the prerevolutionary intelligentsia and former nobles who had been somehow missed before were specially targeted for liquidation. The police came at midnight and "in the presence of his wife," as Bruce Lockhart would write, "took this saintly man into the communist outer darkness from which he never returned." Masha never learned what happened to him, though once, as she was en route from one prison to another, she thought she saw his face in a train window. In Moscow I tried to find out his fate. I asked at the Lenin Library, which had some of his articles, how I could find out more about him. But I wasn't expecting to get anywhere, and I didn't. I wrote to Alexander Solzhenitsyn, who has collected at his farm in

Vermont the most complete archives on that period. He sent back a nice note, saying that he had no information about Nicolai Avinoff. Nika was probably shot, if not on the night of his arrest, then soon afterwards. "What legal expert, what criminal historian, will provide us with verified statistics for these 1937–38 executions?" Solzhenitsyn asks in *The Gulag Archipelago.* "Where is the Special Archives that we might be able to penetrate in order to read the figures? There is none. There is none and there never will be any. Therefore we dare repeat only those figures mentioned in rumors that were quite fresh in 1939–40, when they were drifting around under the Butyrki arches, having emanated from the high- and middle-ranking Yezhov men of the N.K.V.D. who had been arrested and had passed through those cells not long before. (And they really knew!) The Yezhov men said that during those two years of 1937 and 1938 a *half-million* 'political prisoners' had been shot throughout the Soviet Union, and 480,000 *blatnye*—habitual thieves—in addition." From a cell in the Lubyanka Prison, Masha herself watched the records being burned so they would not fall into the hands of the Germans.

After Nika was taken away, Masha waited almost eagerly for the knock at her door, but three months passed before they got around to arresting her. There was a ridiculous inquisition and she was incarcerated in Butyrka, where she came down with malaria and almost died. Then a month in the local jail of Alma-Ata, followed by two years and two months of "free deportation" in the Kazakh village of Addis Ada. It wasn't so bad there. She rented a cottage from a Ukrainian woman named Seraphina. A petty criminal named Fomeech, who resembled a "little stoat," became her devoted servant. When they first got there, she had given him her last rouble. Her old friend, Nadya Shipova, sent her money from Moscow and visited when she could. Nadya's father, Dmitri, chairman of the Moscow city *zemstvo* and a founder of the Kadet party, had died in prison a few years before. Nika had collected his body and buried it at the edge of the city.

Masha's exile ended in May 1941, but she was still not allowed to live in a big city, so she and Nadya moved to the village of Zubsstov, three hundred *versts* southwest of Moscow. A month later, German troops came pouring across the Polish border. Masha, like many Russians who had grown to hate communism, greeted them as liberators. She had always admired German literature and spoke the language perfectly, and had no idea of what Hitler and the Nazis were all about. The S.S. officers were charmed by her culture and enlisted her as a go-between in their dealings with the local populace. Her willing collaboration ended when she watched some German soldiers mow down a line of Russian guerrillas, many of whom were children, as they came charging out of a forest, but she had no choice but to flee with the Germans when the Red Army reached Zubsstov. The women who collaborated and remained were raped and eviscerated. In the city of Vyazma, or what was left of it, General Mittelmeyer was so moved by an ode she had written to the Wehrmacht that he sent her and Nadya to Berlin, where for several years she translated propaganda leaflets that were air-dropped behind Russian lines. In 1944 she sweet-talked a Gestapo officer into letting them go to occupied Paris for a vacation. "The trick was to weave a quick mesh of words in a tone at once propitiating and insistent," she later recounted. Once

in Paris, they got in touch with Masha's nephew, Igor Demidov, and lay low in his villa near Fontainebleau until the
invasion of Normandy.

When I was old enough to start appreciating Masha, she
was already bedridden and in her late eighties. Her hair had
turned snow-white in prison, and since coming to America
she had ballooned to monstrous proportions. I saw her once
standing at her window in nothing but a nightcap. There
were no curves in her body, only folds. She almost always
wore a kimono with the belt tied over her pendulous breasts,
so that they seemed like two pockets filled with sand. She
was a famous eater and a brilliant raconteur. Whole cooked
chickens would mysteriously disappear overnight from Mopsy's refrigerator. She was grand, but had a sense of humor
about herself, like a dowager hippopotamus. I could sit for
hours listening to the stories she told in her rich basso, while
the ashes of her mentholated cigarette—she fitted them one
after another into a long ivory holder, lighted them, and
then forgot about them—broke off and spilled down the front
of her kimono. We grew very fond of each other. Long letters
in French passed between us while I was at boarding school.
In one she railed against the middle-class values of other
émigrés. "All they talk about is each other's pedigrees." She
dedicated to me her English translations of Pushkin. I remember how her eyes would light up when I came to see
her, and she would exclaim "Ach, my dear Panda!" (Panda
is my family name. It was suggested by my round face and
slanted eyes when I was little.)

Masha had the flirtatious eyes of a young woman, and
pencil lines for eyebrows. She reminded me of Cunégonde
at the end of *Candide*, except that her buttocks were still

there. She had seen it all. Nothing could possibly have fazed her.

Her most powerful stories were about the prisons she had known. One, called "The Happy Hour," got published in the *Reader's Digest*. It was about a black cat named Mishka who lived in the Butyrka Prison. In the evening Mishka prowled from cell to cell, looking for food. The inmates would feed him and stuff messages into a little pouch under his tail. The tissues in the pouch listed who was still alive and in good health. Mishka's visit was the big event of the day, "the happy hour." But one evening a guard discovered the pouch, and hanged Mishka in the prison yard as a "counter-revolutionary." Another of her stories, "Scheherazade," appeared in the *New Yorker*. It takes place in the local prison of Alma Ata, where Masha is locked in a cell with fifty prostitutes and murderesses. To stop them from fighting and to keep up her own spirits, she gets the idea of telling them stories. Her mutilated, half-improvised versions of *Ivanhoe, Jane Eyre, La Dame Aux Camélias*, and *The Call of the Wild* are a big hit. Halfway through Conan Doyle's "The Spotted Leopard," one of the inmates, Lucy, learns that she is being transferred in a few hours to a concentration camp, and she begs Masha to whisper the ending. She has to know if the man in the cage escapes. Masha tells her that he does, and as Lucy is taken away, she turns and blows Masha a kiss.

An émigré writer, Prince Paul Chavchavadze, who was a good friend and a distant relative of Mopsy's (through the Bagratids of Georgia), helped Masha make her stories into a book, *Pilgrimage Through Hell*, which was published in 1968.

Masha's adventures weren't over. She became restless at

Mopsy's, and in the last ten years she moved around, or was moved around, a lot. She lived for a time in Sea Cliff, then she went to Sacramento and stayed with the daughter of a cousin named Kitty. Then San Francisco. Then Monterey, where there is a small colony of Russians who are connected with the Defense Language Institute, one of whom is a Panayev cousin of Mopsy's. But Masha wasn't an easy person to have in your house. She ate like six people, and expected to be waited on hand and foot. Eventually she wound up living in Portugal with a shady Russian woman who thought she was rich and more or less kidnaped her. Mopsy got a letter from Masha that said, "I love Portugal and want to live here until I die." Then for months no one heard a thing. Not even a card at Christmas. Masha's sister, Sonya, who lived in Paris, checked with her bank and found that everything had been withdrawn. Zoric offered to fly over and find out what was going on. She took a crash course in Portuguese at Berlitz and landed in Lisbon in January 1971. After two days of sleuthing, she found Masha, very weak and blinded by cataracts, living in a little village on the coast with a pretty Angolan airline stewardess and her three-year-old daughter. The unscrupulous émigré who had agreed to take care of her had absconded to England with Masha's book advance and an enormous pearl brooch Nika had given her. The pearl, held in the claws of a dragon, was more than an inch in diameter. She had been able to keep it in prison by saying it was costume jewelry. The woman had even persuaded Masha to sign a will leaving her everything, including the large, priceless library on Long Island about which Masha had often boasted and which in fact amounted to two shelves of paperbacks. Zoric brought Masha back to Mopsy's house, where she soon lost her hearing, and no longer able to communicate with anyone, she lived in the dark silence of her memories until 1975.

✢ ✢ ✢

My grandfather had three sisters, Nina, Olga, and Zöe. Nina married a Bavarian baron, Peter von Nettlehorst. Zöe married a Russian baron with a German name, Klüge von Klügenau. Olga, the second, and Lyova's favorite sister, married the composer, Thomas de Hartmann, whose second ballet, *The Rose Flower*, with Pavlova, Fokine, and Nijinsky in the cast, was performed before the tsar in 1907. In St. Petersburg de Hartmann explored the relationship of color and sound with the painter Vasilii Kandinski. There was an event called the Yellow Sound that combined his music and some panels Kandinski had painted yellow. De Hartmann became a disciple of the Georgian mystic, G. I. Gurdjieff, and converted his wife. "Mr. Gurdjieff was an unknown person, a mystery," Olga declares in her memoir, *Our Life With Mr. Gurdjieff*, "but whoever came in contact with him wished to follow him, and so did Thomas de Hartmann and I." They fled with their guru to the Caucasus on the eve of the Revolution. Olga became Gurdjieff's secretary. She handled the material plane for him. Thomas wrote scores for his "movements," which required parts of the body to move in unrelated ways, like a child patting his head and rubbing his stomach at once. They made their way to France and bought an old chateau near Fontainebleau called the Prieurie, where many submitted to Gurdjieff's rugged ministry. Katherine Mansfield, terminally afflicted with tuberculosis, went there to die. Olga's parents, the Schumachers, also lived at the Prieurie, though they couldn't stand Gurdjieff. There was an incident in which Arkady Alexandrovitch left the room after

Gurdjieff ridiculed another émigré who had been remembering at great length the excellence of the chocolate in old St. Petersburg. A few minutes later, his wife, Olga Konstantinovna, stormed in and said to Gurdjieff, "I will wager that if someone had brought you your Perrier water five minutes earlier, this wouldn't have happened." Both the Schumachers were tiny and quickly offended by any impropriety.

In 1929 the de Hartmanns broke with Gurdjieff, before he could take over their lives completely, but they continued to practice his teachings. Leaving the Prieurie, they moved into a small house in the poor suburb of Courbevois with the Schumachers. Thomas gave piano lessons and recitals with Olga, who had a fine soprano. They made a record in which Olga sang from the writings of James Joyce set to Thomas's music, but it didn't sell, and they continued to live in "modest circumstances." Zoric saw them in 1933–34 when she came to Paris to study art. Olga Konstantinovna was gaga by then. She kept pirouetting in front of the mirror and prattling about the Polish officers who had danced with her and the twenty pairs of shoes she had once owned. Arkady spent his time sitting in an outdoor café with other ministers of the tsar's government and going over how the Revolution had happened. Thomas, who had kept his head shaved during the twenties, now had long musician's hair. Olga was petite and irresistible in her square beret and elegant black newborn lamb coat. She had the body of a sixteen-year-old. Robert Bien-Aimé, a perfume manufacturer who had married her cousin Vera, was particularly sensitive to her beauty. Bien-Aimé was handsome and full of charm. He mixed the scents himself, and after hitting on Houbigant, he became very rich and bought a fantastic villa in Biarritz.

For the housewarming he engaged the entire Ballet Russe to dance in the courtyard. He drove a Hispano-Suiza, and later bought a second Hispano-Suiza just to follow with the luggage. In a way, he was terribly *parvenu*, and a perfect sugar daddy for Olga.

The Schumachers died before the war. Thomas and Olga left Paris and lived in Montreal, in New York, in Taliesin, Frank Lloyd Wright's commune in Arizona, which is still run on Gurdjieffian principles. Late in the twenties, Mopsy and Uncle sat cross-legged on the floor and listened to Gurdjieff proclaim himself to be Lucifer. Uncle wasn't impressed. He decided Gurdjieff was another of the "swarm of swindling swamis," as he called them. They saw Olga from time to time, but after Thomas died she began to insist on the repayment of twenty-five thousand roubles that she claimed Thomas had lent Lyova "to get out of Russia." Mopsy remembered that they had invested together in a licorice plantation in the Caucasus, but she knew nothing about this loan. Late in the fifties they had a big blow-up over the money and fell out completely. No one was happy about my idea of looking up Olga. All anyone could tell me was that she lived somewhere out West. By chance I met a woman who belonged to a group of Gurdjieff followers that centered around "Madame de Hartmann." She was living outside Santa Fe and not well, the woman told me. "Everything's wrong with her body, but she still has a monumental store of inner energy." She was ninety-six.

A few days after I had written Aunt Olga, a man with a Canadian accent called and said his name was Peter Colgrove and that he was taking care of her. She wanted very much to see me, he said, but she tired very quickly; she had good days and bad ones. I would have to come out and take my chances. I flew to Albuquerque, got in a rented car, and headed east across the old sea floor. It was early in May. The desert was subtly in bloom. Where they could be seen breaking through a low cloud cover, the mountains were heavily sprinkled with new snow. I found the house where I was being put up, in the old adobe section of Santa Fe. My host was a soft-spoken man in his forties who had left an advertising career in New York to immerse himself in the Work of Gurdjieff. We drove to see Olga that evening. She was living in a small house in the Nambé River Valley, an hour from the city, with Colgrove and a young male nurse named José López. Her neighbors were poor chicanos and Nambé Indians. A few doctors from Santa Fe had weekend places down the road. The huge particle accelerator of the Los Alamos Scientific Laboratory, where the atom bomb was developed and a good deal of fusion research is still carried on, sat on a high plateau several miles away.

The house needed repair. Its yard was an expanse of raw grays and red, flecked with rabbit-bush and sloping gently down to a line of willows and Russian olive trees along the Nambé River. Aunt Olga was sitting up in bed. She had exquisitely fine features, with bunches of tight wrinkles around the mouth and long, straight, silver-blond hair. A large metal oxygen tank stood by the bed. She was still frighteningly irresistible, but had wasted away to almost nothing except her will. Her legs hardly raised the covers.

"You have the round face of Lyova," she said in a strong, cultured voice, looking tenderly on the first blood relative she had seen in years. Her accent was French. Her hot water bottle, her glass of boiled water colored with sherry, her sharp, exaggerated cries of agony as Colgrove helped her shift position, were all very European, it seemed to me. We sat quietly. Suddenly her face became bitter and proud. "None of you thought I existed," she said. "None of you cared what happened to me. And your grandmother had that chateau in Napanoch." Colgrove thought it best for her to rest. "In the last two years I've taken her unconscious three times to the hospital," he told me in the living room. He looked like a wreck. Out of earshot, he referred to her affectionately as "the boss" and "her highness," but in her presence she was respectfully Olga Arkadievna. He was somewhere in his fifties, too young to be even her son, and had been her devoted companion for more than twenty years.

In the morning I sat in the living room and looked through some papers that Colgrove set out for me. The childhood chapters of her unpublished autobiography, *What For?*, were unrevealing. Two photographs showed the close resemblance between Kaiser Wilhelm the First and her Wolfert grandfather, allegedly the kaiser's morganatic son by a Polish woman named Labounsky. "The blood is legitimate," Colgrove explained. He had traced back her family tree as far as he could. By noon Olga was strong enough to talk. Speaking French, in which she was more comfortable, she told how her great-grandmother, Josephine Emilie-Louise de Lavalette, had changed clothes with her husband to get him out of prison, how her grandfather had been on the commission to liberate the serfs. But after a while she remembered the unpaid twenty-five thousand roubles, and would only refer to me indirectly, as "him" or "that person." "Tell *that person*," she said imperiously to Colgrove, "that my father toured the prisons with Senator Grott and when he saw the prisoners just sitting there, doing nothing, he had work programs started for them. And he had the death penalty abol-

ished for everything except killing your father or the tsar.
My family were some of the best people in Russia."

Colgrove suggested that we go for a ride in the old blue
Peugeot. They had shipped it over in 1963, he told me, after
driving all over Europe that summer. "We stayed with her
sister in Berlin," Colgrove remembered. "It was a crazy, huge
apartment. The front room was rented to an old countess
who was out of money." Olga sat in front, with a plaid
blanket over her knees, dark glasses, and a floppy white hat
with a purple band. We drove through the desert for a while,
then pulled over to watch the swollen Nambé River run
under the road. "We haven't been here for three years, I
think, yes?" Colgrove said.

"Look, the river is very large," he said when he had gotten
no answer.

"*Il est joli, le petit pont,*" Olga observed.

We continued down the road, past a billboard that said
"Lotsaburger Two Miles" and had been shot to pieces. I asked
what had decided him and Olga to live there. "Olga Arkadievna has chronic bronchitis," he said. "But I don't know
that the dust isn't a trade-off with the damp we wanted to
get away from. We got the idea from D. H. Lawrence, who
came to Taos to cure his tuberculosis. We lived first at Taliesin, where there were Gurdjieff people. Frank Lloyd Wright
became a close friend of Thomas de Hartmann. He thought
that the closest thing to architecture was music."

We drove back to the house and helped Olga onto her
bed. Colgrove served tea. Engraved in Russian on the dented
silver sugar bowl was the word *Kamchatka*. The Wolferts'
estate in Finland, where Olga and Lyova had played as children, had been called Kamchatka, after an ancestor who had

mapped the peninsula. It was one of the few possessions Gurdjieff had let her keep. She asked me to put on a record of her husband's cello concerto. It was a tender, scenic piece of music, with shades of Satie and Debussy, I thought. There was some transitional trumpeting that brought to mind *Pictures At an Exhibition*. In fact, the exhibition that had inspired Moussorgsky was an 1874 retrospective of paintings by Thomas's uncle, Victor Alexandrovitch Hartmann (Thomas added the "de," as many émigrés did, to show that he had been a noble). During the andante, Olga sat up and looked out of the French doors to the high, scudding clouds. The light poured in on her checkered blanket, the apricot-colored irises swayed against the tan adobe wall, the bleached debris of previous tenants lay in the yard, half-buried with sand. "The finale was considered perfect by Casals," Olga said when the concerto was over.

In the fall, when we returned from Russia, a letter from Colgrove was waiting. "I'm sure you'll be glad to know," it began, "that Olga Arkadievna died quietly in her own bed, and that I was with her." In New York my sister Tonia and I went to the memorial service that was held for her at the Russian Orthodox church on Second Street between First and Second avenues. The thirty or so people who came were a mixture of young Gurdjieffians and marvelous-looking white-haired Russians. One, I noticed, had a rolled-up copy of the émigré newspaper, *Novoe Russkoe Slovo*, in his jacket pocket. Tonia and I were the only family.

✠ ✠ ✠

One afternoon, wandering around Leningrad, I found the mauve palace on the Moika Canal that had belonged to the Yusupovs, and opened its huge oak doors. It was now a recreational facility for teachers. The interior was under restoration, with a maze of scaffolding. An old *baboushka* sitting at a desk in the foyer asked what I wanted. I said I just wanted to have a look around. "*Nelzya*," she said. "Absolutely forbidden. Can't you see the building is under restoration?" "But my grandmother danced in the ballroom here. Couldn't I just take a peek?" The *baboushka* repeated "*nelzya*" unbudgingly. "Well, couldn't I at least see the room in the basement where Rasputin was poisoned?" "*Nelzya, nelzya.* There's nothing but toilets down there anyway." "Well, could I please go down and use one of them?" I asked. "Oh, all right," she said. I descended some marble steps to a vast room with a low ceiling supported by numerous columns and arches. A row of porcelain urinals had been installed against one of the walls. Some of the urinals had overflowed, and another old *baboushka*, whose legs were wrapped in strips of felt, was mopping up the mess. I nodded to her and walked around the room. She waited sadistically until she had me trapped in a corner, then with a great shove of her mop she sent a wave of rancid yellow liquid toward me and screamed, "What are you doing here? Get out! Get out!"

That evening, in a freezing rain, I met my cousin, Oleg Markevitch, standing under an umbrella in front of the Marinsky Theater. Vaslav Nijinsky danced many of his famous roles in the Marinsky, until Serge Diaghilev arranged for a private performance, in which, to show the perfection of his dancing form, Nijinsky wore no underclothes. One of the grand duchesses fainted. Nijinsky was dismissed from the Marinsky company and joined the Ballet Russe. My cousin is the son of the conductor, Igor Markevitch, by his second marriage. Igor was first married to Nijinsky's daughter Kira. At sixteen, slim, wolf-faced Igor (or "bird-like and brittle," in Nicholas Nabokov's description) succeeded Boris Kochno as Serge Diaghilev's fourth and last great love. His piano concerto premiered with Stravinsky's *Rénard* at Covent Garden on July 5, 1929. The Markevitches are descended from my great-grandmother Olga Schumacher's sister Mathilda.

I hadn't seen Oleg since 1962, at his father's fiftieth birthday party in Villars, Switzerland. Now he was a tall, aristocratic twenty-two-year-old, who had come to Russia to study at the Leningrad Conservatory. He had invited my wife and me to a recital. Because of the foul weather, only I came.

The Leningrad Conservatory was across the street from the Marinsky Theater. It had been founded by Oleg's great-grandfather, A. N. Markevitch, a cellist, along with the pianist Anton Rubinstein and the composer Nicolai Rimsky-Korsakov. A. N. Markevitch's father, N. A. Markevitch, had been a conductor and a compiler of Ukrainian folk songs. He lived in the same village in the government of Poltava as the composer M. I. Glinka. "Russian classical music began with Glinka," Oleg told me as we hurried into the recital hall. "Today is Glinka's one hundred and seventy-fifth birthday, and the music tonight will all be his."

Oleg and I sat in two seats that were nearer the back than the front, and looked at each other. "You are so Russian," he said to me. "People tell me that," I said. Oleg had spent three years in Moscow, but the conductor he had been studying under had defected to Holland, and he had transferred to the Leningrad Conservatory. "The pianist plays on wood and ivory, the cellist on wood and hair, the conductor on people," he said in English that was remarkably good considering that it was his fourth language (his mother is Italian, he grew up in France, and for the past couple of years he'd been speaking Russian almost all the time). "Paul the Sixth said, 'I am the *serviteur* of Christianity.' The conductor is the *serviteur* of music." Oleg planned to specialize in Russian music. He particularly loved Shostakovitch. "It all ended with him. He was a great composer, but not enough recognized, largely for political reasons. He suffered much under Stalin, was much criticized, and that anguish comes through in his music."

I asked how he liked the Soviet Union. He found the country "a great success, but it's *so* disorganized. The people are adorable. They make up for an inferiority complex by being very proud." I asked if he'd found any relatives. "Yes. One named Ava rang me up a month ago. She wanted me to marry her. She said she had millions of roubles and would split them once we got out of the country. I met her. She was about fifty-five, with short hair sticking out and dyed red, and completely bonkers." I asked about something that puzzled me, the persistence of anti-Semitism. "One would have thought the Revolution eliminated the reasons for it," I said. "It's in the Russian blood," he suggested. "The temperaments are different. The Jew is retentive, while the Russian is expansive. For centuries it has been inscribed in the chromosomes of Russians that there was no repair, no place to go, no *izbah*, no tree, just the sky, as if you had lived for years and years in the sea, like a fish. The Russians are people who are lost in nature and stay where they are. They have no measures. Either they're very happy or they're very sad. That's why they can't live outside of their country. They arrive in Europe and with all those measures they can't breathe."

I was going to ask why, in that case, it was so hard to breathe *here*, but before I could, the concert began with a selection from the opera Glinka had made from Pushkin's poem *Russlan and Ludmilla*. There was a bust of Glinka on the stage, with flowers beneath it. It was clear that everyone in the recital hall had a deep reverence for music. The recital hall was a large, prerevolutionary room that listed slightly toward the left front corner. Maybe some of the reclaimed marsh on which it had been built had subsided. Its walls were white, with rococo trim, like the icing of an elaborate wedding cake, and there was a huge white organ with silver reeds behind the stage. The man who was singing had a booming bass that seemed to fill every square inch of air in the room. I leaned back and looked up at a round mural on the ceiling, in which a group of well-fleshed, rose-complexioned women were sitting on some clouds and plucking harps. For a moment I let myself imagine that we were two young men from the century before, a little more serious than most of our class, that there had been no Revolution to deprive us of our "birthright." I looked at Oleg for some sort of recognition, but he was listening to the music. "Marvelous voices are common in Russia," he turned to me and whispered when the aria was over.

Part Four

Nani and
the Colonel

N ani, my mother's mother, is another of those strong
women with whom our family abounds, who have held it
together when their husbands died early or otherwise de-
faulted at critical moments. Nani was born Nina Mihaelovna
Elaghin. She is a tall, gracious woman of ninety-one now,
and lives in Baltimore. Her people, the Elaghins, were an
old family, emanating from a Roman named Vikenty Zve-

lachony who came to Russia in 1340. The family entered
the nobility in 1605. A wall in the Ouspensky Cathedral on
Moscow's Red Square lists several Elaghins who fell in battle.

Yakov 1547 on the River Sviaga
Peter 1634 at Smolensk
Paul 1634 at Smolensk
Gregory 1634 at Smolensk

The name has such a good Russian ring that it crops up twice
in fiction. While hunting wolves in *War and Peace*, Nicolai
Rostov meets his neighbor, "Ilagin," with whom the Rostovs
had some quarrel and were at law. And in a story of doomed
love by Ivan Bunin, "The Elaghin Affair," a young Hussar,
Coronet Alexander Elaghin, from a "genteel and well-to-do
family," "ten generations of whose ancestors had been in the
army," and, according to the attorney who prosecutes him
at his murder trial, "a locoed wastrel, burning the candle at
both ends," is sentenced to ten years of penal servitude for
shooting his mistress, the bewitchingly beautiful Polish ac-
tress Maria Sosnovskaya, even though it comes out at the
trial that she had been wanting to die for some time, and
had driven young Elaghin half-crazy, until he believed it was
a matter of honor for him to execute her wish.

The most famous actual Elaghin was Ivan Perfilievitch, a
lustrous figure of the eighteenth century—historian, pure
stylist of the Russian language, Mason and count, rusticated
to his estates during the 1750s for his role in a court intrigue,
recalled by Peter III, elevated by Catherine the Great to
senator, then to high steward of her household, then to
Secretary of State—one of the few of her councillors with
whom she apparently didn't sleep—he died, a few weeks

before her, on September 22, 1796. She gave him an island in the estuary of the Neva River, and he built a palace on it. After his death the island changed hands several times and was eventually bought by Alexander I, who commissioned the Italian architect, Carlo Rossi, to expand the palace, to add two stories of white marble columns, a metal cupola and other neoclassical touches. This was Rossi's first big project in Russia. He went on to design many grand structures in St. Petersburg, but the Elaghin palace, as it is still called, remains one of his handsomest efforts.

On a cold, clear morning in mid-September, I went to see it. It overlooks a canal called the Srednaya Nevka, which is lined with former *maisons seigneurales*—some in the style of French chateaux, some like rambling *dachas*, with weathered clapboard and lots of gingerbread—now broken up into apartments. Serge Obolensky wrote about the gay parties he went to in these houses, and of a gypsy singer he was in love with who lived with her band on an island nearby.

In the middle of a road near the canal there was a fine old oak, fenced off by wrought-iron. As I was reading a sign that said the tree had been planted by Peter the Great, a woman passing by said, "Look, it's sick," and pointed to its dead upper branches. Farther along, I recognized the Elaghin palace, set back from the canal by an expanse of lawn. There was no mistaking it from a prerevolutionary postcard Nani had given me. As I crossed the canal on a steel footbridge, a scull glided beneath me, oars sparkling in and out of the water. I passed a formation of elderly people in blue warm-up suits, doing deep knee-bends—Elaghin Island is now a park—then entered an empty playground, with a brightly painted jungle gym, swings, and a billboard that said "Children are our future. To them it falls to continue the deeds

of their father and mother. They will make life on earth
optimal and happy." As I was examining a strange treelet
with willowlike leaves and big axillary buds—perhaps an
oleaster—a red-cheeked policeman, with a walkie-talkie
hanging on his belt, asked what I was doing. Neither old
nor young, I was suspect on a weekday. "My grandmother
was an Elaghin," I said. "I'd like to see the palace." A few
minutes later I was standing before its curator, a scholarly-
looking woman named Dima Nemchinova. We put on felt
slippers over our shoes and walked from the raspberry drawing
room to the circular ballroom to the master bedroom, which
had a canopied bed and a frescoed ceiling. "We are restoring
it room by room, because it is one of the finest houses of the
period," she told me. Blown-up photographs on one of the
walls showed the palace after a Nazi bomb had fallen on it,
and in 1961, when, after ten years, the restoration of the
exterior was finally completed. "During the nineteenth century it was a summer palace for members of the imperial
family," Ms. Nemchinova told me. "The last person who
lived here was P. A. Stolypin, Nicholas II's prime minister."
She didn't mention that in the summer of 1907 there was a
terrific explosion in the Elaghin palace in which forty people
were injured. One of them was Stolypin's little daughter,
whose leg was blown off. Stolypin, for whom the bomb was
intended, was unhurt. Four years later, at a theater in Kiev,
he was successfully done in by an agent provocateur in ca-
hoots with the Secret Police. Stolypin was one of the most
enlightened prime ministers Russia ever had. His brainstorm
was to create a new class of peasant landowners called *kulaks*.
By 1917, when the Bolsheviks were parading the slogan,
"All Land to the Peasants," the expropriation of the nobles
under Stolypin's plan had been going on at the rate of three

million acres a year, and the peasants had already received three quarters of it. The prime ministers after Stolypin were hopeless reactionaries or puppets of Rasputin.

Nani was born in the government of Tambov on December 31, 1890. Tambov is in the central black-earth region, a flat land of vast forests and shallow, circuitous rivers. Tambov was, in Turgenev's words, "the nest of the nobility." Masha's family, the Novossiltsevs, had a twenty-five-thousand-acre estate called Kotchemorova there. All Nani's people were from Tambov. By the end of the last century, dozens of Elaghins lived there. Today, as far as I can determine, there are only two in the whole world. Nani's father Mihail Nilovitch was an Elaghin. So was her mother Alexandra Nicolaevna. They were first cousins. "In Russia, we weren't interested in our ancestors," Nani said to me once. "There were no society magazines. We were all well-born. An officer couldn't be married without presenting the *curriculum vitae* of his bride. Each regiment had a committee to discuss the brides who had been proposed. If they found out the woman wasn't well-born, they called in the officer and said, 'We can't deprive you of your love for this woman, but we can't accept her into the family. Therefore you will have to leave the regiment.' " Nani's father was an officer. He died before she was old enough to remember anything about him, even what he died of. Michael Elaghin left four daughters: Lila, Natasha, Sonya, and Nani. His widow soon married another officer from his regiment, Michael Zhukov; "the family" took care of her. They had a son, Alexander. Zhukov loved the boy so much he had a little grenadier's uniform made up for him and took him often to the regiment. When Nani was seven, Alexander was five, and he was carried off by diphtheria. Dr. Werner, the regimental physician, didn't diagnose it in time or give the injection that might have saved him. Nani remembers that her stepbrother was buried on January 6, 1897, and that the procession to the cemetery was led by several musicians. As the coffin was being lowered into the grave, Zhukov fainted in the snow, and a few days later he was dead of pneumonia. "Mother had a picture of little Alexander lying in his coffin," Nani told me. "Very often, she would take it out and start to cry. We would cry, too, and who wouldn't?" Alexandra didn't marry again. "She was just the most beautiful woman," Nani recalls. "She always took a walk with a parasol after lunch, and she always wore a corset. She had a beautiful figure."

Nani had lost two fathers. It was the start of a long run of rotten luck. Later in her life she would often wonder why she had been singled out for so much pain. But for now, at least, she was a happy child. "We were not glamorous people, just *pameschiki*, landed gentry, who worked with the peasants," she told me. She remembers a small estate called Groushovka. The house had several drawing rooms, a ballroom, a study, lots of bedrooms, lots of dogs and cats, but no plumbing or electricity. Twice a day, water was drawn from a well to fill the toilets, and the children were not to waste it. Not far away was a river that was good for swimming. One of its banks was a melon-field, with canteloupes, watermelons, cucumbers, pumpkins, and squash. The Elaghin girls loved to pile into the *lineika* and visit the old man who looked after their eleven cows. He slept outdoors on a straw pallet, and the sisters would bring him sweets, bacon, cookies. They'd sit around his fire as he roasted kasha and millet and played the balalaika and sang the songs of the village. He always had a melon or two cooling in the river, and he taught them how to tell the sound of a ripe one from that of an unripe one by tapping it with your knuckle, and how to crack it open neatly over your knee. He spread a net and caught crayfish.

The sisters could hardly wait for the hay to be harvested at the end of June. The day before it was to begin, the *prikaschik*, the clerk of their estate, would ride through the village, blowing his horn and proclaiming the hourly wage. Those who wanted to work for the Elaghins came out the night before and slept in the hayloft. "Haymaking was the most charming event," Nani recalls. "The weather was glorious, and the young men and the girls would sing back and forth to each other as they swung their sickles. Haytime was courting time in the village, and the girls would usually be decked out in their finest *saraphans* (high skirts, beautifully embroidered). My sisters and I would give them ribbons we had bought in Moscow months before in anticipation. The huge stacks were driven to the barn, with pretty, buxom girls sitting on them, and laughing at the young men trudging wearily behind. In the evening they would sing wedding songs. One of them played an accordion. There was lots of giggling and romping in the sweet-smelling hay. Many weddings took place after the harvest, some rather hurriedly, but if the man was right, it was not held against them or remembered. The gentle character of the peasants and the beauty of the women were just as Turgenev wrote of them, and in *Eugene Onegin*, Pushkin accurately describes the festivities surrounding haytime. Traditionally, the hay had to be in by June twenty-ninth, the saints' day of St. Peter and St. Paul.

"In July the wheat was ripe. Golden seas of ripe grain stretched on both sides of the road. But this was no time for gaiety. The July harvest was called the *strada*. It comes from

the Russian word for suffering. Everyone over twelve—even
women in advanced pregnancy—left the village and took
part in the *strada*. The survival of each family depended on
it. The wheat had to be cut in ten days, before the thunderstorms of August could ruin it. It was marvelous to see
the men swinging their silver scythes in one long line, and
the women binding the wheat in sheaves, then holding them
up to the wind and shaking them vigorously to free the grain.
I loved to wade into the fields and look at the red and blue
eyes of the poppies and the cornflowers. How shallow I was,
compared to those who were out working in the dust and
the blazing sun!"

In fall, merchants would come and buy the Elaghins'
apples, pears, and cherries. Some of the cherries were saved
to make homemade brandy, *vishniofka*. After the liquor had
been pressed from the fermented cherries, the skins were
thrown into the yard. Nani enjoyed watching the geese and
the turkeys get drunk on them and finally pass out. She also
played a trick on the sheep, removing a low bar over which,
at one point, as they came in for the night, they had to hop.
The sheep would invariably jump as though the bar were still
there. But even she, young as she was, could see that this
life was threatened. "The typical landed gentleman, including my relatives, wasn't much of a businessman," she confessed. "Every morning, lying on a sofa in his dressing gown,
he received his manager in his billiard room or in his *cabinet
de travail*. He agreed to everything that was said, and the
audience ended. The books were brought for his inspection
every quarter, but his natural indolence prevented him from
opening them, and the stack of his "Country Affairs" rose
and rose until at last it was covered with a layer of dust.
Cards, horse races, balls at the marshal of nobility's, wild

parties for men only, with gypsy women and whatnot—that was what interested him. The free-handed *pameschiki* simply wanted to outdo each other. But it couldn't last forever. *On ne peut pas toujours vivre à sa fantaisie.* Before the century was over, many of our neighbors had gone into debt and sold their estates. Those days won't be repeated."

Nani remembers when she was eight going to the wedding of her mother's stepsister, Lisa Elaghin, to a well-to-do *pameschik* named Sinelnikov, who bought Groushovka soon afterwards. Thereafter her mother and the four girls spent their summer visiting with their many relatives. At nine, after passing a stiff exam, Nani was admitted to the Alexandro-Marinsky Institute, one of the best girls' boarding schools in Moscow. The enrollment was limited to thirty students. Religious law, Russian history and geography, French, German, algebra, geometry, physics, calligraphy, cosmography, sewing, and cooking were compulsory. There were classes on Saturday, and if you weren't doing well, you spent Sunday learning something by heart. Speaking Russian at meals was forbidden. Transgressors were pelted with cards that said "*Liebes Kind Vergiss Nicht Deutsche Zu Sprechen,*" or "*N'Oubliez Pas de Parler Français,*" depending on which of the language teachers—Herr Treuer or Monsieur Fontaine— they were sitting with. Nani developed a crush on Professor Savodnik, whose analyses of the Russian classics were known all over Russia.

She excelled at her schoolwork, was consistently first in her class, and was awarded over the years leatherbound sets of Pushkin, Gogol, Lermontov, Turgenev, and Tolstoy. The "august benefactress" of the institute was the empress's older sister, Grand Duchess Elizabeth. "Ravishing beauty, rare intelligence, delightful sense of humor, infinite patience, hos-

pitality of thought, generous heart—all these gifts were hers,"
her brother-in-law Alexander Romanoff writes in his lively
memoir, *Once a Grand Duke*. "Everyone fell in love with
'Aunt Ella' the first moment she arrived in St. Petersburg
from her native Hesse-Darmstadt." Ella took a special interest
in the culinary part of the curriculum. Every Thursday she
would send over her chef, Ivan Ivanovitch, to teach the girls
a new French gourmet meal, which she and her entourage
would consume that evening. Once a year the tsar and his
family would visit. Each student made a present for one of
the imperial children, a painted dish, or an embroidered
doll's dress. In 1904 Nani and several other meritorious girls
were taken to the Kremlin and presented to Dowager Empress
Marie. As she curtsied deeply, Nani tried hard not to stare
at the old lady, whose face was perfectly immobile, like a
mask, and free of wrinkles. It had just been lifted.

In the beginning of 1905, Nani was asked to dinner at
the cream-colored Neskuchny ("Not Boring") Palace, where
Ella lived with her husband, the tsar's uncle, Grand Duke
Serge. While Nani was meekly spooning her vichyssoise,
trying not to slurp, fourteen-year-old Grand Duke Dmitri ran
in and dropped a squawking rooster on the table. Dmitri's
father was Serge's brother, Paul. His mother died having
him, and Ella was bringing him up. Eleven years later, along
with Prince Yusupov and V. N. Puriskevitch, effete Dmitri
would murder Rasputin.

Ella was furious at the rooster prank, but Serge loved it.
Serge was the despotic and widely despised governor of Moscow. A few weeks later, on the morning of February 17, as
he was driving through the gates of the Neskuchny Palace,
a young Social Revolutionary named Kalyayev lobbed a bomb
into his carriage. "Hearing the shuddering blast," Robert K.

Massie writes in *Nicholas and Alexandra,* "Ella cried, 'It's Serge,' and rushed to him. What she found was not her husband, but a hundred unrecognizable pieces of flesh, bleeding into the snow." There was a three-day requiem for Serge. Nani was chosen to represent the Institute at it, and put a wreath on his coffin. His young widow visited Kalyayev in jail and begged him to ask the tsar's forgiveness. Kalyayev refused. Ella became an abbess. A pale beauty in trailing pearl-gray robes and a white veil, she consoled the wounded during the war. Masha, who was running the evacuation center of Moscow's largest hospital, saw a lot of her then. As the conflict dragged on, she heard the wounded curse Ella when they saw her coming with her basket of crucifixes and prayer books. Ella was murdered a day after the tsar, in July 1918, in an abandoned mine shaft in Alapayevsk.

Grand Duke Serge's assassination passed like a small, dark cloud over Nani's otherwise sunny school days. On Sundays she was free to sample pastries and caviar on Tverskaya Street, to take in a ballet at the Bolshoi, to hear the thunderous bass of Chaliapin, to flush in the approving gaze of a handsome young subaltern. "Sentimental feelings were developed rather early in childhood," she told me. "My sisters and I palpitated at postcards of the young grand dukes. At New Year's we filled a punch bowl with water and pasted slips of paper with men's names around the rim. Then we floated half a walnut shell with a lighted candle in it, and stirred the water. The first slip that caught fire would tell your future husband's name. Then, in a group, we ran into the street and stopped men as they passed. 'Tell me, kind sir, what's your name?' Foolish young girls!"

At Christmas, Nani's sisters were released from their boarding schools in Moscow and St. Petersburg, and the family reunited. They stayed with an uncle, Michael Elaghin, who had a mansion on Rzhevsky Lane. He was very rich and jolly and having no children, spoiled his nieces. Nani remembers that in the morning he sent his dog to wake her up. "Uncle Misha played cards and horses," she told me. "He lost so much money at the Moscow race track that its owners endowed a scholarship at the Institute of Languages in his name. When I was around sixteen, he gambled away the house on Rzhevsky Lane, too."

During the twelve days of Christmas Alexandra Nicolaevna and her daughter visited the trees of friends and relatives and exchanged presents. Children got things to eat—satin bags full of nuts and candy, Crimean apples, tangerines and *sanguines* from the south of Spain. Adults got hints—a chocolate bottle for the heavy drinker, candy cigarettes for the chain smoker, an overdressed doll for the vain coquette. Arm in arm, the sisters skated on the Moscow River. On sunny afternoons the whole city took to the ice. It was the duty of the troops who guarded the city to clear it, to provide a band, to build log shelters where you could warm up with a cup of hot chocolate, to light the colored lanterns. Darkness fell early.

The Elaghins were together again at Easter, when all the bells in Moscow pealed at once, and strangers stopped in the street and kissed each other's cheeks three times. Summer was spent in the country—a month at Baron von Dervis's horse farm in the government of Ryazan, a month at the Bezobrazovs' near Tula, a month in Tambov with Uncle Shura (whose young wife fell in love with another officer, got pregnant, and killed herself). The Bezobrazovs threw parties that lasted several days. All the girls slept in the same room. One night the young men snuck in and yanked their sheets away. Once the chaperone caught a few of the young men hiding in the bushes and watching them skinny-dip in the lake. "But there was no sex," Nani assured me. "Just tricks."

Nani watched her older sisters ripen into appealing young women. Lila, a raving beauty, was the first to marry—Captain Nicolai Selivanov of Tambov. Their wedding picture survives, despite a jagged diagonal crack in the negative. Lila, her eyes lowered, has the pure radiance that comes to women at that climactic moment in their lives; moustachioed Nicolai looks like the proudest, tenderest groom who ever took the plunge; Alexandra Nicolaevna—only her head is visible in the lower right-hand corner—smirks gleefully; Nicolai's bald, boisterous commanding officer stands supportively behind the couple in the small, dark-papered room. The Selivanovs had three children rapidly. The second was Nani's goddaughter. Nicolai was killed on the Austrian front in 1915. He bled to death on a hay wagon that was taking him to a hospital. One morning his orderly brought Lila his helmet and sword.

In 1911 Nani graduated number one in her class. Grand Duchess Elizabeth pinned on her the *shifre*, or Imperial Cross—a medal seldom awarded to schoolgirls—and her name was chiseled on a marble plaque in the front hall. That summer, with a young married woman as a chaperone, she set out on the almost obligatory grand tour of Europe. After brief stops in Warsaw and Berlin, they reached Paris, where for six weeks Nani perfected her French at the Alliance Française. The pension where they stayed, on the Rue Cherche-Midi, was full of foreigners. A Chinese man proposed to her. An uncouth American, who put his feet up on chairs and ate bread with his soup, took out his two-way pocket dictionary at the dinner table one evening and said in broken French to the woman who ran the pension, "Your face is all powdered and rouged, but your ears are dirty." Which was true. When Nani walked in the streets everyone from street sweepers on up whistled or made passes at her. At twenty, she was a stately blonde, a solemn beauty with a classic profile, her mother's full figure and proud carriage. People remarked how much she looked like the empress.

By the time the two women got to Geneva they were running out of money. Checking into a hotel on the Rue Mont Blanc (how lucid Nani was to remember even the names of streets after so many years), not far from the railroad station, they bought a small one-burner kerosene stove so they could cook their own meals. One morning the window curtains caught fire. Unable to find a shop with the same material to replace them, they paid the bill and quickly boarded a boat to Lausanne. On to Zurich, Salzburg, Innsbruck. One afternoon in Vienna, as Nani was looking into the window of a pastry shop, two officers with gold epaulets approached and started speaking to her in German. "Who are you, beautiful lady?" one said. Nani didn't answer. "You know, we have a custom in Vienna," he continued, "of taking foreigners for a ride and showing them our beautiful city." In the nick of time the chaperone appeared. The officers clicked their heels and left. From Vienna the tourists returned to Moscow. The grand tour had lasted two months.

Joining Natasha and Sonya, Nani ended the summer in the Crimea. Natasha was timid and rather plump. Sonya was getting lots of attention from a Moscow district attorney. She was an enchanting blonde with cheeks so red they looked as if they had been painted with beets. The Crimea at that time of year was full of people from the north—elderly valetudinarians who had come to take the cure at one of the many mineral springs, divorcées who had come from Moscow and St. Petersburg in long dresses and wide-brimmed Crimean hats for a fling with the tall, strong Tatars who lived in clean white villages, each with a minaret, along the Black Sea coast. At Yalta the sisters tasted grapes on the vine, moodily watched the purple waves flashing on the gray pebbly shore. At Livadia, where the imperial family was in residence, they glimpsed the four grand duchesses—Olga, Tatiana, Maria, and Anastasia—coming out of a shop. Slightly younger than the Elaghin girls, they seemed terribly exposed outside the palace grounds. At Anapa, another coastal resort, the girls checked into a pension whose proprietress, a Frenchwoman named Mademoiselle Mabit, introduced them to a handsome young engineer, Eugene Korotkevitch.

A graduate of the polytechnic institute in St. Petersburg, thirty-year-old Korotkevitch was working in the rich new oilfields near Baku, on the Caspian Sea. He had come to Anapa for a holiday. He and Nani were immediately attracted to each other. He took her to the casino, to dinner and music in the park. Some nights she returned to her room barely before dawn; it was hard to part. "Believe me, there were kisses," she reminisced. When it was time for the sisters to go back to Moscow, Korotkevitch took them to the station and gave them each a box of chocolates. Nani gave him a gold ring with a small green stone called a chrysoprase. Slipping it on, Korotkevitch said, "As it squeezes my finger, I will think of you." They corresponded. He proposed by letter, then appeared in Moscow. They went to the Bolshoi, and afterwards to dinner. He suggested they continue to a night club he knew where one could rent a private room stocked with champagne and fruit. "I told him, 'Nothing doing.' He said 'I can't marry you yet. I couldn't subject you to the life we have in Baku. We live in barracks. It's rough and dangerous. There are *ingushi*, bandits who lie in wait when we cross the mountains with the payroll.' "

Korotkevitch returned to the oilfields, and the passionate correspondence resumed. One morning Nani got a letter that said only, in an illiterate scrawl, "Mr. Eugene Korotkevitch was killed by *ingushi*." A few months later, his mother called on Nani. She had found Nani's letters, and wanted to return the chrysoprase ring. "My son was killed by an *ingush* who shot him through the window while he was asleep, thinking he had the payroll," she told Nani. "Before he died, Eugene managed to get up and open the door. By the river the police found an outfit that the men who work on the oil rigs wear. They think the *ingush* put it on to get past the guards. They think my son's maid may also have been involved. In a few weeks they caught the bandit and hanged him. But what good does that do?"

Tears were in Nani's eyes as she got up from the table and went into the kitchen to make coffee. We'd been sitting there for several hours, she telling me about her life, I writing in longhand on yellow, legal-sized notepaper. Nani was forty when she started to learn English, and she speaks it with a Russian accent. Sometimes the word she wants in English won't come, and she'll say it in French. Once she complained that her English was *arabique*. "But fortunately, I am not senile," she said to me. On the table, for inspiration, she had put old medals and photographs, yellowed calling cards, photocopied pedigrees, and other memorabilia. Once she got up and with her hands on her hips did a little *kolomeika* around the living room. The *kolomeika* is a Ukrainian jig. She wanted me to see how good her figure had been. It was

still good, and that fall she was a few months shy of eighty-
nine. Her living room looked on the courtyard of an old,
genteel apartment house in the Roland Park section of Baltimore, where she had been living since she retired over
twenty-five years earlier. The courtyard had a cement pool
with red carp and *nenuphars*, as she called water lilies. The
building was Mediterranean Tudor: exposed exterior beams,
beige stucco, red tiles. It had a European flavor, like Nani's
flat, like Nani herself. She lives frugally, switching off the
lights when she leaves the room, snipping coupons from the
newspaper, eating like a bird. People have begun to do her
shopping and to fill her prescriptions, but she won't take
money from anybody.

Before Korotkevitch died, she acquired another suitor,
a captain in the empress's Crimean Guards named Boris
Adamovitch. They had met in Nicholas Novossiltsev's garden. The Novossiltsevs—bastard Stroganoff progeny, way
back—were, like the Elaghins, a large and visible family in
Tambov. Masha was a Novossiltsev. Nicholas Novossiltsev
was the adjutant to a general who had stolen his wife, leaving
him with their two children, Natasha and Sasha. Sasha was
in cadet school and doing poorly in French. Nicholas had
asked Nani, a friend of the family, to help him out. One
afternoon she and Sasha took a break from studies and went
into the garden, and there were Nicholas and Boris Adamovitch rallying superbly in white flannels on a grass tennis
court. Boris was dark, dashing, debonair, devilishly good-
looking with that extinct virile, moustachioed cavalry-officer
John Gilbert-Prince Matchabelli sort of handsomeness. Boris
was a couple of years older than Nani and had already been
married. He had run off to Finland with his colonel's wife.
She was a great beauty and everyone in the regiment was in

love with her. Eventually she got bored with Boris and went on to someone else.

Boris was my grandfather. His family, the Adamovitches, were descended from Monvid, a grand duke of Lithuania. Monvid died in 1341. One of his descendants was named Adam; hence Adamovitch—"son of Adam." By the seventeenth century we find a cluster of Adamovitches living in Chernigov, a government in the western part of Little Russia: Anton is a colonel of the Kiev Cossacks, Simeon is arbitrating a religious difference with Moscow for Hetman Skoropadsky's Cossack host. At the beginning of the nineteenth century, Efrem Grigorievitch appears. A doctor in the Preobrazhensky Regiment, he marries twice and fathers twenty-four children. His ten sons are famous in Russian military history because they all die with the rank of general or admiral. Leonid Efremovitch becomes a knight of all orders of the empire (with his cross of St. Vladimir, his cordons of Saints Anne, Stanislav, and Alexander Nevsky, and all his other decorations, he must have looked resplendent) and marries an Apraxin (Kitty of *Anna Karenina* was an Apraxin). One of the sons of Victor Efremovitch ran a military academy in Sarajevo, the Yugoslavian town where World War I was precipitated. Another became in exile a respected literary critic, and made the mistake of crossing a fellow émigré writer, Vladimir Nabokov. Nabokov writes in an introduction to his story "Vassily Shishkov":

To relieve the dreariness of life in Paris at the end of 1939 . . . I decided one day to play an innocent joke on the most famous of émigré critics, George Adamovitch (who used to condemn my stuff as regularly as I did the verse of his disciples) by publishing in one of the two leading magazines a poem signed with a new pen name, so as to see what he would say about that freshly emerged author. . . . The Russian original . . . was acclaimed by Adamovitch in his review of that issue with quite exceptional enthusiasm ("At last a great poet has been born in our midst," etc.). . . . Adamovitch refused at first to believe eager friends and foes who drew his attention to my inventing Shishkov; finally, he gave in and explained in his next essay that I "was a sufficiently skillful parodist to mimic genius." I fervently wish all critics to be as generous as he. I met him briefly, only twice; but many old literati have spoken a lot, on the occasion of his recent death, about his kindliness and penetrativeness. He had only two passions in life: Russian poetry and French sailors.

Michael Efremovitch, the fourth son and Boris's father, distinguished himself at Balaclava and in the Turkish wars and married Elizabeth Marchenko, a composer of military marches. Elizabeth's mother was a Hlopova—a name recognizable to most Russians, because her ancestor, Maria Hlopova, almost became the first Romanoff empress. The story is told in Rimsky-Korsakov's opera *The Tsar's Bride*. Briefly, this is what happened: Shortly before 1613, it was decided that Michael Romanoff, who was about to become tsar and found a dynasty, would marry a Russian girl; it would be like symbolically marrying Russia. So his ministers traveled far and wide and returned with five hundred of the most beautiful and eligible women of the realm, who were by slow elimination reduced to a hundred, then to ten. The finalists and their families were installed in tents around Michael's palace, so he could get to know them. He chose Maria Hlopova, who was vivacious and had a good sense of humor, though she barely met the height requirement. But one evening

Saltykov, his minister, got into an argument with Maria's uncle about whether Russian swords were better than Turkish ones, and it got so violent that Saltykov decided to sabotage the marriage and joined forces with Michael's mother, Martha, who wanted her son to marry a Dolgoruky. When Maria came down with a bad cold, Saltykov and Martha persuaded Michael that she was sickly and would die within the year. Michael broke off the engagement and Maria, losing all her privileges, was banished to Tobolsk. During the next seven years various German and Swedish princesses were brought to Michael, but he kept thinking about Maria. At last he sent a delegation from the Church to Tobolsk. They reported that Maria was in perfect health. Michael was at once furious and delighted; he banished Saltykov and had Maria brought to Moscow in a triumphant procession. But his mother still promised to lay a curse on the marriage if it went through. Eventually Maria got fed up and went to Nizhni Novgorod, where she lived for the rest of her life. Michael married a Narishkin. Their grandson became Peter the Great. Boris liked to tell the story of how he had come within a hairsbreadth of being a Romanoff.

He had a number of other interesting tie-ins. Efrem's first wife, a Princess Dervlitt-Kildeyev, was said to be directly descended from Juchi, the oldest son and field commander of Genghis Khan. The princess had pronounced Tatar features. Boris told the story that when she and her husband quarreled their relations would say, "The East and the West are at it again."

"The flirtation with me and Boris began almost immediately," Nani remembered. When Boris learned he had a rival, he stepped up his attentions. "He was handsome and

kind, a great lover and a great spender. I was embarrassed
by all the flowers and perfumes he showered me with. His
Cossack orderly knocked at my door almost daily. Knowing
that I collected miniature ivory elephants, once he sent me
five." Boris told some good stories. One was about meeting
Gregory Rasputin the previous summer in a corridor of the
imperial palace in Livadia, and throwing his glove at the
"holy devil's" feet. Not grasping that he was being challenged
to a duel, Rasputin gave Boris a strange, supercilious look
and walked on. Nani wasn't sure she believed the story,
however. In the first place, Rasputin was *neduelnii*. Only
nobles were "duelable." Secondly, Rasputin was the most
powerful man in Russia. If one of the empress's guards had
pulled a stunt like that, he would have been in deep trouble.
Boris explained that he had seen Rasputin tear off his clothes
and dance obscenely at Yar, a Moscow nightclub that was
famous for its heartrending gypsy chorus. When he heard
Rasputin boasting to strangers of his influence over the tsar,
and how the empress called him Christ, he had decided to
duel him at the first opportunity. Yar was a favorite haunt
of young officers and pleasure-bent Muscovites. Once Boris
told Nani about a party he had gone to there for a young
Hussar who had just been promoted. One of his comrades
had gotten drunk and started to fill a piano with champagne.
"What do you think you're doing?" the manager asked.
"Making an aquarium," was the reply. A homesick ensign
who was barely eighteen had removed his shirt and started
pasting himself with postage stamps. "Send me home to
mother," he sobbed.

Grand Duke Alexander in *Once a Grand Duke*, describes
how it was in Russia, and at Yar, that year—1913:

The remaining three hundred days of peace were filled with gambling, sensational crimes, and a rather significant epidemic of suicides.

That year they danced the tango. The languorous tempo of its exotic music sounded from one end of Russia to another. The gypsies cried, the glasses clinked, and the Rumanian violinists, clad in red, hypnotised inebriated men and women into a daring attempt to explore the depths of vice.

At five o'clock in the morning—the endless winter night was still glaring through the high Venetian windows covered with frost—a young man with drunken gait crossed the polished dancing floor of the nightclub "Yar" and stopped in front of a table occupied by a beautiful woman seated with several elderly gentlemen.

"Listen you," shouted the young man, leaning against a column. "I will not stand for it. You have no business remaining in a place like this at such an hour of the night."

The woman sneered. They had been divorced for eight months. She saw no reason for taking his orders.

"So it's like this," said the young man somewhat more quietly, and fired at her six times through the pocket of his tuxedo.

The notorious "Prasoloff case" . . . exposed revolting orgies taking place in the millionaire set of Moscow. Two witnesses committed suicide before it was their turn to testify.

The outbreak of war provided a welcome moral lift. Six-foot-five Grand Duke Nicholas, the tsar's uncle, was put in charge of the troops. He was no statesman, he had no idea why so many Russians were discontented, but in battle he was fearless. Grand Duke Nicholas was Boris's godfather, and there was no question in Boris's mind—or in that of any Russian in uniform—what he had to do. This was what they'd all been waiting for. "The declaration of war found us on a boat trip along the Volga and Kama rivers, at a time when we were very much interested in each other," Nani recalled. "But regardless of all that, he sent a telegram to his uncle Mitrofan asking him to use his influence and get him sent at once to the front." Mitrofan Marchenko, his mother's brother, was head of the Nicolaevsky Cavalry School in Petrograd (the West Point of Old Russia)—and his influence was considerable. In two weeks Boris had been transferred to the Kuban Cossack Regiment and was on his way to the Austrian front. Nani, who had been putting him off for nearly a year, was suddenly alone. "He didn't have to go, but he acted like the heroes in *Cid,* Corneille's *classique,*" she wrote me once. *"Quand il faut choisir entre devoir filial, patrie, religion, leur passion amoureuse et l'amour passent toujours au* second place. *C'est le devoir qui triomphe toujours. Mais on garde des souvenirs heureux."*

Boris was a superb rider; he had won a collection of silver cigarette cases at jumping meets. He took both his horses with him to the front—dappled gray Beauty, who was strong and high-strung, and would throw anyone but a superb rider; and small, dark brown Duckla, who seemed to second-guess what you wanted her to do. At first, though both sides suffered heavy losses, the Russians won victory after victory. They pushed through to Krakow. In the devastation near Lambey, Boris found a barefoot boy bawling by the corpse of his Austrian father. He put Ivas Schram, as the boy was named, on his horse and took him north with the regiment. Ivas was only six, and became a sort of mascot. The Cossacks even made him a little uniform. Late in 1915 Boris caught a piece of shrapnel in the stomach that knocked him off his horse. He was taken to a hospital in the small town of Slutsk, a hundred miles behind the lines. From his cot he wrote to Nani and told her that he had been wounded and that he wanted her to come and marry him. Under such circumstances, vacillation seemed unpatriotic; she came. Boris sent a special car to pick her up in Moscow. The road to Slutsk happened to pass through the town of Mogilov, where Eugene Korotkevitch was buried. Nani had the car stop at the cemetery and asked the keeper to show her his grave. After a good cry for her first love, she returned to the car, and they continued. Boris had been very good to Nani when Korotkevitch was killed. He had even offered to go to Baku and find out what had happened. But Nani had said she already knew all that she wanted to know. Then Boris had pressed her gently against him and said, "Very often, someone's sorrow is another's happiness."

Nani and Boris were married on October 25, 1915, in a small church near Baronovichy, where the tsar was headquartered. It was a brief military service. There was no reception or honeymoon. No family, no other women were present. Nani herself had needed a special pass to be there. Boris's commanding officer, Colonel Zvechintsev, gave her away. Everyone drank a champagne toast, then left the newlyweds alone in a little house Boris had gotten for them. It was quite nice in Slutsk. The house had a lovely garden. As Boris recovered, he put on weight, and his face puffed up. It would take him three years to recover his looks and his strength. But after a few months he was well enough to become involved in activities that he wasn't allowed to talk about.

In the summer of 1916 they were sent to Moscow, and

from there to Kharkov (Mopsy's birthplace), where Boris was to interrogate captured German officers. They took Ivas Schram, the Cossack orderly (whose name Nani has forgotten), Beauty and Duckla. On a trip to Sebastopol, Boris brought Ivas to his sister, Tanya Schwarz. She and her husband, a captain in the Black Sea Fleet, had no children, and they took Ivas in. In Kharkov Nani saw a lot of Tamara Gagarina, whose husband had been a classmate of Boris's in cavalry school. One afternoon they took a walk in the zoological park with a doctor, who had just given Nani a checkup. Nani stopped to watch some monkeys. "Choose some other objects to admire," the doctor said, "or your child will grow to look like them." Nani was pregnant with my mother.

In Kharkov Boris was promoted to colonel. That was as high as he would get in the chain of command before his military career, like thousands of others, was abruptly terminated. To Nani, he is still, and will always be, "the Colonel."

The news from the front was getting worse all the time. There were shortages of everything: arms, ammunition, food, clothing, men, morale. In the end fifteen million Russian soldiers would be called up, and only twelve and a half million would return. In October, new orders were cut for the Colonel. He was to go recruiting in southeastern Siberia, where there was great untouched manpower. Nani and the Colonel, his orderly, and her Lithuanian maid Margaret boarded the trans-Siberian express at Moscow. They were given the last compartment at the back of the train. It had a big picture window and a porter who cooked their meals. For two weeks they traveled across Russia in style. They reached Sretensk, a thriving town of ten thousand on the Shilka River, at the beginning of November. It was already so cold that Nani couldn't wear earrings because the metal would have frozen her earlobes. The country around Sretensk was something like Montana—endless larch forests, open steppe, mountains in the distance. It teemed with fish and game.

The Colonel took stock of his raw material: Siberian Cossacks, ex-convicts, exiled settlers, peasants (who were mostly fundamentalists, Old Believers), and Buryats, the nomadic natives of the region, who practiced a mixture of Buddhism and shamanism. They were a disparate lot, but they had one thing in common: no one had the least desire to fight in a war that was thousands of miles away and had nothing to do with him. So the Colonel had no luck recruiting. Privately, he had begun to have doubts about the war himself. He had seen his comrades mutilated, and for what? What glory was there to being cannon fodder? He was just as glad to be out of it.

Both he and Nani fell in love with Siberia. "It is the most peaceful, wonderful land, and I would like to live there again some time," Nani told me. "You could get a whole salmon for five kopecks. Pound tins of caviar and sealskin coats were only a few roubles. We were just west of Manchuria and north of Mongolia, and there were lots of Chinamen in Sretensk. They were splendid farmers, and perhaps splendid spies, too. In the middle of winter they delivered fresh vegetables—carrots, beets, turnips, cauliflowers—which they had buried in their cellars in clean, dry sand. They trapped and froze grouse and partridges, which infuriated a sportsman like the Colonel. They smeared their faces with goose fat against the cold. Every Chinaman's house was lighted by electricity. I was surprised when I got to America to find that Siberia was ahead of New England in that sense. My house in New Hampshire didn't get electricity until 1945."

The Colonel spent most of his time hunting. He had an English pointer called Rolpa and two black Gordon setters, with yellow rings around their eyes. The female was named Scripka—Violin—because of the shrill, high-pitched barks with which she announced game. Bonzai, the male, was stupid and got killed by wolves on the frozen Shilka. The Colonel hunted bear with three Buryats. One probed likely cavities with a long-handled pitchfork. If there were growls from within, the Colonel and another Buryat fired into the den. Then the third Buryat crawled inside—it was the most perilous moment of the hunt—to see if the bear was alone, and if it was still alive. Once the Buryat shouted, "It's *lyudno* (many people) in there." That day they shot a mother, a yearling, and a cub. In a few years, when he was a refugee and short of cash, the Colonel would use the skins to pay a doctor for delivering his son. Sometimes he went hunting alone. Killing a cow or a horse, he waited in a tree, sometimes all day, for wolves to come. Once when he was crossing the steppe he ran into three Hunhusi. The Hunhusi were Manchurian bandits who preyed on prospectors. All the settlements around Sretensk were fortified against them, and the radio was always warning about them. As the three Hunhusi were drawing their long, two-handed swords, the Colonel pulled out a revolver and shot them.

On March 15 Nicholas II abdicated. "We were shocked and puzzled," Nani told me. Sretensk was in the heart of Prison Land, and soon the town was flooded with inmates who had been released from the surrounding penal colonies by order of Prince Lvov. Many had been imprisoned for trying to overthrow the monarchy, and this was what they had been waiting for. "Revolutionary committees formed at once," she went on. "They started inquiring about the Colonel, and told us we had to leave. 'Where do we go?' we asked. 'That's your problem,' they said."

They took the train west. Margaret, who had fallen in love with a railroad worker, stayed in Sretensk. She baked plenty of *suhari*, zwiebach, and packed them in tins for the journey. It was rumored that in central Russia people were starving. The station at Chita, the first big city, was in chaos. "A group of awful revolutionaries came aboard, grabbed the Colonel and our baggage, and told me to stay put. The first bell rang. The second bell rang. Just before the third bell, when the train would leave, I became hysterical, and the Colonel returned. 'Don't worry,' he said. 'We have to stay here for a while.' " He took her to a hotel. She was seven months pregnant by now, and her legs became so swollen after that scare that for several days she couldn't get up from bed. From her window she could see the main square, which was filled with people. Periodically some hate-filled dema-gogue would get up on a barrel and urge them to take revenge on their oppressors. After a lengthy interrogation, the rev-olutionary committee of Chita decided to let the Colonel go. The head of the committee, who had an eyepatch, had served with the Colonel at the front. For old times' sake he signed papers that allowed them to continue.

Before they reached Irkutsk the Colonel took the pre-caution of removing the insignia from his greatcoat. Even so, as they left the station, crossed the frozen Angara River on planks, and entered the city, people could see that they were aristocrats and gave them dirty looks. Irkutsk in those days was like Manaus at the height of the Amazon rubber boom. A few of its citizens had become very rich from gold and furs, and among them (as with the Brazilian rubber barons) it was a status symbol to have their laundry done in

London—a round trip of nearly a year. The city was utterly devoid of self-consciousness. Pigs wallowed in its streets. Gaudy palaces and wretched hovels stood side by side. Nani and the Colonel found others of their class in the same predicament, not knowing what had happened, where to go, or what to do. With another colonel and his wife, they rented a large furnished house from a woman whose husband was in Kamchatka, buying furs. The house had a big white tile stove that burned oak and maple. Inside, it was so hot the women wore summer dresses. Nani hardly went out. It was bitter cold, there were violent people in the streets, and she was due any time. The Colonel went hunting whenever he could.

On May 6, Nani delivered a fine baby girl. They named her Nina Tatiana—Nina after Nani, Tatiana after the Colonel's sister, Tanya Schwarz—and hired a hefty Siberian wet nurse. There is a photograph of my mother, soon after she was born, in the arms of her *kormilitsa*, who is wearing the traditional wool skirt with gold braid, the embroidered blouse and pearl tiara.

The Colonel learned that as a wounded veteran under thirty-two he was eligible for a program that trained military prosecutors at the Judicial Academy of St. Petersburg. He took an entrance exam—Nani helped him brush up on grammar and punctuation, to which he'd never paid much attention, and he was accepted. The train ride to Moscow, in July, was very different from the trip out. At every station, people tried to get on, but the cars were already so full that some of the passengers were even standing in the bathrooms. Many of the people at the stations were drunken deserters who called themselves Red Heroes. By now no one wanted to prosecute the war. Soldiers at the front had started fraternizing with the enemy, defying their officers, and walking home singly and en masse. Some joined General Kornilov's abortive attempt to overthrow Kerensky, who had taken over the Provisional Government from Prince Lvov. Many were attracted to Bolshevism. Some, for no clear reason, fired on the train, shattering the windows. Nani huddled with her baby in a corner of their compartment. There was no food except the *suhari* they had brought with them and, at some stations, cooked meat, butter, and eggs people held up to the windows.

After nine days of this they reached Moscow. Natasha was there to meet them. Thin and hungry-looking, she was taking courses at the Institute of Languages. Sonya was at the Polish front, nursing the wounded. It was her job to write the next of kin when a patient died. "Being so beautiful," Nani told me, "it was hard for her to survive." Lila was in Souzdal, not far from Moscow, with her three children. Their mother was in Tambov. "Sad to say," Nani said, "I would never see any of them again." Natasha said they could stay with some friends of hers if they gave them some of their bread. There were no street markets in Moscow anymore, and food was scarce. Nani still had plenty of *suhari*. They spent the night in Natasha's cramped flat and in the morning, leaving most of their *suhari* with her, they caught a train to Sebastopol, where the Colonel's mother and sister were living; his course didn't begin until August. Tanya greeted her brother with crushing news: the day before, their mother had died, with a sweater she had been knitting for little Nina in her hands. As the widow of a general (her husband had died in 1912), Elizaveta Konstantinovna had been receiving a comfortable pension. With dark eyes and hair, in her sixties, she had still been conscious enough of her looks to think that men were always noticing her. She had called her son by the affectionate diminutive Borisyuk, and died of kidney trouble.

Tanya and her husband lived in an apartment building for naval officers. Captain Schwarz was from an old Navy family; his uncle, an admiral, had invented the system of flag signals that is still internationally recognized. Tanya was seventeen years older than her brother, but they were very close. "She was an *Amazonka*, who rode horses like a man," Nani told me. "She and her father had ridden together all over the Crimea and were known as magnificent riders." Tanya kept several horses in the stables of the apartment house. She had eleven Persian cats and spoke several languages. Nani got along with her beautifully. Ivas Schram, the war orphan, was a bright, adorable eight-year-old by now. Tanya had started him mucking out the stalls. He had slept in the kitchen at first. Then she promoted him to the hallway. Now he sat at the table. Ancient Anna Williams, who had taken care of the Colonel when he was little, completed the household. Anna Ivan'na, as everyone called her, hated England because she was the illegitimate daughter of some high British official who had sent her to Germany to be trained as a governess. She was in charge of the meals, and was delighted to have a new baby to look after (Mom's wet nurse had gone back to Siberia).

On July 16 there was a rising at Kronstadt, the naval base at Petrograd, in whose construction the Colonel's uncle Dmitri (one of the famous sons of Efrem) had played a large role. Six thousand Bolshevized sailors in the Baltic fleet mutinied, and Kerensky rushed in a division of cavalry from the front in time to put down their threatened *coup d'etat*. It didn't take long for the sailors of the Black Sea Fleet to "start misbehaving," as Nani put it. In the south of Russia, the Red Terror began several months before the actual Revolution. It began when the sailors, fired by news of the Kronstadt rising, started killing their officers and chaplains. From Tanya's window, Nani saw angry sailors and longshoremen leading their unfortunate victims at gunpoint and dragging them down the white marble steps at the harbor, where, in happier times, the officers of visiting foreign navies had received a gala welcome. Most of the men who were to be killed were thrown on barges, taken out a mile or so, and with rocks tied around their necks, dumped into the sea. By September the Borah—the terrific wind that comes in off the Black Sea during the winter months—had started to blow, and the women shielded their faces and leaned into it as they stood waiting for their husbands' bodies to wash ashore. It was forbidden to bury the bodies, but many of the widows, at great personal risk, put them in plain wood boxes covered with red cloth and conducted secret funerals.

Once comrades came to Nani's building looking for officers, and took away the man next door. Nani remembers how pitifully his children screamed, "Leave our father. He has done nothing." The comrades were especially vindictive toward cavalry officers because of Bloody Sunday—January 22, 1905, when the tsar's cavalry cut down hundreds of peaceful demonstrators in front of the Winter Palace. But they passed over the Colonel because Tanya's cook's boyfriend was a sailor. With food on ration, Nani shared hers with the man, and when the comrades came, he went to the door and said, "These are good people." That was in November, after the Revolution. Everything in Petrograd had fallen apart, and the Colonel had made his way south, along with thousands of other officers who were joining General Anton Denikin's Volunteer Army.

Once while the Colonel was still in Petrograd the Cheka had entered the apartment. They claimed to be looking for firearms, which were illegal for anyone but them to have, but they were really after food and valuables. Anna Ivan'na had hidden ninety-five thousand roubles, a jewel-encrusted scimitar, and other things they didn't want to lose under the mattress of my mother's crib. When the agents entered the baby's room, Anna Ivan'na said, "If you wake my baby, I'll make you stay all night and take care of her," and shooed them out.

General Denikin later estimated that between 1918 and 1919 the Cheka put to death a million several hundred thousand in south Russia. But the Whites hung, garroted, and even buried people alive, too; it is still arguable which side committed the most atrocities. "The smell of blood was in the nostrils of the Russian people," George Stewart writes.

At the beginning of 1918, on St. Bartholomew's Eve, the Cheka gave the order to slaughter all former nobles on the Crimean coast. Nani and the Colonel fled to Novorossisk, where it was relatively safe, and where until a few months before his uncle Leonid had owned a cement factory, several villages, and thousands of acres. They joined Baron Alexander Nolken, General Denikin's liaison in charge of foreign relations, and headed up the Kuban River on his yacht. Nolken's wife was the sister of the Colonel's comrade-in-arms, Vsevolod-Pouschine, who had died on the Austrian front. Also aboard were the widow of V. N. Purishkevitch, her two daughters, and their governess. A champion of the extreme right who had helped kill Rasputin, Purishkevitch had been murdered a few months before on his estate in Poltava, and from his widow they learned that the Colonel's aunt Nadezhda, who lived next door to the Puriskevitches, had been killed while she was having dinner with her three sons and a cousin, Anna von Felkersan, who had the misfortune to be paying a visit.

The Colonel arranged for his family to stay in the Cossack village that his orderly came from, and he returned to Novorossisk to help with the White counteroffensive. For Nani this was a blissful interlude. There was plenty of food in the village—*blini*, pancakes with sour cream, *aladi*, a borshchlike soup with meat in it—and for the first time since the summer before, she ate well. Like the Ukrainian peasants, the Cossacks were prosperous and independent. They had their own cattle, wheat, and poultry. Many of the elders were Old Believers. When it was time for a young man to go to war, his father gave him a horse and the saber and dagger *his* father had given him. All the men in the village, except the elders, had joined the Volunteer Army.

After a few months the Colonel returned and said that things had quieted down, and they could go back to Sebastopol. The Naval Authority, or what was left of it, had put him in charge of port security. His job was to see to the needs of foreign ships, to fight fires, and to protect the warehouses, which were full of arms, provisions, and special sturdy silk to make flags with. He had several dozen men under him and three launches at his disposal.

No sooner had they settled back in the Naval Apartments than word spread that the Germans were on the way. They were marching from Kiev, twenty or thirty miles a day. There was no one to stop them. Trotsky had declared the war over in February, the Russian army had joyfully demobilized, and the Crimea was now, as of March 3 and the signing of the Brest-Litovsk treaty, part of the Ukraine—in theory independent, but in truth a German satellite. "One spring day in 1918," Vladimir Nabokov explains, "when the pink puffs of blossoming almond trees enlivened the dark mountainsides, the Bolsheviks vanished and a singularly silent army of Germans replaced them. Patriotic Russians were torn between the animal relief of escaping native executioners and the necessity of owing their reprieve to a foreign invader— especially the Germans. The latter, however, were losing their war in the West and came to Yalta on tiptoe, with diffident smiles, an army of grey apparitions. . . ."

The Germans entered Sebastopol on May first. The city was in terrible confusion. The Red sailors had tried to evacuate the fleet, but having killed their officers, couldn't navigate the ships. Many had run aground in the harbor, and the sailors in them had returned to shore and melted into the population. Nani and the Colonel had taken chairs and a supply of milk for the baby and had hidden in a coal cellar for several days, along with two other families. Captain Schwarz and Tanya had escaped to Constantinople on his ship. The Colonel would never see his sister again. Nani would find her when she visited Istanbul in 1936, living in severe poverty in a one-room flat, teaching foreign languages to Turkish medical students. Schwarz had died two years earlier. Anna Ivan'na had gone mad, and died soon after they reached Turkey. But Ivas Schram grew up, went to Robert College, an American institution in Istanbul, and became an engineer. His three children—all professionals— live there today.

After they came out of hiding, Nani and the Colonel went to their apartment and found that it had been commandeered by a German colonel. "But he let us stay, and when he found that I spoke German, he was very nice to us. The food situation improved because a colony of Germans who had been farming outside Sebastopol for decades showered the occupying troops with produce they had been hiding. Easter came, and the German colonel brought us dozens of eggs. But for most of the people in Crimea there was even less food than there had been before, because each German soldier was instructed to send food every two weeks to his own starving family."

The Germans left in November. Under the terms of the armistice, they had to evacuate all the parts of Russia they had occupied in the spring. Late that month, the French came. Nani remembers going to the harbor and throwing flowers to French sailors as they walked up the white marble steps. Everyone thought they had brought food and arms—that help had finally come, and the Reds would be crushed—but the sailors had come with nothing but cases of wine, profound war-weariness, and a susceptibility to Bolshevik propaganda. With no more precise instructions than to "make common cause with patriotically thinking Russians," they rudely requisitioned Nani's crystal wineglasses, and offered women five-pound sacks of flour to sleep with them. Some were so hungry they accepted.

The seventy thousand French, Algerian, Greek, and Senegalese left hastily in April 1919. The Red Army had broken through at the Isthmus of Perekop, at the neck of the Crimean peninsula, and General d'Anselme gave the order to evacuate in forty-eight hours. Panic spread among the civilians, who knew what would happen when the Reds arrived. Thousands lined the docks, begging the French to take them along. As they were leaving, the French pillaged

Sebastopol one last time, sank thirty submarines, and put out of commission as much of the Black Sea Fleet as they could. "Under wild machine-gun fire from the shore," Vladimir Nabokov and his family escaped on the *Hope*, a small, shoddy Greek ship carrying a cargo of fruit. "I remember trying to concentrate, as we were zigzagging out of the bay, on a game of chess with my father—one of the knights had lost its head, and a poker chip replaced a missing rook," he wrote. As soon as the guns of the French cruisers were out of range, the local Soviet of Workmen and Peasants' Deputies took over Sebastopol. Not a few who had been left behind committed suicide. The Colonel hadn't even tried to join the exodus. He wasn't ready to leave Russia. He thought the Whites still had a chance.

In part he was right. The Whites rallied not long afterward and drove the Reds from the peninsula, or back into hiding. Then the "perfidious British," as Grand Duke Alexander called them, came. They were playing a waiting game, promising support and recognition to both sides, and above all, keeping open the shipping lanes to the oil fields at Baku. For the rest of 1919, Denikin's victorious advances secured the south of Russia for the Whites, and the British were vociferous backers of the counter-revolution. The regional government at Simferopol, at the center of the peninsula, which had been set up after the armistice by old Kadets like M. M. Vinaver and Vladimir Nabokov senior, started to make sense out of the chaos. It would be the last experiment in liberal democracy on Russian soil. "A brash, hectic gaiety associated with White-held towns brought back, in a vulgarized version, the amenities of peaceful years," Nabokov *fils* had observed before he left. "Cafés did a wonderful business. All kinds of theaters thrived." They thrived, perhaps, because life itself was theater of the absurd. Nothing was serious, permanent, or believable anymore.

The Colonel was still in charge of port security, and in the summer they moved to a villa on Gallandia, an island across the bay. "A porch ran the length of the house," Nani remembered, "and overlooked a park with gorgeous allées of roses and lilacs. Palm, banana, walnut, almond, and peach trees were on the grounds, and there was a vineyard with all kinds of grapes—white, rose, green, pink, dark red. In February everything blossomed—hibiscus, magnolia, bougainvillea. They were magical surroundings. You could see the mountains across the bay coming right down to the water. Their bases were green with cypresses and eucalyptus, and for most of the year their summits were capped with snow. The sea had the soft, warm, lilac hue that Chekhov described. The days were hot and sultry, but at night it got pretty cold."

Nani bought a cow and a goat that she milked herself; having a maid would have been too conspicuous. She served four o'clock tea on the porch, with hot chocolate and fresh cottage cheese, almost every afternoon. British officers often dropped by with tins of fruitcake. They loved sport, and asked the Colonel to let them play cricket in the field behind the house. The Colonel took them hunting for *valdschnepf*, as he called woodcock, and for quail camouflaged among the gray-brown rocks on hillsides. When Rolpa, his bird dog, spotted a bird, she gracefully raised her left leg and froze in a *stoika*, or pointing position. If the bird didn't fly up right away, Rolpa scratched the ground a little, and when it finally did, one of the hunters would shoot it out of the air. The Colonel bought Nani a light lady's gun called a *plume*. She went out with him once, but didn't like it. Sometimes he took the fireboat way out, dropped a few grenades into the sea, and netted the fish that floated to the surface. Nani pickled them with tomatoes in vinegar.

If the British were useless and devious as allies, Nani at least found them the most congenial of the three "liberators." She picked roses and lilacs to send to the officers' mess, and they invited her and the Colonel for lunch, followed by boat races on the bay. There were formal evenings, too, which Nani adored. "At that time, I was young and good-looking," she told me, "and I loved to dance." With her white gloves and long dress, her classic features and full figure, she attracted a stream of British and Russian officers. They approached with a bow and a click of the heels—Hussars in scarlet uniforms, blue Uhlans, yellow Cuirassiers, white Kavalierguards. "I danced the waltz, the *quadrille* (it had seven parts), the *mazurka* or *hongroise*, the *pas de quatre*, and I still know the steps by heart. The Colonel hated how vivacious I became on these occasions, but I knew that if I was a mummy, no one would ask me. He hated to dance. To get out of going, he once feigned a toothache. The next time it was a headache. I got the picture, and the third time I left him at home and went with a girlfriend. After that, he was cured. He always went, but stood at the back of my chair, as if guarding me. *Ce n'est que l'amour qui fait naître l'amour.*"

The captain of a British dreadnought, the *Canterbury*, who hunted regularly with the Colonel, was particularly attentive to her. On Easter Sunday, 1920, he watched the Russian officers kiss her three times on the cheek; the next day he came to her in the barn, where she was washing the teats of Mashinka, her cow, and stammered, "I want to wish you Happy Easter, too."

"But Easter is over," she said.

"Well it isn't for me," he said, and pulling her to him, kissed her on the mouth. "I'm going to tell you something in confidence," he went on before she had a chance to recover. "In the autumn Russia will fall. The White cause is lost. Lloyd George and Buchanan, our foreign secretary, have persuaded the Crown to recognize the Soviets. We are the first country to do so. My dear Nina Mihaelovna, I'm terribly fond of you—the only reason I listen to your husband's interminable stories is so I can be with you—and I'd hate to see you get caught up in this mess. Admiral de Roebeck, our high commissioner in Constantinople, has cabled General Denikin urging him to abandon this unequal struggle and offering him and his followers hospitality and a refuge in Great Britain. In three days we are leaving for Malta. There is trouble in Turkey with the Kemal Pasha. I want you to come with me. I have a big property in Britain and will be only too happy to let you have the gatehouse. I will take you, your nurse, your baby, your cow, your pigs, your goat, and (after the animals, with a noticeable slackening of enthusiasm) your husband, with me now on the *Canterbury*. This is a serious proposition, and I beg you to think it over."

Nani gave her husband the news that the British were pulling out, but she didn't mention the kiss, because the Colonel would have killed the man. "We decided together that we would stay and see it to the bitter end. But we sent on the *Canterbury* a trunk with our linen and silver, a samovar, and six icons, which the captain promised to deliver to whatever ship we took for our escape. He was true to his word. Months later, when we were anchored in the Bosporus, the trunk arrived along with some cakes and sardines, and

a sweet note that said how sorry he was we hadn't taken his
offer. Perhaps I missed *l'affaire de ma vie*, but I still loved the
Colonel. Those boats on the bay, though, those little white
triangles of straining cloth—they were beautiful."

Denikin had resigned command of the Volunteer Army
in March, and Baron Peter Wrangel, the only one of his
generals who was still committed to the struggle, found himself in charge of a hundred and fifty thousand mouths to feed.
Scarcely one sixth of them could fight. The rest were
wounded or sick or refugees who had attached themselves to
the army. There was no bread, coal, clothing, arms, oil, or
harness for the artillery. There was a dearth of "the most
necessary fatty substances," Wrangel would later remember.
"Drunkenness, abuse of authority, pillaging, and even assassination had become frequent at the centers where the
units were stationed."

The news that the British were withdrawing their support
was the final blow for the Russian army, as Wrangel renamed
his ragged troops. After that he had no illusions of being
able to win. He only wanted to save the honor and the lives
of his men. Half of them had typhus, and the healthy ranks
were plagued with desertion. Cossacks were laying down their
arms by the regiment and joining the Greens—barbaric bands
of pillagers who had deserted from both armies. The south
of Russia became a wasteland strewn with dead men and
horses, and broken-down vehicles. Long files of prisoners
stumbled along so dejectedly they only needed a couple of
guards. Refugees by the thousands, with their valuables in
bundles, streamed toward the coast. Money was worthless.
The White government "had no alternative but to turn to
the promiscuous use of the printing press," Peter Kenez
writes; but no one would take the one hundred and seventy-

six billion paper roubles it ran off in 1920. The new roubles had only slightly more currency than Romanoff roubles or Kerensky money. The region reverted to a primitive barter economy, centering on brandy, barley, and wine; but everything that could be eaten was hoarded and speculated on. In the summer they had to leave the villa on Gallandia— it was too fancy a place to be found in. They took Mashinka and the goat and moved to a former estate nine miles from Sebastopol. It had belonged to Nani's friend, Tamara Gagarina, who was still living in the big house and seemed to have lost her mind. Nani hardly recognized the gay, ethereally lovely woman she had left in Kharkov. Tamara's husband had been killed by the communists. She didn't care what happened anymore.

The Colonel hired an illiterate woman from the interior to cook and clean house. She could be trusted not to denounce them, but he wasn't sure about the former gardener and his wife. He made a deal with them: they could have whatever milk the cow and the goat gave, after what Mom needed. Disguised as peasants, Nani and the Colonel took trains to outlying villages to buy food. Bread, meat, and sugar were on ration, and it was hard for anyone with an aristocratic appearance to get anything. "We traded shoes and clothing, especially the Colonel's shirts, for kasha, bacon, flour, potatoes, vegetables. The peasants had stopped taking their goods to the city because the money they got for them was worthless. A slice of beef was going for eight thousand roubles. Many were laying up their food for the winter and wouldn't sell at all. As the cold set in there was a shortage of fuel. Coal shipments had stopped the year before. People were tearing down fences and even breaking up their furniture to stay warm. I forgot what real coffee and tea tasted like. I made a tea of dried carrot, apple, and quince skins, and brewed coffee from wheat and ground acorns. It wasn't bad at all. I pasted crackers made of flour and vegetable skins to the surface of our wood stove. They weren't tasty, but we ate them anyway." Early in October, Nani discovered that she was pregnant again.

One day Rolpa wouldn't get up. She always came when the Colonel whistled. The Colonel found her lying under the dining room table, swatting at her muzzle as though she were pestered by flies. The Colonel leaned down and felt that his dog was burning with fever. Suddenly Rolpa got up and bolted out of the room. The Colonel ran after her and about a mile from the house he found her lying in the road. He took the death of his favorite dog worse, it seems, than the loss of his property and position.

On the twenty-sixth of October they went into Sebastopol. Life was going on as usual. The shops were crowded with customers, though there wasn't much to buy. The theaters and cinemas were packed. Trotsky was leading the Red Army to the Isthmus of Perekop, but Wrangel gave a press conference assuring everyone that the lines of defense were impregnable. On the twenty-eighth Nani and the Colonel were foraging in a cornfield when a hay wagon with people they knew passed. They were all crying. The Colonel asked what was wrong. "Haven't you heard?" one of them answered. "The Bolsheviks have broken through at Perekop and are murdering everyone in their path. They've gotten hold of a train and will probably be here tomorrow." The White cause had succumbed to uncontrollable historical and natural forces. On top of being outnumbered three and a half to one (Trotsky had a hundred and thirty-three thousand men with him and twice as many rifles and machine guns as

the Whites did), the defenders at Perekop had been exposed
to the worst frost in years. On October 29 Wrangel gave the
only sensible command left. "I now order the evacuation
and embarkation . . . of all those who are following the
Russian army on its road to Calvary: that is to say, the families
of the soldiers, the officials of the civil administration and
their families, and anyone else who would be in danger if
they fell into the hands of the enemy. . . . May God grant
us the wisdom to endure this period of Russian misery and
to survive it."

By pretending to launch an attack on Odessa, Wrangel
managed to slow the Red advance and bought time to get
the ships ready. Many were in no condition to put to sea.
All foreign vessels docked on the peninsula were detained.
Instructions about the evacuation were posted in every town
by October 30, and long trains of wagons, with people sitting
in them or trudging beside, began to converge on the ports
of Sebastopol, Feodosiya, and Kerch. Boris cashed in at a
bank war bonds he had bought in 1914 and received a
hundred and fifty thousand roubles for them—the going price
for six cans of condensed milk, if you were lucky enough to
find them. Nani packed her jewels, her astrakhan coat, her
best silk dresses, and the blue velvet album of family photographs, and gave the rest of her possessions to the gardener's
wife, who burst into tears and told her how sorry she was.
At the port they joined a line three blocks long, but the
admiral of the fleet, a friend of the Colonel's, boarded them
right away and let them take their suitcases, which the others
had to leave. "As our ship was pulling out someone threw
a bomb and immobilized it," Nani remembered. "A few
people were killed, and many were wounded. We managed
to transfer to the *Kronstadt*, a big, strong repair ship. They

put us in the machine room with fifty others. In the confusion we were separated from our suitcases. From the deck the Colonel saw some Cherkesi—Georgian mountaineers—on the dock, about to make off with them, and running down the gangway, he said, "Ah, gentlemen, how wonderful! You've found our luggage."

"On the fourteenth and fifteenth of November," George Stewart writes, "a hapless armada of one hundred and twenty-six ships of all sorts, ranging from passenger steamers, transports, men-of-war, and destroyers, to one tiny lightship, streamed out of Sebastopol, Feodosiya, and Kerch. They bore 145,693 persons, of which thirty thousand were women, seven thousand were children, and one hundred thousand were soldiers of all services in the Russian Army. With what agony of spirit did many strain their eyes for the last gleam of light over the slate-colored waters." Some of the ships were in tow, but Wrangel could congratulate himself that they were all watertight. "You can leave with your head held high," a municipal councillor told him as he stood on the bridge of the *Weldeck-Rousseau*, the last ship to leave. Wrangel was also pleased that the recent cold spell had broken, and that the sea was as calm as a mirror. But on the evening of the fifteenth thick fog set in. The wireless operator on the *Kronstadt* kept getting messages that didn't make sense about which way to go. He suspected they were from communists. At about ten o'clock the *Kronstadt* collided with a Bulgarian vessel—their allies coming belatedly to the rescue. The *Kronstadt* escaped with a slightly bent prow, but the Bulgarian ship was so badly damaged it had to be abandoned. Now there were more than a thousand people on the *Kronstadt*. Some were washed from the deck during a storm later in the night. No one slept. A priest led them in a Te Deum,

and they could hear thousands of other voices in the fog—
people on the other ships, singing for all they were worth.

The refugees anchored in the Bosporus on November 19
and remained there a week, while negotiators ashore tried
to arrange somewhere for them to go. No one was allowed
to leave ship. Once a day the crew handed out a slip of paper
that could be exchanged for a slice of bread and a cup of hot
water; and that was it for the next twenty-four hours. A few
managed to get ashore, among them a cousin of Masha's,
Prince Alexis Scherbatov, now president of the Russian Nobility Association in New York. "We had good connections
in Constantinople," he told me as we sat among the association's genealogical and heraldic tomes in a small flat on
east First Street. "My brother-in-law got us off. Bribery was
possible." It would have been perfect for Nani and the Colonel to have joined the Schwarzes in Constantinople, but it
couldn't be arranged. Instead, they were transferred to another ship, the St. Vladimir, and for almost three months
they tossed in the Dardanelles while the negotiations continued. The problem was that no country would have them.
Conditions on the ships were appalling. "The French sent
dried beans and corn flour from Tripoli, but they were full
of worms," Nani told me. "From time to time the American
Red Cross came aboard and treated the sick. They gave each
child an egg and a spoonful of sugar and distributed a loaf
of bread for every eight people." Turks would sail up to the
ships in saics and hold up food. The refugees would tie gold
and jewelry to strings and lower them from the portholes,
and the Turks would replace them with bread, figs, sardines,
halva, and oranges. Those who had nothing to trade watched
the lucky ones eat. Some began to steal. Nani's baptismal
cross and a gold watch of the Colonel's were snatched from

them. No one had soap or fresh water, of course, to wash his clothes. After about a month, Nani found a louse in her brassiere. After two months everyone was covered with them. After two and a half months she came down with typhoid fever. Twelve people in the room died of it, and their bodies were thrown overboard. Others were sick with cholera or scurvy. My mother got whooping cough from several other children who had it. Each night the rats grew bolder. Nani had to suspend the food from a pipe.

At last a representative from the League of Nations came aboard and asked everyone which country they wanted to go to. Nani said France—the Colonel's brother George and his uncle Mitrofan were in Paris. But the man said that France was having a terrible time recovering from the war and was full of Russian refugees and was accepting no more. "How about the United States?" the Colonel asked. The man ex-plained that America was trying to stem the tide of immi-grants to its shores and had just put in effect new laws that were particularly strict about East Europeans. That year Pres-ident Harding signed a bill that would become known as the Johnson Act. It limited the annual number of immigrants who would be admitted from then on to three percent of those who had entered in 1910. It set quotas by nationality: no more than two hundred thousand from northern Europe, no more than a hundred and fifty thousand from southern and eastern Europe. Destitute Slavs were at the bottom of the list. But the man from the League of Nations told them that Rumania and Bulgaria would be glad to have them. Nani was less than thrilled. "Who wants to go there?" she said. "I'd rather stay on the ship. Just put us off somewhere where it's warm."

By the end of January the fate of the flotilla had been

decided: twenty-five thousand were transferred to refugee camps at Gallipoli, Turkey; fifteen thousand were put on the Greek island of Lemnos. Fifteen thousand went to Tchatldja, near Constantinople. Thirty thousand were placed in Serbia, Rumania, Bulgaria, and Greece. The thirty ships of the Black Sea Fleet and the five thousand crewmen sailed on to Bizerte, in Tunisia, where the ships, as previously agreed, were given to France in return for the help it had given during the evacuation. They included seven of the fastest destroyers in the world. The crewmen were invited to migrate to the state of São Paulo, Brazil. Those who accepted were dismayed to find themselves welcomed not as colonists, but as peons. Former members of the Russian army fought in the war between Bolivia and Paraguay in 1932. Others, as if they had not had enough of civil war, fought in the conflict that broke out in Brazil that year. Like the spores of a giant puffball, the participants in the greatest diaspora from Old Russia scattered to the wind. Many drifted to Paris, the émigré center in the twenties. Today they can be found almost anywhere. There are two in my home town. I know of several in Montreal. "The ship" is famous in émigré annals. One evening my parents were sitting in the deep armchairs at the Explorers' Club (my father was voted in as a result of his butterfly work on Jamaica) and chatting with the astronomy historian, George Mikanovsky, when the conversation turned, as it often does when White Russians are together, to the question, "How did you get out?" "I was on the famous last ship," Mikanovsky said. "I was born in Yalta in 1920, and was of course too young to remember a thing about it. But my mother told me. She was not a technological person and was notoriously vague about names and dates, but she was vivid about her tribulations on that ship."

On the twenty-seventh of January, 1921, Nani and little Nina's saint's day, they and the Colonel and about twenty others were put ashore at a Yugoslavian fishing village named Senj. Nani still had a fever, but it was abating. Nina was thin and still coughing. Yugoslavia means "the land of the southern Slavs," and at that point it consisted of Serbia, Croatia, Dalmatia, Slovakia, Slovenia, and Montenegro. Senj was in the Croatian part, and it welcomed its new citizens bravely. A man named Dr. Feretich started speaking to them in Yugoslavian, which no one understood. He switched to German, and Nani interpreted it for the others. There were two large tubs, divided by a partition. Dr. Feretich wanted them to strip and get in. "Are you girls deloused yet?" one of the men shouted over the partition, and everyone laughed. It was the first time in a long time any of them had laughed. Dr. Feretich explained that washing their clothes wasn't enough. They had to be ironed, especially the seams, if all the lice were to be got rid of. He also warned them not to eat too much at first, and gave them each four hundred dinars. The money, he explained, was in recognition for the late tsar's kindness in allowing Croatians to be educated in Russia. Nani bought bread, kolbasa, a bar of chocolate, and some oranges, and they had a feast, after which they fell into a delicious sleep on the floor of the fortress.

The next day, with a couple from the ship named the Samodayevs, they rented a two-room cottage. For the first time, Nani had no one to help her with menial work. She cooked on a primus stove, scrubbed and pounded laundry on a washboard, and like all the women of Senj, lowered her bucket into the public well and carried it home. Nani had chosen the Adriatic, hoping that its warm climate would help her daughter's recovery. Senj had been described to her glamorously, as being on the Austrian Riviera (it *had* belonged to Austria before the war), but it was a godforsaken hole, with steep, narrow streets and sudden gusts from the sea that blew up the priest's robes and the women's dresses as they came down from church. Sometimes in the night and early in the morning earthquake tremors would make dishes rattle and crash to the floor. The only communication with the outside world were packets that went to Sušak and Crikvenica, fairly large market towns up the coast, every day or so. My mother was almost four when she arrived in Senj; she was there for three years. "Maybe it was just a crummy little fishing village, but for a child it was a wonderful place," she told me. "The Adriatic was so handsome. I remember swimming in it with some of the other refugees, when an octopus wrapped itself around my knee. Can you imagine anything more petrifying?" She remembers water snakes in a garden, getting stuck in a mulberry tree, horrendous thunderstorms. "When we got there, Yugoslavia was deep in Serbo-Croatian problems. Once at the market in Sušak I watched a woman leaning down to take out her *portemonnaie*, and a dagger fell out. Even the women were ready."

Dr. Feretich stopped by often to see how they were doing. While Nani was still suffering from typhus, she had asked him to prescribe a tonic. He had said, "All you need is food." And from then on, every Sunday after mass, his two daughters would bring her a slice of beef. "It was such a kind gesture," Nani told me, "and so gracefully arranged, that when I left Senj, I gave the doctor four plates made by Kuznetsov at the Imperial Porcelain Factory, showing boyars against a blue background."

Nani got a job teaching French and German at the local

guimnaziya. Her salary was less than what a Yugoslavian citizen would have made, but at least some money was coming in. Their landlord died, his daughter inherited the house and asked them to leave. They moved to an awful basement—"a charming place—oh, brother—it had an earthen floor, and sheep bleating through the wall," my mother recalls. Meanwhile, Nani's time was coming. The marriage was beginning to show the strain. "When the horror story started, Father was totally unequipped to cope with it," my mother explained. "He had been trained to be a magnificent horseman, and that was it." The Colonel refused to stoop to menial work. Any kind of work, in fact, went against the grain of a Russian cavalry officer. In Paris, Nani would find old comrades of his playing bridge in cafés while their wives taught school or took in sewing. It was the Russian woman who summoned the strength and enabled their families to survive in exile. The men, as my mother put it, were "absolute rotters." The Colonel did know something about geology, veterinary medicine, and firearms, but he was poor at languages. When he was five years old he had made the mistake of biting Anna Ivan'na on the wrist, and their relationship during the rest of his childhood had never improved enough for him to learn English from her—a fact that he would ultimately have deep cause to regret. Their neighbor in Senj was a forester named Balič. The Colonel tried to pretend he knew something about forestry so he could get a job with him, but it didn't work. Soon after his son was born, the Colonel went to Sušak and found room and board in a beautiful villa that belonged to a rich young widow for whom he did odd jobs. "He was a great ladies' man," my mother explains. "He couldn't stand our one-room existence in Senj. I met the widow once. She was a fascinating upper class type, a gay lady from Fiume. I remember her taking me into her garden, pointing to an old man who was deep in thought, and saying, 'That's the great Italian poet, D'Annunzio.' "

My uncle Mike was born on the twenty-seventh of May, after a difficult labor that lasted all night. Mom stayed with Mrs. Balič until it was over. Mrs. Balič told her to keep looking at the sky for the stork. Mom picked flowers, pinching the whole stem as children do, and Mrs. Balič arranged them in a dish. Early in the morning, they heard frail screams in the basement. Nina ran in, looked suspiciously at the window, which was shut, and asked how the stork had got in. Nani laughed and explained that she had opened the window. The Colonel cabled his godfather, Grand Duke Nicholas, and asked if he would do the same honor for his son. The grand duke had gathered at Antibes a group of émigrés who recognized him as the Pretender to the Russian throne. He cabled back and said he would be happy to. A General Philimonov stood in for him at the christening. Mrs. Samodayev was Mike's godmother.

For Nani, on her own now with two small children, life was grim. A good bit of her salary went to a teenager who babysat while she was teaching. Supper was the eternal cup of tea and slice of bread to fill the stomach. She allowed herself a quarter pound of beef a day. By denying herself, she was once able to send food to her mother and sisters through the Quakers. She didn't write them directly for fear of exposing them. But she got a postcard from the Quakers saying the package had been delivered; and that was the last contact she ever had with her family. One evening, while grading papers on her trunk and rocking Mike's cradle with her left foot at the same time, she fell asleep. In the morning she found that she had scribbled all over one of her student's papers with red pencil. "I'm sorry," she told the boy when she handed back his homework. "My daughter got hold of it."

There was no one to help when Nina got diphtheria. Senj had no serum. The doctor who was bringing it from Crikvenica was delayed by stormy seas. Nani hung the room with steaming towels and plied Mom with warm water, sugar, and milk, and prayed on her knees with tears running down her face for the Good Lord to save her daughter. At one point Mom was so congested she started to gag. Instinctively Nani opened her mouth, stuck a finger down her throat, and fished out a huge chunk of *makrota*. (*Makrota*, phlegm, is one of those vestigial words of Russian that was still used in the family when I was growing up.) After this desperate maneuver Nina's temperature dropped. When the doctor finally arrived, he looked at the *makrota* and told Nani that she had undoubtedly saved her daughter from choking to death.

The Colonel had gone on to Paris by then, but knowing little French he hadn't been able to find a thing there, and being too proud to sponge off relatives, he continued on to Belgium, where a certain Cardinal Mercier was helping White Russians enter the United States illegally. Through the cardinal he signed as a deckhand on the *Leviathan*, a freighter that was bound for New York, and when it docked, he and the rest of the crew jumped ship. Nani got a letter from him postmarked Port Washington, New York. It said that he had been hired as the pheasant-keeper on a huge estate on Long Island belonging to a man named Harry Guggenheim. Guggenheim had gotten rich from mining out west and in Chile. He had *two thousand* pheasants. The Colonel said he was doing fine. He had even bought a Model T for two hundred fifty dollars. He promised to send a picture of it in his next letter. (The schmuck, Nani seethed when she read this. Here we are, practically starving, and he buys himself a car.) They would not see each other for seven years. Nani journeyed to Zagreb and was told there that it was useless even to apply for an immigrant visa to the United States.

After two years at the *guimnaziya*, the principal told Nani that if she wanted to keep teaching, she would have to pass examinations in Yugoslavian literature, language, history, and geography. He showed her some sample literature questions. "I'm sunk. I haven't even heard of any of these writers," she said as she looked them over. "Not even our greatest writer, Peter Preradovič?" "Well, yes," she said (the Preradovičs were distant relatives of the Colonel, on the Serbo-Croatian side of the family). So she crammed her head with birth and death dates of authors, names of heroes of Yugoslavian classics, rules of Croatian grammar (which was more or less like Russian grammar), boundaries of countries that no longer exist. She journeyed again to Zagreb and presented herself at the *realschule* where the examinations were being given. "I dressed beautifully," she recalled, "so at least my appearance wouldn't be faulted. I thought I'd faint when I saw the questions. Compare the main characters of two Yugoslavian novels I've never heard of. The second question was like the first. The third was explain the importance of the boundaries of Croatia. I wrote about a page. The fourth was about prevailing winds. I told them what it was like living in Senj. I said I was sorry I couldn't write more or better—'consider me like a twelve-year-old child'—and signed my name. The next day I had to teach a class on Croatian subordinate clauses in front of the minister of education. I wrote on the board this sentence: The table that I saw yesterday in the living room was absolutely gorgeous. They were kind to me. I passed the essay questions with a *dobro*, and the grammar class with a *veamo dobro*, and they gave me a teacher's certificate."

Her living was now assured, but it was lonely for her in Senj. She longed to be with her husband. Selling some bracelets at the beginning of 1924, she set out for Paris with her children; maybe there she could find a way of getting to America. As they passed through Italy, the country seemed in a kind of euphoria. Mussolini was at the helm, and police were everywhere. They searched Nani carefully when she crossed the border at Trieste. "Everyone was so afraid *il duce* would be assassinated."

All Russia was in Paris, it seemed. Ex-princes were doormen, generals waited on tables. Half the taxi drivers were former soldiers of the Russian army. There was even a publication called *Le Chauffeur Russie*, which came out once a year. In 1921 Dr. Fridtjof Nansen, the League of Nations' high commissioner for refugees, had calculated the total number of Russian émigrés at a little less than a million. (Considering that there were more than two million people in the Russian nobility at the time of the Revolution, and that many who escaped were not nobles, that leaves about a million who didn't get out and probably suffered the same fate as Nika and Masha.) I talked about the exodus with Prince Teymuraz Bagration, executive director of the Tolstoy Foundation in New York (and my remote cousin). The Tolstoy Foundation is a clearinghouse for newly arrived émigrés—not just White Russians (of whom there are not many left), but Tibetans, Hungarians, anyone without a country. "The aristocrats went to Paris, London, Rome,"

Prince Teymuraz told me. "The intellectuals went to Berlin, Vienna, Prague, and the Baltic states. The peasants and Cossacks went to the Balkans. Quite a few got out to Manchuria and Shanghai. Most of their descendants are in California. Many have Chinese features."

At first Berlin and, to a lesser extent, Prague and Belgrade, were the big émigré centers. But during the twenties everyone went to Paris. By 1932 there were four hundred thousand Russians in France, and the great majority were in Paris. "The Fifteenth Arondissement was a ghetto, with about a hundred and fifty thousand unassimilated Russians," Serafim Miloradovitch, editor of Paris's main émigré paper, *La Pensée Russe*, told me when I stopped at his office on the way to Russia. "They had their own opera, two theaters, two lycées, two dailies, thirty-three churches, numerous political parties and literary reviews, one of whose contributors, Ivan Bunin, got the Nobel prize. Today their children and grandchildren can be found *dans tous les domaines*: journalists, architects— even the secretary of the Elysée is a man named Andronikov. And that was only the first wave. After the Second World War, a lot more Russians, who had been freed from German prison camps but refused to be repatriated, came to Paris. And now that it's somewhat easier to get out, we're getting a third wave. Five to seven thousand, I would say, have come to Paris in the last few years."

George Adamovitch, the Colonel's younger brother, had escaped to Paris with his wife, two children, and parents-in-law. He had been a cavalry captain. His father-in-law had been a general. Now he was a short-order cook. Madame Krizhanowsky, his wife, was making women's hats. She found Nani a room to rent from a coiffeur she knew. The coiffeur gave Nani the once-over and said, "You have the looks, the

figure, the complexion; why not try modeling?" Nani's modeling career lasted two days. Every time she stepped down
from the ramp she was propositioned. Her boss hinted that
if she wanted to keep the job, she'd have to start accepting
the offers. This wasn't what she'd banked on at all, so she
quit. She went to the American embassy to apply for an
immigrant visa, and learned that the restrictions against Slavs
were even tighter now. That year President Coolidge put
into effect that National Origins Quota Rule. From now on
only two percent of the number of people who had entered
the United States in 1890 would be let in annually: 150,000
in all, with 130,000 from northern Europe and only 20,000
from southern and eastern Europe. The vice-consul told her
that the yearly quota of Russians who were being let in from
France was only fifteen, and that there were four hundred
and nineteen applicants ahead of her. It looked hopeless,
but she added her name, Mike's, and Nina's to the list.

For five years she went at least once a month to the
embassy. The news was always the same: there was no news,
but they would let her know as soon as they had some. She
tried tears, but the process was unmoved. She rented a garret
in Le Raincy, a suburb on the Seine et Oise, twenty-six
kilometers from Paris. Across the street was a private clinic
called La Louisianne, run by nuns. She got a job as a night
attendant there: no pay, just tips—the French way. Most of
the patients were dying of cancer. She would become fond
of one of them, then the patient would die, and leave her
some money. "It was a *cauchemar*," she recalled. "It hurt my
pride, as a lady, to take *pourboires* from sick people." But
the sisters were very nice to her. They heaped her dinner
plate with double portions, so she could take the leftovers
home in the morning; they saw that the children were visited

by Père Noel—that Nina got a doll, Mike a train, and each a bag of candy and nuts, and a small pair of shoes. When the war came and Nani was safe in America, she would repay the nuns with Care packages.

During the day Nani slept. Mom played in the garden with Mike and ZaZa and Josette Le Outre. There were two old maids in the building. One had adopted Josette, who was Mom's age; the other looked after ZaZa, the retarded daughter of a prominent Parisian. ZaZa would die of tuberculosis when she was seven. The garden was tremendous. Mom remembers the smell of its flowers—stock and giroflets—hunting for Easter eggs in the garden and standing in it on May 21, 1927, when Charles Lindbergh flew over in the *Spirit of St. Louis*. "The airport where he landed wasn't far away. I remember seeing the floodlights on his plane and thinking, 'Please God, let him be able to land—he must be so tired and hungry,' and hearing the shouts when he came down. The next day his face was on every front page. When I met him at Igor Sikorsky's years later, I told him how I had watched him come into Paris from a garden in the *banlieue*, and he was touched." Because she had to take care of Mike, Mom couldn't go to school. Nani taught her French and Russian grammar. She learned to read from novels of Gogol and Tolstoy. She still reads omnivorously.

Later that year the Colonel came for a visit. Now they were four in one wretched room, heated by a coal stove, with a hotplate in the closet. "He and my mother were like strangers," little Nina observed. "You could see it wasn't going to work out. Mother had become more straightlaced and uptight. I don't think she took the Revolution in a good way. I don't think she was a good sport about it—after all, she was only one of thousands. But she was magnificent to keep us alive." The Colonel went back to America after a week or two. Soon afterward a spot of tuberculosis was discovered on one of Nani's lungs, and she had to stop working. From then on they lived on what the Colonel sent them.

Nani had little to do with other émigrés. In her fallen state she didn't want to see anyone. Her only contact with other Russians was at the Cathedral of St. Alexander Nevsky, a handsome example of nineteenth-century eclecticism on the Rue de la Rue. In its dark interior, with life-size icons and candles flickering in a haze of incense smoke, the faith was kept, the old protocol was still observed. Former nobles bowed or curtsied as former grand dukes and duchesses entered and took their places. Mom remembers seeing the Duchess of Kent and her two sisters, who were Greek princesses, there. "Everyone held their breath, they were so beautiful." "The singing there brought tears to my eyes," Nani told me. "There were some real artists in the choir. Once I even heard Chaliapin again." The cathedral was locked on the weekday I went to see it, but I hunted up the custodian, a bearded old man who spoke a thick Slavic French as he limped up the white marble steps to let me in. Father Obolensky had just died, he told me, but the church was still going strong. I lit a candle in front of the Kiot du Régiment Préobrazhensky de la Garde Impériale, in honor of my ancestors who had served in it.

Some of the congregation were still actively scheming to retake Russia in the twenties. Their leader was General Kutepov, who had been the military governor of Sebastopol at the end of the civil war, and the Colonel's immediate superior. Kutepov wrote stirring right-wing pamphlets and sent anti-communist subversives into the Soviet Union. Serge Obolensky, who collaborated with him for a while, describes him as "a big man in every sense of the word, physically powerful, and clear-headed as to what he was doing and what he might accomplish." Nani was shocked to hear that he had been kidnaped on a street not far from the cathedral. The mystery of his abduction was unsolved until one of the perpetrators surrendered several years later. Kutepov had been chloroformed and dragged into an ambulance by three Cheka agents dressed as gendarmes. They had driven him to the coast, where a Soviet freighter was waiting offshore to take him to Russia. He was to be tortured until he revealed the names and roles of everyone else in the movement. Luckily for him, the dose of chloroform was too large, and he died en route. Two of the agents were shot for bungling the job. The third escaped and went into hiding.

There were some bright moments during their stay in France. Once Nani took the children to Vimines, a village in the wine-growing section of Savoie, in the French Alps. It was good mushroom country. Another time they went to Deauville, a fishing village in Normandy, and stayed in a pleasant thatch-roof cottage. Breakfast was crêpes and fresh cider. The tide was tremendous. When it had gone out the children would try to catch the shrimp caught in the tide pools, but never could—they were like rockets—and watched women rake half-buried flounders out of the mud. Mom and Mike had ice cream about twice a year. They couldn't get over the abundance of it in America.

They always spent Christmas with the Colonel's uncle, General Mitrofan Marchenko. The white-haired aristocrat had had a full life. As military attaché to the court of Emperor Franz Josef he had overheard the kaiser tell the Austrian emperor at a reception about his plan to invade Russia. In October 1917 his students at the Nikolaevsky Cavalry School had been the last group in Petrograd to hold out against the Bolsheviks. Masha describes smuggling food to them when the school was surrounded. Somehow Marchenko and his wife escaped and, with a price on his head, fled to Persia dressed as peasants and carrying as much of their wealth as was portable. They became tobacco growers, importing strong black leaf to France, where it is appreciated, and quickly prospered. In 1919 they passed through Sebastopol. The Colonel arranged their passports to Paris, where they had had an apartment since before the war. Now Uncle Mitrofan was the editor of two newspapers, *L'Economiste Française* and *Le Financier Français*, and a stringer for *The New York Times*. Before he died, he would receive a supreme honor: election to the Académie Française. His salon was often filled with socialites, writers, and prominent Russians. "The émigrés talked on and on about what might have been and about the ins and outs of the Kerensky regime," Mom recalls. "All the furniture was covered, in the Russian fashion, with white linen sheets. Madame Marchenko, a Pruchenko, was enormously wealthy. She had an ancient maid who had been a serf. Imagine. I'm old enough to have known a freed serf." The Marchenkos had no children and were prepared to do anything for Nina and Mike, but Nani didn't exploit the relationship. Uncle Mitrofan called Mike Kapelka, "Little Drop." He wrote a book that predicted the energy crisis.

George Adamovitch and his family were always there at Christmas, too. "Uncle George was completely unaffected, and he wasn't ashamed to do menial work," Mom recalls. Mike can still repeat a dirty joke about Catherine the Great and a sickening war story his uncle George told him. According to the *Chernigov Book of Nobility*, he served in the

Primorsky Cavalry Regiment and "was contusioned." But
before that happened, he told Mike, his regiment was ordered
to kill everyone in a section of Poland where a large, secret
offensive was soon to be carried out. Fulfilling its instructions
to the letter, the regiment wiped out an entire hospital—
German and Allied wounded and even the nurses—and when
they had finished, they were told that the offensive had been
canceled. In the thirties Uncle George moved to Berlin and
started a restaurant that became very successful. No one has
heard from that side of the family for decades.

Harry Guggenheim had two sisters in Paris, and one afternoon they invited Nani to tea. Learning of her plight, they
offered to pay her way to New York and back; there was
nothing to stop her, while her application was still in limbo,
from going as a tourist for six months. But Nani refused: if
she was going to America, it would be for good. She and
her children each have their own version of how they finally
got their immigrant visas. Here is Mike's: "Mother's approach
to the consul in Paris was sobbing and hysterics, which was
exactly the wrong thing to do. You have to treat hemorrhoidal bureaucrats on their own hemorrhoidal level."
(Bearded Mike—a confirmed bachelor, inveterate pipe-
smoker, and for many years copyeditor with the Baltimore
Sun, had few heroes. One of them was H. L. Mencken, and
his observations often smacked of that acerbic populist.) "We
were living in a suburb that caught it in both wars. Fortunately there was a Catholic priest there (who did his best to
convert us) and he wrote a very well-phrased letter to President Coolidge. In his most distinguished act as president,
Coolidge, by executive order, had us admitted." Nani, however, claims the letter was never answered. According to
Mom, through the two old spinsters who lived in their build-

ing they met a woman named Madame d'Este, whose husband was president of the French stock exchange. "Madame d'Este fell in love with Mother and what she was going through and introduced her to two powerful American women, Miss Elvina Neezer and Mrs. Coudert Garrison. Miss Neezer was a friend of Coolidge and wrote to him in our behalf. Before we left, she sent us boxes and boxes of clothes. Except for her, we could still be poor and languishing in Paris, as plenty still are." But Nani told me that none of the strings that were pulled worked. According to her, it was purely a process of attrition. "Many of the applicants ahead of us dropped out, and our number kept advancing until, early in 1929, it finally came up." Nani was called to the embassy and was asked to prove that she had a good character, wasn't affiliated with the Communist party, and wasn't carrying any trans- mittable diseases. The examiner was really tough. "You speak Russian, French, and German, Mrs. Adamovitch, but no English. Who will take care of you?" "My husband," she said, and produced a letter from Harry Guggenheim stating that the Colonel was steadily employed. "But he's not a citizen," the examiner objected. "You need an American citizen to be your sponsor." "Don't worry," Nani said. "I'm intelligent. I know what the good life is. I'll become a lady's companion. I'll tell her what clothes to wear." The man frowned, but in the end he approved their visas.

On March 14, 1929, having crossed the English Channel and reached Liverpool, they set out for Boston on the *Cedric*, a British steamer on the White Star Line. Nani had sold a necklace so they could go first class. "I wanted to wash out all our unhappiness," she explained. On board she made a lasting friend—Mrs. Charles Fayerweather of New Lebanon, New York. Mrs. Fayerweather knew the Franklin Roosevelts intimately, and years later she would take Nani to lunch with Eleanor at the White House. My mother and father were married by then. Nani noticed that the small portrait Mopsy had made of the President in 1943 was hanging in the Oval Office, and she explained that the artist was her son-in-law's mother. Eleanor stiffened and said nothing.

Mom recognized her father waving from the dock, but the reunion was marred by Nani's criticism of his hat. Both children remember that it wasn't such a bad hat, a sportsman's felt cap with a long pheasant feather stuck in it. But Nani was shocked by his appearance. He looked so shabby, so common. "How could I introduce him to Mrs. Fayerweather, who was so anxious to meet him, after all I'd been telling her?" The Colonel had left the Guggenheims and was working for an elderly textile heiress named Mrs. William Harcourt Amory, who had a stone castle and a good deal of land in Dublin, New Hampshire. She had made him superintendent of the place. He was happy enough with the job, but Nani wasn't. "During all those years in America, he had made nothing of himself," she complained to me. Nani expected him to be working in a bank by now, or at least an insurance company, not just drifting from gamekeeping to groundskeeping positions. Mom understood her father better. "Mother wanted him to be urban, but he would have perished in the city. He was an outdoorsman."

Mrs. Amory had given him an enchanting cottage to live in. She was "a bit stiff, but very high class," Mom recalls, "and she always wore a black velvet ribbon around her neck." In June Mrs. Amory's grandchildren came for the summer. She hired Nani to teach them French. They went on picnics, which Mrs. Amory ruined for Nani by forbidding her to pick mushrooms. It was a major cultural clash. Nani had never encountered Anglo-Saxon mycophobia, and she didn't know what to make of it. In his book *Russia, Mushrooms and History*, Gordon Wasson suggests that certain peoples, like the British and their stock, are mycophobic because their ancestors, before converting to Christianity, worshiped mushrooms; they had to develop artificial taboos. Others, like the Russians, to whom fungi never had religious significance, were left free to become rabid mycophiles. Nani wondered if she ought to cook up a batch of the delectable chanterelles that littered Mrs. Amory's woods and cure the woman of her idiotic squeamishness, but in the end she just shook her head and stayed quiet. Mrs. Amory took a great liking to Mom and Mike. She wished that some of their lovely European manners would rub off on her grandchildren, and encouraged them to play together. The grandchildren were far better English teachers of Mom and Mike than French pupils of Nani; they grimaced at having to repeat *bleu* and *rouge* as if the words were spoonfuls of cod liver oil.

In the fall Mrs. Amory closed the castle and returned to Boston. The Colonel stayed on and kept an eye on the place. With a scholarship from Mrs. Amory's church, Mom entered the eighth grade at St. Mary's School in Concord, New Hampshire, and though it was the first school she had ever gone to, she had no trouble keeping up with her peers. Nani stayed in Cambridge, Massachusetts, teaching French at the Haskell School in the morning and at Concord Academy in the afternoon. On Friday she took the train up to Dublin. Things were quite pleasant until the cottage caught fire one morning in January 1930. No one knows exactly how it happened. The sheriff later found plenty of cracks in the chimney through which flames could have eaten. The chimney was all that remained. Even before the Colonel's gunpowder went off (he kept a supply for refilling his own shells), the fire was out of control. Eight icons Nani had been saving to put Mike through college burned up. One had been given to the Colonel by Grand Duke Nicholas. Others had been in Nani's family for generations, passed on at weddings or christenings. The blue velvet album of family photos was lost. So was the suitcase in the closet full of silver and jewelry. The linen, too—everything she'd managed to bring through their ordeal, except her diploma from the Alexandro-Marinsky Institute, a pair of diamond earrings, Mom's baptismal cross, and a couple of spoons and rings, went up in smoke. That fire really undid her. It was the last straw. There was clearly no end to what she was being made to suffer, she concluded, and the suffering was absolutely unredeeming.

They left Dublin in a cloud of bitterness. The Colonel got a job in Fitzwilliam, working for a rich man named Morgan, who had a Scotch pine nursery. He was in charge of a crew that took the trees down and sawed them into boards. The pay wasn't bad, and Morgan threw in a nice house. But Nani was mortified that her husband was now just a woodcutter. Shortly after they moved, Mom remembers a terrible fight in which the Colonel confessed that he was involved with a nineteen-year-old woman, and asked Nani for a divorce. They separated. Nani kept the children, and from then on she pretended that the Colonel no longer existed. She never remarried, or even dated another man, though she was still a stunning woman and had plenty of opportunities. One morning, after I had left Baltimore and was going over my interview notes with her, there was a letter from her. "Important," it said. "Please put these lines somewhere at the end of my sad story. You see I had no bitterness after all, and still think about the happy times I had with him. In Russian the poetry is beautiful. You know how *arabique* my English is, but I will try to translate:

> *Forgotten are the tender kisses.*
> *Passion sleeps, and love has passed.*
> *The joy of a long-awaited meeting*
> *No longer stirs my blood.*
> *My heart is weighted down with sorrows*
> *But the murmur of happiness has not been stilled.*

Nani picked up an old thirty-acre farm in Richmond, the next town, for four hundred and twenty-five dollars (the asking price was four hundred and fifty). The house needed work but was fundamentally sound. They spent the summer fixing it up, and in the autumn she took the children to Baltimore and began what was to be a twenty-four-year teaching career at the Bryn Mawr School. The school was in an enormous building on Cathedral Street. The classrooms had high ceilings and were full of Greek statues. The headmistress was Edith Hamilton, an arresting woman in her sixties who wore long black dresses and her white hair in a bun. Miss Hamilton had not yet written her famous book, *The Greek Way*. "Edith made the most academically difficult school for girls in the United States the most popular school in Baltimore, a city where many of the parents not only did not care whether their daughters learned anything or not, but in some cases, felt it a great mistake for them to do so," wrote her former student and longtime companion, Doris Fielding Reid. Mom, who went into the ninth grade at Bryn Mawr, remembers Miss Hamilton vividly. "Her eyes bored through you. You could feel the power of her intellect." Mom's classmates were friendly and full of life, not cold and cliquish like New England girls. She felt more at home in Baltimore than anywhere they had lived; they all did. "We blended in joyously with the gracious southern life," Mom told me.

In some ways, Baltimore was an ideal place for exiled Russian gentry to start over. The people of that city held qualities like breeding and background in higher esteem than wealth. Some of its own best families had fallen on hard times, and this was nothing to be ashamed of. It was perfectly obvious what sort of Russians they were, and that Madame, as her students had begun to call her (old students still come up to her in the supermarket—prim, fortyish women now in madras skirts—and tell her how many children they've had; to them she is still Madame), had never stopped holding her head up. The old South and Old Russia, moreover, were kindred souls. Both were languorous rural existences, full of dogs and horses and devoted servants, and Old Russia would probably have slipped into genteel oblivion just as content-edly as the old South if it had been allowed to do so. Nani was charmed by the Maryland countryside and by what went on in it. It took her back to her childhood in Tambov.

Several ladies of society—Mrs. Lennox Birckhead, Mrs. Tilghman Pitts, Mrs. Bruce Cotten—decided to take the poor family under their wing, and saw that Mom had the life of a typical southern girl. She was invited for weekends to great brick mansions in Green Spring and Worthington valleys. She watched point-to-point races, danced at hunt balls. At sixteen she was already blossoming into one of the celebrated beauties of the day. (I'm not just bragging about my mother. Baltimoreans used to ask Mike and Nani if they were any relation to *the* Nina Adamovitch.) With several Bryn Mawr classmates, she "earned extra pennies" modeling at the Hotel Belvedere and on the runways of Hutzler's and Hoschel-Kohn's, department stores that used "society girls" to enhance their prestige. The main event of the social season was the Bachelors Cotillon, at which the eligible young ladies of Baltimore were presented to society. It was a lavish affair, whose every move was worked out months in advance. The debutantes received detailed instructions along with their engraved invitations.

Black Brothers, florists, and a corp of assistants will receive the flowers only at the Maryland Ave. entrance. Put each debutante's name on her flowers and keep them together until asked for. When ready to enter the ball room each debutante should claim her bouquet from Mr. Black, and have one of the footmen provided by the Cotillon for the purpose, assist her in carrying her flowers into the ball room when she enters.

The flowers may be placed anywhere in the ball room, as the managers have provided wire receptacles and will appreciate it if the debutantes will have their flowers placed therein, thus adding materially to the presence of the ball room.

None of the Ball Room Boxes can be reserved except by occupying them.

Mom came out at the 1936 Cotillon. She was the first foreigner to do so. You were technically supposed to be related to a member of the Cotillon, but because of her looks, background, and powerful sponsors, the requirement was waived. She wore the dress in which her aunt Marchenko had been presented to the court of Nicholas II, but that evening she felt as if she had no Russian blood at all. "We all wore white," she recalls, "and both sexes had on white gloves. Everybody you ever knew sent you flowers. A tall, elderly man with gorgeous white moustaches—his name was Mr. Penniman, and the Pennimans were one of Baltimore's most aristocratic families—cut in and asked if I wasn't so-and-so's daughter." That evening she felt completely Baltimorean, and Baltimore, on its side, was captivated by her.

After her debut, and even after she had married and moved away, the press wouldn't leave her alone. She was as hot copy in Baltimore as Uncle was in Pittsburgh. "Nina Adamovitch was having a beautiful time dancing on the terrace in a pale blue dress." "The skiers who dashed in after an afternoon on the hill were Nina Adamovitch and Medi Slinlguff." The clippings fill a scrapbook, and have started to yellow after almost fifty years. One reported that she was "a great-granddaughter of Ivan P. Elaghin, *oberhoffmeister* of the court of Catherine the Great" (actually, Ivan P. Elaghin had no children, and our precise connection to him has yet to be established). Another claimed that Nani would have been a princess in Old Russia, but had relinquished her title when she became an American citizen (in 1936). "Whether this will mean," the article continued, "that her attractive daughter, Miss Nina Tatiana Adamovitch, come what may, can never claim the title of princess we are not sufficiently familiar with royal customs to state, but by inheritance this debutante of the past year is descended from the Princess Gagarin, her great-great-grandmother, and from the lady's husband, General Boris Adamovitch of the Russian Imperial Army, but it seems not to worry her very much." Nani denied ever having given this, or any information, to the papers; it appears they *wanted* her to be a princess.

Little Mike watched his older sister preparing to go out,

and decided he wanted nothing to do with society. Nani enrolled him in a dancing class, but the first day he and a friend jumped out the boys' room window, and never returned. He did well at Boys' Latin and Johns Hopkins and went into newspaper work. He lived until his death in 1988 in a brick row house "on the slum boundary of the exclusive Guilford residential district, thereby paying one-third the taxes." "There's only one rule in this house," he was fond of saying. "If anybody goes hungry or thirsty here, it's his own goddamn fault." His friends tended to be from all walks, taxi drivers, longshoremen, regular guys who like to go hunting and fishing and drinking. "Baltimore society is much too boring to confine yourself to the people in the studbook," he explained. Far from having nostalgia for the *ancien régime*, he once recited to me a bit of doggerel in his favorite bar:

> *Tsar, Tsar, wherever you are,*
> *Although the Reds may abhor you,*
> *We're going to restore you.*
> *Tsar, Tsar, Tsar.*

"Just like the Bourbons who learned nothing from experience. Mother still thinks he could do no wrong. She couldn't see the writing on the wall. Neither could my father. They were like the poor bastards in Rhodesia and South Africa."

Every summer until 1950, Nani and the children would go up to the farm in Richmond. She called it Hootor Elaghin (a "hootor" in Russian was a poor man's country estate) and planted a flowerbed in the shape of an *E*. "They were gloriously spent days," Mom told me, "with memories of *shashlik*, mint juleps, and Cossack songs." I can remember tagging along on some of the almost daily mushroom sorties, though I was only four when Nani sold the place. Because the minute, wind-blown spores of mushroom rise to great height, they are immune to the ocean barriers that keep most plants from migrating, and the prize edible species of New England—the chanterelles, the boletes, the morels—are the same as those in Russia. Mushroom gathering was one activity a displaced Slav could enjoy undiminished. Like Pine Bush, Hootor Elaghin was usually brimming with boisterous fellow-exiles. Mstislav Dobuzhinsky, a frequent guest, sketched Mom in a sailor suit. He had designed sets for Diaghilev's Ballet Russe, and had been one of Vladimir Nabokov's favorite tutors. "He made me depict from memory, in the greatest possible detail," Nabokov wrote gratefully, "objects I had certainly seen thousands of times without visualizing them properly: a street lamp, a postbox, the tulip designs on the stained glass of our own front door." Gratian Yatsevitch, head of the arsenal in Watertown, Massachusetts, was there a lot. So were hulking George Shapavaloff, a former aviator, now owner of a garage in Cambridge; Princess Lila Galitsin, who would be one of Mom's bridesmaids; Elizabeth Artzybashev, whose husband did covers for *Time* magazine. A writer named Hutchins Hapgood lived up the road. He was a protégé of the journalist Lincoln Steffens and a practitioner of the new "social realism," which saw "murder as tragedy rather than crime, a fire as drama instead of police news, a pushcart as pageant and not a street nuisance," as Moses Rischin writes in an introduction to *The Spirit of the Ghetto*, Hapgood's affectionate documentary study of the Lower East Side. Sadly, Rischin goes on, Hapgood's "tendency to idealize and sentimentalize alcoholism and sex doomed him to an amiable bohemianism that was much valued by his friends, but rendered him creatively ineffectual for the last thirty years of his life." Hapgood was a great fan of Nani. He had covered the Sacco and Vanzetti case, and wanted to write her story, but she wasn't at all interested. She recalls him as a "nice little drunk." One evening he appeared at her door, reeling and in pajamas, with an arm around Eugene O'Neill. Nani refused to let them in.

One man who was always welcome at Hootor Elaghin, though, was Colonel Alexei Lvov. Lvov had been in charge of the Imperial Train; his grandfather, a composer, had written the old Russian national anthem. During the civil war he had been forced to watch as his wife and daughter were executed, and had himself twice been brought up before firing squads, but each time something had distracted them. A person meeting Lvov would never have imagined the hell he'd been through. He was such a gentle, jovial soul, a devout Theosophist and strict vegetarian, and always talking about the teachings of Krishnamurti. On sunny days he would borrow a blanket and practice yoga in the nude in a clearing of Nani's woods. In Boston, where he worked in the Oriental section of the public library, old Lvov, with his magnificent white moustaches, his radiant blue eyes and splendid physique, could often be seen jogging shirtless, even in the dead of winter, and blowing kisses to women who gaped from their apartment windows. He was such a distinctive character that Thomas Wolfe knew him by sight and describes him in *Of Time and the River*: "Another was an old man with a mad, fierce, handsome face and wild strewn hair of silvery white, who never wore a hat or overcoat and who muttered through the streets of Cambridge, over the boardwalks of the Harvard Yard, in every kind of weather; winter was around him always, the rugged skies of winter sunsets, red and harsh to frozen desolation of old snow: in street and yard and gutter,

the harsh, interminable, weary savagery of gray winter." I
have a dim image from boyhood of this kindly old man
visiting us in Westchester County and starting, but not finishing, the gargantuan task of cataloguing Uncle's books. He
sang a song about the nightclub Yar, where Nani's now-
unmentionable ex-husband had often caroused. That was
Colonel Lvov.

Lvov appointed himself Mom's guardian. She was the
same age as the daughter he had lost. He insisted she read
War and Peace (he, too, had an ancestor in the novel), and
encouraged her to write poetry. There were two young men,
both Russians, he wanted her to meet. One was a baron,
the other was named Nicholas Shoumatoff. Lvov had met
my father, then a junior at M.I.T., at Prince Toumanoff's
pheasant farm in Peterborough, New Hampshire. Pa was a
fine pianist, and they discovered they had a lot more to talk
about than music. Lvov kept building up Mom and Pa to
each other, but Mom wasn't interested in meeting him.
"Please don't introduce me to any more poor, stricken Russians," she begged Lvov. Lvov praised Mom's literary sensibility so highly to Pa that Pa got the idea she was what
was then known as a "Radcliffe girl," a sexless intellectual
with wire-rim glasses.

But nothing could have been farther from the truth. After
several years in Baltimore Mom had gone to New York to
try to get on the stage. She was living at 47 West Forty-
third Street in a three-story brownstone called the Rehearsal
Club, much like the rooming house made famous in *Stage
Door*. For eight dollars a week, aspiring young actresses got
room, breakfast, and a buffet supper there. "Men weren't
allowed across the threshold after eleven," she recalls. "One
of my roommates was Jayne Cotter, who eventually changed

her name to Jayne Meadows. I remember her stuffing her bra with Kleenex, and both of us laughing because she couldn't get the bosoms even. Her sister Audrey, who wanted to be an opera singer, was there, too. Their father was a minister, and they had grown up in China. Phyllis Thaxter, the daughter of a Maine judge, was another of the boarders. So were Jeanne Crain, a redhead, and some of the Rockettes. We were all so poor we kept borrowing each other's stockings." Mom almost got into a production of *Saint Joan*, starring Ingrid Bergman, when one of the cast got appendicitis, but the doctors managed, by a new technique, to "freeze" the inflamed organ. She went briefly on the road with a show called *Claudia*. An MGM talent scout offered her a screen test, but "he was so sleazy I never looked him up." She shortened her name to a more American-sounding Nina Adams, and perfected a clear, well-spoken English. Waiting for her big break, she worked as a salesgirl at À La Vieille Russie, a Fifth Avenue shop that specializes in old Russian artifacts. "It was so depressing to see all these old Russians coming in to sell their cigarette cases," she recalled. "Once the owner took me into the back room, opened the safe, and showed me a necklace of emeralds and black pearls. 'Do you want this?' he said. But he wouldn't have given it to me anyway." She got into store modeling. The Tailored Woman hired her for the whopping sum of thirty-three dollars a week, good money in the late Depression. She went out a lot and had scads of beaux. Once she had a date with Admiral Byrd. She received eight serious proposals. One, from a member of one of Philadelphia's top families who has since died from drink, she nearly accepted. But as for getting on the stage, "I didn't make out at all."

Colonel Lvov was worried about her. After Mom had

been at the Rehearsal Club about a year, he wrote Mopsy, whom he had met by then, about this enchanting young girl living alone in New York and modeling, about whom he was terribly unhappy. Mopsy was having a Russian Easter party at Hidden Hollow for a hundred and fifty people in a few weeks and invited Mom, who accepted. Pa, it was arranged, was to pick her up at Manhasset, but having been at the Stork Club till three the night before, she missed her train, and came out on a later one. "When we finally met, he'd had to make the trip twice, and was livid." Mom recalls that she had on a navy blue dress spattered with white butterflies. (What attire could have been more appropriate? Pa wouldn't let her throw it away for thirty years.) On her head was a straw hat shaped like an overturned flowerpot, with a spray of flowers to one side. Under her arm was a best-seller about the antebellum South: *Gone With the Wind*. It was April 28, 1940. Pa had graduated from M.I.T. with a degree in mechanical engineering, and had taken a job with the General Electric Company in Bridgeport, Connecticut, for twenty-eight dollars a week. With him in the car was a sweet old émigré named Misha. Misha was the art director of the Lion Match Company in Long Island City, which employed many émigrés. He was married to a woman named Milochka, who was the adopted daughter of a first cousin of Grandmother's named Countess Tolstoy (in fact, it was rumored that Milochka was the countess's own child by her Tatar groom). Milochka talked and dressed like a man, with pants tucked into high black boots, and dangled her cigarette from the side of her mouth; during the war, she had served as a nurse in the trenches. She died before Misha did, and he, lost without her, took some pills and killed himself soon afterward. I was given his medals and his gold watch. I was about ten. My parents thought I was old enough to have a watch, but I wasn't. One morning, in the heat of a snowball fight with some other boys waiting for the school bus, the watch, which had a stretch band and fit loosely on my little right wrist, flew off and shattered against the drugstore wall.

Pa drove (to resume the story), but kept looking back at Mom, and, according to her, several times he nearly went off the road. At the party she was immediately surrounded by admirers, and he had no chance to talk to her. When she said it was time for her to go, a dozen young men stepped forward and offered to take her home. Pa shouldered his way through and said, "I'm sorry, gentlemen, I brought Miss Adamovitch, and it's my duty to see her home." He drove her all the way to the Rehearsal Club. On the way they spoke French. Pa kept using the familiar *tu*. "Don't you think it's rather daring for you to *tutoyer* me when you hardly even know me?" she protested. Pa stopped the car, leaned over, and kissed her. "There," he said. "Now we can call each other *tu*, *n'est-ce-pas?*" It was one of the most forward things he'd ever done.

They met for lunch in New York a few days later. She had just stepped off a runway at Town and Country, and recalls accidentally dipping the price tag on the cuff of her dress into her soup. Pa took her into Central Park and proposed. She didn't say yes, and she didn't say no. Nani didn't like him at first. She thought that he was too *muzhikavat*, that he looked too much like a peasant. But she had not yet approved of any of her daughter's suitors. In June Pa visited Hootor Elaghin and wrote in the guestbook:

Although I have known but this beautiful summer,
I don't feel myself at all a newcomer,

And look forward again to washing the dishes.
I leave with all my very best wishes.
My thoughts will fly back to Hootor Elaghin,
And myself, with the swiftness of a toboggan.

The courtship went on for a year and a half. Pa wrote her passionate letters from Jamaica, where he was collecting but-terflies with Uncle. Once Uncle came out on the porch of their hotel, where Pa was writing her in the light of a full blue moon. "Must you take so long over each word?" Uncle asked impatiently.

War broke out in Europe again, and it seemed unpatriotic for her to keep him dangling any longer. They were married in Baltimore on November 29, 1941. In her column, "Belle Brummel Views the Town," Rosalind White describes the nuptials of the belle about whom she had written so often before:

Right in the midst of the pre-Cotillon excitement . . . the debutantes in a flurry, parties practically every hour . . . there were two weddings of note.

One was the Shoumatoff-Adamovitch marriage, uniting two old families . . . the blonde, very lovely Nina, looking nothing less than ethereal in her white satin and tulle, and her mother, Mrs. Nina M. Adamovitch, quite lovely in the receiving line at the reception in dark blue with brilliant embroidery forming a panel in the bodice.

Mrs. Lennox Birckhead, in whose house the reception was held, wore a striking model of shirred leaf-green crêpe while her daughter, Mary, was in lamé.

Viewing the gifts, among which was a silver portrait me-dallion of the Czarina, which the Czar gave to the bride's father and which he, in turn, gave to his daughter, was Mrs. J. Clarke Matthai and her daughter Adelade, soon to be a bride herself. . . .

They had just finished their honeymoon when they heard on the radio that Pearl Harbor had been bombed. He joined the navy two years later, and leaving Mom with my year-old brother, he would spend much of the next two years on an escort carrier in the Atlantic.

✢ ✢ ✢

When I was growing up, there were two green sacks in the attic. (I was the second child, a classic postwar baby, born in November, '46.) One sack contained hundreds of mushy letters Pa had written to Mom during the war. The other was stuffed with old Russian paper money, wads of imperial roubles that my grandfather Lyova Shoumatoff had brought to America on his purchasing mission for the Zemsky Union. When he got here, of course, the Revolution had taken place, and the money was worthless. I used to hold up the large bills to the window and examine their watermark. The five-hundred-rouble notes were cool black and watermarked with the dapper figure of Peter the Great, suited in armor. The hundred-rouble denominations were called *katerinkas*; they showed a bust of Catherine the Great, a formidable woman with white hair who reminded me of Aunt Masha.

More than anyone else in my childhood, it was from maudlin, aristocratic Masha that I got the greatest blast of the old country. I was fascinated by her rings. There were eight of them. Each had a past, and whenever we met, I would ask her to tell me about them. One of Masha's rings had a large fake pearl. She told me it had been a gift of the

Aga Khan, who had invited her and Nika on his yacht while
they were honeymooning on Lake Como. Eventually Masha
confessed that the ring in fact came from a thrift shop on
MacAllister Street, San Francisco. But such niggardly details
were never important in Masha's stories. "If that's not the
way it was, that's how it ought to be told," she was fond of
saying.

Sometimes Alika would come up from the Bronx, and we
would get another blast of the old country. Among my first
memories is one of spreading a scoop of sour cream with my
spoon in a bowl of Alika's *borshch*, and unenthusiastically
watching it curdle between floating slivers of beets and carrots
and impermeable beads of broth, while Alika is standing over
me and saying in her grating, irritable whine, "*Yesh, Yesh,*"
which meant "Eat." Another Russian word I learned from
Alika, trying a different tack—the soft sell—was *vkustno*,
delicious. In fact, Alika's *borshch* was delicious. Years later,
when she was ninety, I got her recipe. Our first son had just
been born. Alika had known four generations of us and had
taken care of two, and it just wouldn't have been right for
her not to be there. Zoric drove her up from the small Russian
colony outside Lakewood, New Jersey, where she has been
living for years. While we were in the Finast, shopping for
borshch ingredients, an ancient Italian man came up and
shook her hand like an old friend. "You're old. I old," he
said to her. "I older than that," Alika said, and waved him
away.

Back in the kitchen, she got down to business. "Fresh
beets boil and cover preferably day before," she explained.
"A little lemon keeps fresh. Cut them and cabbage wash
good and cut in big pieces. Two carrot or three I cut, little

celery, three onions, two potatoes. Cook about three hours."
Real *borshch* like Alika's tastes better each time it's heated
up again.

Her real *tour de force*, though, is *galubtsy*. "Take not very
hard cabbage and cut round the rest and after put in kettle
boiling water. When soft, dump in strainer and spray cold
water. I already have cooked rice and ground meat and lotsa
onions, pepper, salt, egg sometimes and mix good. Make
patty on leaf, roll up, and tie with string. Spray tomato soup
or *borshch* juice. Cover tight and boil on slow fire about two
hours."

As children, we were of course more interested in Alika's
sweet dishes: *sirniki*, crêpes filled with cottage cheese and
topped with sour cream; crispy cookies of twisted russet dough
sprinkled with confectioner's sugar, the making of which
filled the kitchen and involved the whole family. My brother
recalls that they were called *hvorosti*; I don't. Here are the
Russian words we knew when we were children:

posmotri   look
pozhaluista   please (i.e., cut it out)
spasibo   thank you
zdravstvuitie, milii   hello, dear (so-and-so)
Christos voskresye   Christ is risen
Voistenno voskresye   Indeed he is risen
uzhasno   ghastly, vulgar (Mom's term for the sort of person
        who wore loud Hawaiian shirts, the Rodney Dangerfield
        type; very similar to Baby's term, "una," short for
        "unattractive")
kabusar   a piece of dried nasal mucus
makrota   phlegm

Those were the main ones. And of course we heard Russian
being spoken a fair amount. At least once a week Pa would
get on the phone with Mopsy and they would have a good
long chat in Russian (she always called him Goula; that was
another word we knew, though we didn't know it meant
little dove). We became quite good at getting the general
gist of what they were talking about, even if we didn't understand most of the words. Certainly the sound of Russian
was not strange to us. When I started studying it in college,
I had an overpowering sense of *déjà entendu*.

There were some Russian artifacts in the house: photographs of our ancestors, the moustachioed men in uniform,
the regal women in court gowns, and of Shideyevo, its big
white columns rising out of a sea of poppies, and Mopsy, a
young woman then, standing out front. There were several
pieces of imperial china in a cabinet, with the double eagle
on them, several icons in the bedroom, and a big brass
samovar. There was a lot more in a converted barn behind
the house. The barn was like a museum. Most of the things
in it had been collected by Uncle. He had built up a fabulous
library on Russian art, popular and religious. When we
moved to London for several years, the books were shipped
for safekeeping to the Firestone Library at Princeton. James
Billington referred to them when he was writing his monumental survey of Russian culture, *The Icon and the Axe*.
Some of Uncle's books were three feet tall, with color plates
of men and women in regional costume, and dated to the
early nineteenth century. Some were the genealogies with
which he had been able to trace himself back to Cleopatra.
Most of the books were in Cyrillic. To us they were mysterious, untouchable (the most valuable ones were kept behind sheets of clear plastic or locked in a safe); the knowledge

they contained was beyond us. They were Uncle's books, and Uncle himself was like a god to us, someone on a much higher plane. The walls of the barn were covered with his paintings and drawings: pencil sketches of Nijinsky and Rachmaninoff, a caricature of his old schoolmate Nichvalodov, in the turban of a Persian emir; Blakeian grotesques and apocalyptic fantasies; flower paintings in styles varying from Old Dutch to Cubist. His roses, with Old World butterflies hovering over them, the Ukrainian steppe in the background, and the sun breaking through mountainous cloud formations, were as delicate and beautiful as music of Mozart. One wall was devoted to his Tibetan studies. I was particularly fascinated by a portrait he had made of the last king of Ladakh in 1912. The left eye was crossed, Pa explained to me, because the king of Ladakh had been considered too exalted a being to look on ordinary people with both eyes. The eye had been trained to focus on his nose since childhood. The portrait was done with a stipple pen in the pointillist style. I couldn't get over how whenever you looked at it from up close, it looked like a jumble of scratch marks, but when you stepped back a few yards, a man fell into place. In fact, all of Uncle's paintings made a deep impression on us children. No one we knew had a barn like that. It made us feel proud and special.

But apart from the barn, our childhood was like that of anyone else who was reasonably well off and grew up in north-central Westchester County during the fifties. Mine can be conveniently divided into a stamp-collecting phase, a fishing phase, a butterfly-collecting phase, and a rock-climbing phase. Looking back on it, I realize that it was my father who got me into butterflies, and that that interest was a family tradition going all the way to Vladimir Panayev in the early nineteenth century. But it wasn't an especially Russian tradition; it had grown out of the Victorian interest in natural history; I could have had butterfly collectors in my family just as easily if I had been of English stock. In fact, I didn't particularly think of myself as being Russian at all when I was growing up, and I don't think having originated from that part of the world made any great difference. My parents were part of the local gentry, but Pa was a lot more interesting than the men who commuted to Wall Street and swatted golf balls on the weekend, and Mom had more to her than the women who tooled around in gigantic ranch wagons and sashayed down to the post offices in black velvet riding helmets. We belonged to the country club, worshiped at the Episcopal church, and went to the local private school. There *were* several disconcerting incidents. Once, at the height of the McCarthy era, while Mom was weeding the pachysandra in front of the house, a son of one of our neighbors (not seeing her there) spat on the fence and muttered, "Russians." And once at school some boys kept calling my brother "Red." He started to cry, and Mom had to come and take him home. But that was their problem. If they didn't know the difference between Reds and the kind of Russians we were, that was their problem.

I don't know if these incidents, the result of our living in a conservative exurb during a reactionary period, had anything to do with it, but there seemed to have been a decision, when we were growing up, to downplay our heritage. The most important consequence of this decision was that we were allowed to lose the Russian language and the Orthodox faith (my parents were already sufficiently Americanized to have lost interest in mushrooms, so that lore wasn't passed on either). In this respect we conformed to the American pattern of shedding one's ethnic origins as quickly as possible. I can also remember thinking how unfair it was for Mom to criticize, as she did sometimes, the way Nani talked—not always grammatically, and with a fairly thick Russian accent—when Nani couldn't help it. Now I see that Mom was just conforming to this Americanization pattern; and as immigration historian Marcus Lee Hansen has observed, "what the son wishes to forget, the grandson wishes to remember."

But in many respects our family deviated from the pattern, in which, typically, the first generation acts as a bridge, and never fully makes the psychological transition from the old country, but sacrifices itself in the hope that its children will make good, will attain at least "professional" standing. Mopsy and Uncle made the transition effortlessly, it seemed, or they had so much style that it didn't matter what country they ended up in. We, the grandchildren, are their pale descendants. It would be useless to pretend that there has not been considerable slippage; that my life is not coarse-grained and loose-ended in comparison with theirs; that with respect to my "aristocracy," I am not like a garden let go. And (another important respect) when we became curious about our roots, we had no trouble finding them. They were still barely beneath the surface. Pa had kept meticulous archives, and as we grew up, each of our files duly thickened. It gave him great pleasure to do this. Our family, he once told me, was "like an organism, made up of people, living and dead, who are dear to us."

Both my brother and I went to boarding school in New Hampshire. My brother at that time seemed almost the reincarnation of Uncle: thin, high-strung, a brilliantly gifted artist, and, already in his teens, interested in Tibet and Zen and Eastern things. He designed sets for the school plays and starred in them; made drawings for the *Horae Scholasticae*, the literary magazine, and published precocious essays with titles like "Buddhism, America, and the Orient." He wore pajamas to chapel and was forever raking leaves on the weekend, to work off demerits for being so incorrigibly unconventional. I worshiped him. By the time I got to St. Paul's he was already at Stanford, majoring in Chinese; after two years there he transferred to Pembroke College, Oxford.

I was always the better student; I found that I could beat him that way. At St. Paul's I had two passions: Greek and squash; reading Homer in the original and working off excess energy against the spattered walls of the squash courts. Because I maintained a certain average I was periodically awarded scrolls that hailed me, in Latin, as a *puer optimae spei*, a young lad of great promise. My roommate, Cummins, had an enormous collection of jazz records and claimed, at thirteen, to have read the complete works of Dostoevsky. We would go to New York on vacations and, flashing fake I.D.'s (mine said I was the crown prince of Afghanistan) at the doors of nightclubs, get in to hear Thelonious Monk or Cannonball Adderly live. At the end of my third form (ninth grade) year, my father took a job in London, and for the next six years I commuted glamorously to Europe every summer on the *Queen Elizabeth*, the *France*, the *Arosa Sky*, and other now-extinct ocean liners.

One spring vacation, for some reason, I stayed in New York, holed up in an apartment of Zoric's near the Midtown Tunnel with a yard or so of nineteenth-century Russian fiction. For two weeks running I did nothing but read, hardly pausing to eat or sleep. It was the most intense literary experience in my life, and also the first time I really felt Russian.

To this day, if you asked me which writers are most important to me, I'd say Pushkin, Gogol, Tolstoy, Dostoevsky, and Chekhov. I'd already read *Lolita* for the sex a few years before, marveling at all the long, beautiful words I'd never heard of. That summer Nani and I made the crossing together. I think it was on the *Flandres*. I soon fell in love with a girl on the boat. She was going to Sarah Lawrence and was four years older; a creature out of *Franny and Zooey*, she would have a breakdown a few years later. Nani loved to go on cruises; since retiring she had gone to Casablanca, to Palma de Majorca, to Madeira and the Canary Islands. She had been a wonderful grandmother to us when we were children; now for the first time she and I were together as grown-ups. She was very proud of me—at the top of my class, as she had been, in one of the best schools in the country—and it made her feel young and happy to see me running after this pretty Sarah Lawrence girl, who spoke good French and picked right up on what a remarkable person Nani was. One afternoon, while Nani and I were having tea in our deck chairs, with plaid blankets over our knees, I asked her how my grandfather, the Colonel, had died. I had been led to believe that he was dead, but had never heard the details. Nani told me a moving story about how he had fallen through ice and drowned during a skirmish with the Bolsheviks somewhere in Siberia, and we both watched the wake in silence.

In fact—I didn't know this until much later—the Colonel was still alive. After he and Nani split up (apparently the affair with the nineteen-year-old fizzled) he built an *izbah* across the street from Nani's farm, on the edge of a brook deep in the woods. Its walls were made of thick, unpeeled hemlock logs. It had a fireplace and a Dutch oven, two upstairs bedrooms, and a large trellised window. He lived there until he went broke several years later and had to sell the property.

During the thirties the Colonel was often seen in Richmond and Fitzwilliam with a handsome woman from Boston who rode sidesaddle. Once he appeared with her at Nani's and asked if he could borrow the photographs she had of him as a young officer. Mom, about fifteen, said to him (according to Nani), "Let her see you as you are now, not as you were then," and closed the door on them. Although he was no longer married to Nani, and presumably no longer in love with her, he is known to have become so enraged at a local who was making advances to her somewhere around that time that he challenged the man to a duel. He was well-liked, I have learned, at a small colony of Russians in Truro, Cape Cod, which he visited from time to time. He hunted a great deal; it is said that he shot one of the largest black bears that was ever seen in southwestern New Hampshire. One of his hunting buddies, a robust, tweedy man named Watson, had lost his right eye and had a special rifle made so he could sight with his left eye and still shoot from his right shoulder. The Colonel was quite knowledgeable for an amateur geologist, and sometimes took interested parties to remote moonstone deposits he had found in the woods.

In 1937 the Colonel was invited by an ousted Latin American government to help train an army in preparation for a counter-coup. He almost went, but the negotiations fell apart when the government refused to pay his girlfriend's way.

When America entered the war, the Colonel was eager to be of help. He wrote a letter to "His Excellency General Arnold, Chief of the U. S. Air Force," offering to develop "a new branch of service—the air or glider cavalry." His idea was that if there was a strike force of "light-weight horses" attached to hang-gliders by "a suspensory harness similar to those used to load horses on board a ship," they could float over the mine fields, and alighting five or ten miles behind the enemy's position (on each horse, of course, there would be a man armed with an automatic rifle, a tommy gun, and a brace of hand grenades), they could do some real damage. The letter was signed "Boris d'Adamovitch, Colonel of Imperial Cavalry and Cossacks, Former Commanding Officer of Kuban and Tchutsk Regiments, and Chief of Army Guard of Port of Sebastopol." Like Thomas de Hartmann, he had begun to affect the noble particle. The letter, as far as we know, was never answered.

As he grew older, he did anything he could. That's how it is in New Hampshire. You can't be that choosy. He worked in a tannery. He worked in a box factory. He worked on the roads (and went coon-hunting with one of his Highway Department colleagues). He reloaded people's empty cartridges, and there was some demand for his superb penmanship, though he could never write grammatical English or spell correctly. He kept abreast of world developments and discussed them with several other interesting recluses in the area. The fiercely independent editorials in the *Richmond Community Newsletter*, "published when the spirit moves," could always be counted on to set them off.

When he was seventy-five, the Colonel applied to the Peace Corps. He went to Keene and spent a whole day taking exams and passed them all. "I feel like I've just been run over by a truck," he said to Mike, who was visiting the night he came back from Keene. Notified that he had been accepted for duty in Africa, he elatedly started to equip himself. He bought a safari jacket, a big-game gun, mosquito netting against the tsetse flies. One day a second letter came from

the Peace Corps, saying that he hadn't been accepted after
all. The last few years of his life he was in despondent and
rather pathetic condition. Finally Guy Packard, the Richmond police chief, notified Mike that he was unable to take
care of himself, and Mike came up and put him in the
Westmoreland State Farm for the Aged. The Westmoreland
State Farm for the Aged, Mike told me, was "not a nice
place." He died there on January 8, 1965.

When I first learned that during all those years I was at
St. Paul's, my grandfather was living in a shack not far away,
I felt as if a terrible trick had been played on me. But as I
grow older, I think I begin to understand the cover-up of his
existence, and am more able to forgive it. I was still a vul-
nerable *puer optimae spei*; to have known him at that stage
might have taken the wind out of my sails. And the Colonel,
for his part, apparently had no interest in knowing his
grandchildren.

Late in the summer of 1970, having got the directions
from Mike, I visited his last camp. It was on a narrow paved
road that went on and on through the trees and smelled of
tar; the black seams between the slabs of concrete were oozing
in the heat. His land was opposite a Veterans' Hall and so
overgrown that from the road the three shacks, connected
by a boardwalk, weren't immediately visible. Behind the
shacks were eight doghouses. The Colonel had surrounded
himself with dogs—huskies, spaniels, hounds. Once when
Mike came up to see him he had just acquired a mutt. "What
do you want that mutt for?" Mike asked. "Watchdog," he
said. "He needed a watchdog like a hole in the head," Mike
told me. "Whenever you came near the place the other dogs
barked their heads off." I peered through the window of a
toolshed whose eaves were curved, Russian style. The tools

he had used for filling cartridges were still on his workbench. Near the toolshed was the foundation hole of a larger building, the one he and Leon Amadon, the local carpenter, had built together, which burned to the ground in the early sixties. Toward the end of his life the Colonel was plagued by fires. After his main house burned, he moved into a well-built, insulated fiberboard shack, but about a year later that, too, went up in smoke, even though Mike had provided him with a fire extinguisher. "That extinguisher worked fine," he reported to Mike, "as long as it lasted." As a result of the second fire, he had a stroke.

I have a photograph Mike took shortly before he died, in which an old man in a cap and checkered shirt, shriveled beyond recognition from the dashing young cavalry officer Nani fell in love with and married, is cupping a sprig of spruce almost worshipfully, as if it were a candle at church. As I look at the photograph I think of the things Mike has told me about him, how he wasn't easily impressed by people, how he had two senses of humor—a Rabelaisian one and a subtle one. This old man looks at peace. Maybe he found more peace in this country than Nani did. She never relaxed her standards, never stopped aching for that beautiful, charming world in which she was a child and a young woman. He looks in this picture as if he had successfully transferred his affections and his allegiance to the New Hampshire woods.

Near one of the doghouses I spotted a mushroom with a tawny cap, and a stout, rather sinuous white stalk, which instead of flaring into gills, supported a firm white under-surface of minute spores. I pulled it gently from the earth, and circulating it slowly below my nostrils, drank in its dank, woodsy bouquet. I ran trembling fingers over its cap, which was moist and glabrous ("destitute of pubescence" in Louis Krieger's classic, *The Mushroom Handbook*), but not viscid. It was a *Boletus edulis*, the cèpe of France, the *byelii grib*, or white mushroom, of Russia, whose flesh is more succulent than the tenderest filet mignon. If the Colonel had been alive, it would not have gone unpicked. I pocketed it, and when I got home, sauteed it in butter and ate it for him. I would not see another edible bolete until ten years later, in some pine woods near Poltava. It was a Saturday morning. That evening we were turning back—taking an overnight train to Moscow and flying home. It was my last chance to go mushroom-picking in the Soviet Union.

I had known the Russians were mycophiles, but I wasn't prepared for the fact that *everyone* in the Slavic parts of the U.S.S.R. is an avid and savvy mushroom buff, that *everyone* takes to the woods on Saturdays, unless he has a wedding to go to. Mushroom-picking is virtually the national pastime, and Ukrainians are no less fanatic about it than Great Russians. I had no trouble persuading Alexei Isaschenko, head of the Intourist bureau in Poltava, to *hodit' po griby*, to go looking for mushrooms with me. We met at about seven. "We have to get an early start," he had said. "By noon the good ones will all be gone." We drove about twenty miles north of Poltava. The farther from the city, the less competition, Alexei explained. We passed through Dikanka, a hamlet immortalized in Gogol's charming collection of early stories, *Evenings on a Farm Near Dikanka*. The hamlet was awash with banners. It was the thirty-fifth anniversary of the day the Nazis had pulled out of Poltava. "They carried off a million tons of our black earth, and two and a half million of our people to concentration camps," Alexei said angrily. The memory of the occupation was still like yesterday. In prerevolutionary times everyone in Dikanka had worked for the Kotchoubeys, who had a fabulous house, designed by Korinfsky, the same architect who did Shideyevo. There is an Andrei Kotchoubey, a little older than I, on the board of the Russian Orthodox Theological Fund in New York. The fund throws a ball each year at the Colony Club and with the proceeds gives scholarships to needy applicants to Orthodox seminaries.

Every Slav has his special, secret mushroom place, but Alexei figured that since I was leaving that night and probably wouldn't be back in the near future, it was safe to show me his. Looking behind him to be sure we wouldn't be seen making the turnoff, he gestured to an unobtrusive logging road that led into some pine woods. We drove along for about half a mile until we were in deep forest, and Alexei indicated for me to cut the motor. He handed me my equipment. It was very simple: a plastic shopping bag and a kitchen knife. Then he produced a bottle of vodka and two cups, which he filled. "To our success," he said, and tossed his back. He filled them again and we kept making toasts, to each other's families, to peace between our countries, until the vodka was gone. Alexei was about forty, short and balding, a good communist I'm sure and a man of deep sincerity. His speech was slightly faltering, a third-degree stutter, not a real head-thrower. He wore a dark beret, a long coat over a blue warm-up suit, and city shoes. He entered the woods purposefully, with long, healthy strides and eyes to the ground, and I fanned out to his right.

I would have guessed that the orange-barked conifers had been planted in the fifties. They had grown to around thirty feet, and the floor beneath them was a springy mat of golden needles, several inches thick. They had been planted over many square miles, and beneath them there were mushrooms every few feet. The most abundant species were the familiar, gregarious, deadly *Amanita muscaria*, known as the fly agaric in the English-speaking world, in France as the *tue-mouches*, and in Russia as the *muhomor*. The bright cap, ranging from yellow to scarlet (here it was a deep cadmium orange) and speckled with white warts, is unmistakable. "Bad," Alexei said, turning one over with his shoe. "I know," I said. "We have an acquaintance who wanted to experience its high in the sixties and doesn't seem to have come down yet." *Amanita muscaria* is the world's oldest hallucinogen, the God-narcotic *soma* of the Rig-Vedas, the inebriant of Siberians, who drank its active principle, muscarin, in the urine of their shamans before they went hunting whales. "The old people know how to prepare it, and eat it after long boiling," Alexei told me.

The second most common fungus in the forest was a nondescript brown one Alexei called the false *maslyata*. It wasn't good, but in a hollow where the pines gave way to low shrubs we found the real *maslyata*. "See, the pores are firmer and more yellow, and the cap is easily peeled. Our first trophy," Alexei said, and plopped it into my bag. "Last month we could have collected ten kilos minimum. Now they are fewer." I found another real *maslyata* but Alexei stopped me as I was about to add it to the first. He sliced off the base of the stem, and the cross-section was riddled with worm-holes. Then he sliced off the top of the stem, and there were still worm-holes. Then he cut the cap in two, and it had been eaten from within. "This is no good," he pronounced, and punted it. "Basically, if the mushroom is good, worms eat it. If it isn't, they don't. Worms eat the good mushrooms and leave the bad ones. That is the first rule my father told me. If the rabbits eat it, if the toads eat it, it is good. But if it is old, even if it is good, it is not good." A sudden gust of wind, as if confirming the truth of his words, brought a rain of golden needles down on Alexei's beret and shoulders.

We found a few chanterelles, called "little foxes" because they are rusty orange like the coat of a red fox. We found *Russula* in abundance, ranging in cap color from crimson to faded lilac green. Alexei said they were called "without prepare" because one ate them raw with salt. We found a burial ground with weathered Orthodox crosses akimbo, the median death date around 1935. We found two men thinning a younger, denser part of the woods with short-handled broad axes. Alexei picked up a branch and used it like a metal detector to probe likely mounds in the pine needle floor. Many mushrooms were inspected, but few made the grade. For the most part it was slice, slice, slice, punt. As the vodka wore off, the wind started to get to me. Howling around the trees, it sounded like wolves. We found two grizzled old men up on the roof of a prerevolutionary schoolhouse with the flap of their fur hats down over their ears, and got directions from them. We picked some late asters for our wives. We found our first white mushroom, growing in moss. "This is the *mokhovik*," Alexei said. "*Mokh* means moss. It has a larger cap than the *dorovik*, which is the most prized of the white mushrooms. On a good Saturday in September you can find forty *mokhoviks* and *doroviks*." Plop. We found honey mushrooms, the delectable parasites of oak and beech, or *opyata* as Alexei called them. We found puffy little sklerodermas— edible when young, but not prized. We were two Russians walking in the woods.

UNCLE ON A LEDGE AT LAKE MINNEWASKA.

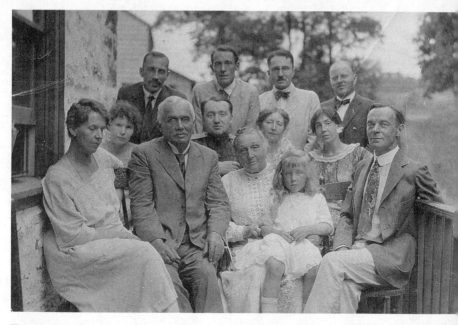

THE ÉMIGRÉS AT PINE BUSH. MOPSY IS SECOND ROW RIGHT, WITH
UNCLE AND LYOVA BEHIND HER.

ALEXANDRA NICOLAEVNA WITH HER GRANDCHILDREN AT
PINE BUSH (LEFT TO RIGHT): ZORIC, BABY, AND
NICHOLAS (MY FATHER).

Hunting mushrooms. Lyova is second left, wearing the
straw boater.

Pine Bush. Prince Lvov with his famous beard, on left.

Lyova operating the tractor at Pine Bush.

René Fonck, the French flying ace (third left). Lyova on extreme right.

ONE OF SIKORSKY'S FIRST PLANES IN THE YARD AT OLD WESTBURY.
Courtesy United Technologies Corporation

Lyova (third left) next to Igor Sikorsky (fourth left), three days before Lyova drowned.

Mopsy and FDR.

THE UNFINISHED
PORTRAIT. *Courtesy The
Little White House*

MOPSY (FRONT ROW, LEFT) ON THE REVIEWING STAND WITH GRAND
DUCHESS MARIE (THIRD LEFT).

NYANYA SKUNKS, UNCLE'S
PAINTING OF HIS FIRST
IMPRESSIONS OF AMERICA.
WOOLWORTH BUILDING IN
BACKGROUND.

MY FATHER
HUNTING
BUTTERFLIES IN
JAMAICA, C.
1931.

SHOUMATOFF'S HAIRSTREAK (*NESIOSTRYMON CELIDA SHOUMATOFFI* COMSTOCK & HUNTINGTON).

THE FAMILY AT HIDDEN HOLLOW (LEFT TO RIGHT): BABY, A GOVERNESS, MOPSY, MY FATHER, UNCLE, ZORIC.

ONE OF UNCLE'S LATE ROSE PAINTINGS, WITH A *PARNASSIUS* IN UPPER RIGHT.

UNCLE NEAR
THE END
OF HIS LIFE.

OLGA AS A YOUNG WOMAN.

Masha.

Thomas de Hartmann and Olga in Paris.

Olga and me. New Mexico, 1979.

Nani, 1978.

Nani, age 4.

THE ELAGHIN PALACE, FRONT VIEW, TAKEN FROM A PRE-REVOLUTIONARY
POSTCARD.

RURAL RUSSIA IN NANI'S GIRLHOOD. *Courtesy*
Paul Rodzianko

Nani at 15 (second left on wagon), visiting Uncle Sasha Elaghin.

A skating party. *Courtesy Paul Rodzianko*

The Elaghin sisters (left to right): Natasha, Nani, Lila, Sonya.

The wedding of Nani's sister Lila to Captain Nicolai Selivanov (second left).

The oil fields at Baku. *Courtesy Paul Rodzianko*

The Colonel (center) during W.W.I.

White Army cadets during the civil war. *Courtesy Paul Rodzianko*

Nani in Russia.

The Colonel in Sebastopol, wearing the Kuban Cossack uniform. To his left is the British captain who admired Nani.

WHITE ARMY SOLDIERS AT THE FRONT. *Courtesy Paul Rodzianko*

BOARDING THE SHIPS TO LEAVE RUSSIA, 1920.
Courtesy Paul Rodzianko

MY MOTHER AND MIKE IN SENJ.

NANI AND HER CHILDREN IN PARIS.

GENERAL MITROFAN
MARCHENKO.

Nani in Baltimore.

MY MOTHER DURING HER
MODELING DAYS. THE
PORTRAIT IN THE
ADVERTISEMENT WAS DONE
BY MOPSY.

MOPSY'S PORTRAIT OF
MY FATHER DURING
THE WAR.

MOPSY'S PORTRAIT
OF ME, 1973.

THE COLONEL AND MIKE IN NEW HAMPSHIRE, 1930S.

THE COLONEL JUST
BEFORE HE DIED.

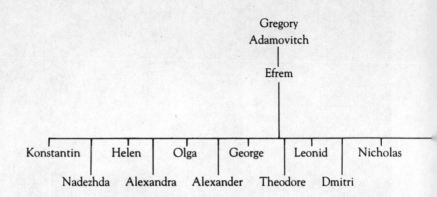

Gregory
Adamovitch

Efrem

Konstantin	Helen	Olga	George	Leonid	Nicholas
Nadezhda	Alexandra	Alexander	Theodore	Dmitri	

✠

*The
Elaghin-Adamovitch
Line*

✠

Linda Upton   *m.*

Natasha

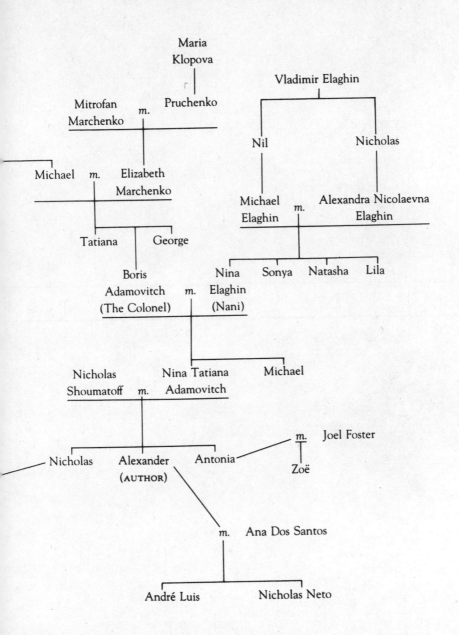

Notes and Acknowledgments

The main sources of the material in this book, transmitted in both oral and written form since I was a child, are, of course, my two grandmothers. This is their story, and it has been a privilege for me to hear it from them, not to mention to be their grandson. Everyone in the family has been extremely generous with time and information. At the head of the list is my father, who inherited and expanded Uncle's archives, and my sister, Tonia Shoumatoff Foster, who during the 1970s gathered a tremendous amount of information about Uncle; many of her informants have since died.

My mother, Aunt Zoric, Uncle Mike, brother Nick, cousin Victoria, and French cousins Igor and Dmitri Markevitch and Nina Budin have also been of inestimable help. I did not show the manuscript to anyone for verification or approval before it was published, except an early draft of "Shideyevo" to Mopsy, Zoric, and my father, and an early draft of "Nani and the Colonel" to Nani. For any errors that may have thus resulted I am very sorry.

I want to thank Joe Kanon for urging me to take on this project and for seeing it through to the finish, William Shawn and Robert Bingham of *The New Yorker* for their editorial counsel, Serge Troubetzkoy and Alexis Scherbatov for advising me on points of Russian history and culture. I am grateful to Paul Rodzianko for letting us reproduce his wonderful family photographs; to the Little White House in Warm Springs, Georgia, for permission to run the unfinished portrait of FDR; to United Technologies for contributing early photos of the Sikorsky Aero-Engineering Corporation; to Andy Singer for photographing two of Mopsy's miniatures; to Zoric for giving us access to the paintings and photographs in her possession; to Mr. and Mrs. Thomas Daly for bringing me Olga de Hartmann's family memorabilia after she died (several of the photographs are reproduced). As I look back over the text, I see numerous debts which should be recognized specifically. I hope my collaborators will forgive any inadvertent oversights.

In the first part, "Mopsy Leaves Us," I got the *charmante soirée* anecdote partly from Tonia, partly from an article about Mopsy that appeared in the Sunday magazine of *Newsday* on December 5, 1976. Masha's book, the main source about her life and Nika's, is *Marie Avinov: Pilgrimage Through Hell*, by Paul Chavchavadze. The friend of Uncle's who was covered with butterflies, Blanche Matthias, told me the story in San Francisco in 1969, and subsequently gave me important insights into his character and Grandmother's. John Walker's remarks about Uncle's paintings come from an interview Tonia had with him.

In "Shideyevo" the information about the Ovinoffs comes from the *Kharatei Novgorodian Chronicles* and the *Novgorodian Chronicles, I and II,* translated for me by my father; several genealogical books of Uncle's; and Vladimir Gurmin, vice-director of the State Museum in Novgorod. The historical background about Novgorod comes from G. Vernadsky's and V. Klyuchevsky's monumental histories of Russia; B. Rubakov's *Early History of Russia*; Nicholas Riasanovsky's *History of Russia*; Francis Dvornik's *The Slavs in European History and Civilization*; Sir Donald Mackenzie Wallace's *Russia*; Ted Spiegel, an authority on the Vikings; and our well-informed Intourist guide, Nadya. Mopsy showed me the story of the Avinovskaya icon in two books she had, *Slava Bogomateri* and *Zhity Svyatikh*. The information about the hodigitria position can be found in Vladimir Soloukhin's *Searching for Icons in Russia*. Vladimir Nabokov mentions his disdain for the double *f* in *Speak, Memory*. Marshal B. Dividson wrote about the real motives of the Russian fleet during the American Civil War in *American Heritage*. There is a long entry on General Alexander Avinoff and his antecedents in the 1895 *Russian Biographical Dictionary*, and a nearly complete genealogy of the Avinoff family in the 1896 *Collected Genealogies of Noble Families*. I read about the Azov line in Vernadsky and in B. H. Sumner's *A Short History of Russia*, and about Catherine the Great's trip through Little Russia in Henri Troyat's biography of her and in Sumner. I learned about Ivan Kotlyarevsky's friendship with Andrei Lukianovitch at the Kotlyarevsky Museum in Poltava, and about Taras Shevschenko's visit to Shideyevo from the memoirs of Andrei Fyodorovitch's granddaughter, Alexandra Myelnikova, *Vospominanie o Davno Minuvschii i Nedavnem Bylom,* Moscow, 1899. Mopsy was the source of most of the Shideyevo material, supplemented by correspondence with Tanya Smirnoff-Makcheeff, conversation with Zoric and Alika, and Masha's and Miss Whishaw's books. The material on Vladimir Panayev comes from Uncle in the March 1920 *Études de Lépidoptérologie* and from Henri Troyat's biography of Nikolai Gogol. The anecdote about the Bagrations comes from Fitzroy Maclean's *To*

Caucasus. Uncle's catching of the cabbage is told in Elizabeth Moorhead's *Pittsburgh Portraits.* I found an exhibit of local butterflies in Poltava's Museum of Local Lore and took down their names. My father commented on the dual nature of Uncle's eyesight in an obituary he wrote for *Lepidopterists News.* Nicholas Nabokov's description of the *lineika* appears in *Bagazh.* Uncle related his expedition to the Pamirs in the same article in *Études de Lépidoptérologie,* and his trip to western Tibet in the *Pittsburgh Record.* The anecdotes about the rare flea and the sixty-course dinner were told by Geoffrey Hellman in his profile of Uncle in the August 21, 1948, *New Yorker.* Vladimir Nabokov, Sr's., *The Provisional Government,* Alexander Kerensky's *The Prelude to Bolshevism,* Bruce Lockhart's *The British Agent,* and Alan Moorhead's *The Russian Revolution* had information about the Kadet party and the Constituent Assembly, and Nabokov and Lockhart told of Nika's involvement with the attempt to set up a democracy in Russia. I learned about *zemstvos* from Geroid Tanquary Robinson's *Rural Russian Under the Old Regime,* from Henri Troyat's *Daily Life in Russia Under the Last Czar,* and from Sumner, Wallace, and Vernadsky. Boris Menshutkin's *Russia's Lomonosov* had information about Johann D. Schumacher. J. Lucas-Dubreton tells the story of Lavalette's escape in *Récits d'autrefois.* I am grateful to Claire Heskestad for tracking down the story in France. James Billington discusses the art of Kandinski and Malevich in *The Icon and the Axe.* Hellmann tells about Uncle's lunch with the tsar and the German envoy. Moorhead describes his first trip to America. Anatol Bourman describes Nijinsky's dancing in *The Tragedy of Nijinsky.* I read about St. Petersburg before the Revolution in John Reed's *Ten Days That Shook the World* and in Moorhead, and talked about it with Norman Armour. The excerpts from John Rickman's journal are taken from Geoffrey Gorer and John Rickman's *The People of Great Russia.* The agricultural data about Poltava come from Theodore Shabad's *Geography of the USSR.* The state of the Ukraine after the Revolution is described by Vernadsky, Moorhead, Sumner, and Michael Hrushevsky in *A History of the Ukraine*.

In "George Vashington Bridge" I am grateful to Paul Rodzianko for sending me Irina Tatischev's memoirs. Nabokov's phrase comes from *Speak, Memory*. I talked about the days at Pine Bush, Napanoch, and Yama Farms with Mopsy, Zoric, my father, Blanche Matthias, Claudia Lyon, and Alika, and read a short memoir by Mrs. Sarre furnished by my sister. Boris Brazol's careers are described in John J. Stephan's *The Russian Fascists* and Norman Cohen's *Warrant for Genocide*. All mycological material comes from Louis C. C. Krieger's *The Mushroom Handbook*. My father told me Lyova's ghost story. Hellmann describes Uncle's visit to the White House with Prince Lvov. Most of the anecdotes about Yama Farms come from Mopsy's unpublished memoir, *Out of My Paintbox*. The information about the Sikorsky Aero-Engineering Corporation, Lyova's connection with it, and the Merrick days is from Mopsy, Zoric, my father, Igor Sikorsky's *The Story of the Winged S*, the August 8, 1926, *New Yorker*, Duncan Woodman, and Henry Lanier. My sources on the unfinished portrait and events leading to it are *Out of My Paintbox* and a scrapbook of clippings Mopsy had. The memoirs also describe her painting of Prince Yusupov, Grand Duchess Marie, and Presidents Tubman and Johnson. My father tells about the meeting of Uncle and B. Preston Clark and about William J. Holland in his unpublished account, *Two in the Bush*. Hellman writes about some of the names Uncle gave new species. For material about Pittsburgh and Uncle's years at the Carnegie Museum I am indebted to John Walker's *Self-Portrait with Donors*, to Moorhead, conversation with Graham Netting and Anna Tauber (who also sent me material from the natural history museum's library), to Johnny Bauer, to John Brindle of the Hunt Botanical Library, and to Tonia's interview with Anne Catherine Bannon, Mr. Krautworm's niece. The Jamaican expeditions are described in *Two in the Bush* and several articles by Uncle in the

Carnegie Magazine. Hellman and Uncle in the *Carnegie Magazine* describe the quest for *Parnassius przewalskii*. Thomas C. Emmel assesses Uncle's contribution to lepidopterology in his book, *Butterflies*. The monograph by Uncle and Walter R. Sweadner is "The Karanasa Butterflies, A Study in Evolution," Annals of the Carnegie Museum, February 10, 1951. He elaborated his ideas on what a natural history museum should be in the *Carnegie Magazine*. Archibald Roosevelt talked to Tonia about his friendship with Uncle. Mrs. Edwin Bechtel described his meeting with Edith Sitwell in a letter to Tonia. For the section on Olga de Hartmann I am indebted to Thomas de Hartmann's *Our Life with Mr. Gurdjieff*, to James Webb's *The Harmonious Circle*, to Peter Colgrove, Zoric, Dmitri Markevitch, Mopsy, and to Jean Sulzberger for getting me together with my long-lost great-aunt. The career of Igor Markevitch is discussed in *Bagazh* and in Richard Buckle's *Diaghilev*.

In "Nani and the Colonel" Serge Obolensky describes his courtship of the gypsy girl in *One Man in His Time*. The material about Ivan Elaghin comes from Troyat's biography of Catherine. The assassination of Stolypin and his land reform are treated in Wallace, Sumner, Moorhead, René Fülöp-Miller's *Rasputin, the Holy Devil*, and Robert K. Massie's *Nicholas and Alexandra*. Troyat's *Daily Life* provided some background for Nani's childhood memoirs. A long article about Maria Hlopova appeared in *Novoe Russkoe Slovo*. Prerevolutionary Siberia is described in George St. George's *Siberia, The New Frontier*, and in A. I. Dmitriev-Mamonov's and A. F. Zoziansky's 1900 *Guide to the Great Siberian Railroad*. Crimea during the civil war is dealt with in Vernadsky, *Speak, Memory*, Grand Duke Alexander's *Once a Grand Duke*, George Stewart's *The White Armies of Russia*, Peter Kenez's *Civil War in South Russia—1919–1920*, and General Baron P. N. Wrangel's *Always with Honor*. Paris in the 1920s and the émigré statistics are treated in Stewart. The information on the National Origins Quota Rule comes from Keith Welden's *Becoming American*. Louisa Spenser reminisced about Mrs. Amory, John Train told me about Gordon Wasson's theory on why Russians are mycophiles. Doris Fielding Reid's memoir of Edith Hamilton appeared in *Greek Heritage*, Nabokov's reminiscence of Dobuzhinsky in *Speak, Memory*.

Note to the Vintage Edition

This new edition was vetted in 1989 by Zoric and my father. Some of their addenda and corrigenda are incorporated in the text or entered as footnotes. It was impossible to include them all without entirely rewriting the first two-thirds of the book.

Mopsy's autobiography, *Presidential Memoirs*, is in press at the University of Pittsburgh.

Index

ABOUT THE AUTHOR

Alex Shoumatoff, a staff writer for *The New Yorker*, is the author of seven previous books, including *In Southern Light*, *The Mountain of Names*, *Florida Ramble*, and *African Madness* (all available from Vintage). He has an abiding interest in the Third World tropics and the relationship between man and nature. He is the father of two boys and now resides in Mexico City.

Also by

Alex Shoumatoff

African Madness

Brilliantly written, filled with horror, sadness, and a sense of wonder,
these four essays take us to Rwanda, to reconsider the life and savage
death of the primatologist Dian Fossey...to Madagascar, an endangered
Eden of impossible life forms...to the Central African Republic, to the
trial of "the emperor who ate his people"...and across tropical Africa in
search of the origins of AIDS.

Florida Ramble

Alex Shoumatoff travels from the boardwalk of Miami Beach to an Indian
enclave on the Tamiami Trail, with stops at a migrant farm workers' camp
and what may be the original site of the Garden of Eden. The result is a
lushly descriptive and quietly surreal book in the traditions of Jan Morris
and John McPhee.